Race and New Religious Movements in the USA

ALSO AVAILABLE FROM BLOOMSBURY

The Bloomsbury Companion to New Religious Movements,
edited by George D. Chryssides and Benjamin E. Zeller
The Bloomsbury Reader in Religion, Sexuality, and Gender,
edited by Donald L. Boisvert and Carly Daniel-Hughes
New Religious Movements, Paul Oliver

Race and New Religious Movements in the USA

A Documentary Reader

EDITED BY
EMILY SUZANNE CLARK
AND BRAD STODDARD

BLOOMSBURY ACADEMIC
LONDON • NEW YORK • OXFORD • NEW DELHI • SYDNEY

BLOOMSBURY ACADEMIC
Bloomsbury Publishing Plc
50 Bedford Square, London, WC1B 3DP, UK
1385 Broadway, New York, NY 10018, USA

BLOOMSBURY, BLOOMSBURY ACADEMIC and the Diana logo are trademarks of
Bloomsbury Publishing Plc

First published in Great Britain 2019

Cover design: Maria Rajka

Cover image: 8th August 1946: Father Major Jealous Divine (1874–1965), also known as
George Baker, and his bride Edna Rose Ritchings © Keystone/Stringer/Getty Images

A catalogue record for this book is available from the British Library.

A catalog record for this book is available from the Library of Congress.

ISBN: HB: 978-1-3500-6396-9
         PB: 978-1-3500-6397-6
         ePDF: 978-1-3500-6400-3
         eBook: 978-1-3500-6399-0

Typeset by RefineCatch Limited, Bungay, Suffolk
Printed and bound in Great Britain

To find out more about our authors and books visit www.bloomsbury.com
and sign up for our newsletters.

Brad Stoddard dedicates this book to Jerry and Louise Little, with love.
Emily Clark dedicates this book to her students.

Contents

Acknowledgments

The editors would like to thank their editor at Bloomsbury Press, Lalle Pursglove, for her editorial expertise and support of the project. We would also like to thank Lucy Carroll at Bloomsbury for her valuable advice on permissions and editorial knowledge. We are grateful to the anonymous reviewers who read earlier drafts of the manuscript. They also thank their colleague Jeffrey Wheatley who provided feedback on the manuscript, along with Allison Isidore and Ryan Geary.

Being a documentary reader, securing permissions was quite a task. In this regard, the editors would like to thank the *Journal of American Folklore*, Earl K. Long Library Special Collections, Jesuits West Archives, Christopher B. Stewart, PhD (of Woodmont Archives with the International Peace Mission Movement), Marie Silvia, Fielding M. McGehee, III, Rebecca Moore, Lise Tiano, and Pascal Riché. Additionally, Linda Schearing, Judith Weisenfeld, John Crow, Adam Gaiser, and Mattias Gardell were helpful regarding primary and secondary sources.

Permissions

The editors are grateful to the following sources for permission to reproduce in this book material previously published elsewhere. We have made every effort to secure the permission of relevant parties, but if we have inadvertently missed any relevant permissions then we will move to rectify this at the earliest opportunity.

Chapter 2: The Code of Handsome Lake
All excerpts from Arthur C. Parker, *The Code of Handsome Lake, the Seneca Prophet* (Albany: University of the State of New York, 1913). In public domain.

Chapter 3: Conjure
Excerpt from Jacob Stroyer, *Sketches of My Life in the South, Part I* (Salem, MA: The Salem Press, 1879), 42–45. In public domain.
Excerpt from William Wells Brown, *My Southern Home: or, The South and Its People* (Boston, MA: A. G. Brown & Co., 1880), 72–81. In public domain.
Excerpt from "The 'Hoodoo' Superstition," *Rocky Mountain News* (Denver, CO), Sunday, December 11, 1887, page 18. In public domain.
Excerpt from Zora Neale Hurston, "Hoodoo in America," *The Journal of American Folklore* 44.174 (1931): 326–327. Reprinted with the permission of the American Folklore Society.

Chapter 4: The Church of Jesus Christ of Latter-Day Saints
Excerpt from 2 Nephi 5:1–34, Book of Mormon. In public domain.
Excerpt from "Sanitary Report—Utah Territory," *Statistical Report on the Sickness and Mortality in the Army of the United States* (Washington, DC: George W. Bowman, 1860), 300–304. In public domain.
Excerpt from "Joseph Smith, the Prophet," *Young Woman's Journal* 16.12 (December 1905), 551–553. In public domain.
Excerpt from Official Declaration 2, Doctrine and Covenants, The Church of Jesus Christ of Latter-day Saints. Reprinted with the permission of the Correlation Intellectual Property of The Church of Jesus Christ of Latter-day Saints.

Chapter 5: Spiritualism
Excerpts from *The Spiritual Telegraph*, vol. 3, edited by S.B. Brittan (New York: Partridge & Brittan, 1843), 202, 492, and 571. In public domain.
Excerpt from Robert Hare, *Experimental Investigation of the Spirit Manifestations* (New York: Partridge & Brittan, 1856), 138. In public domain.

Excerpts from Emma Hardinge Britten, *Modern American Spiritualism* (New York: The Author, 1870), 401, 481–482, and 485. In public domain.

Excerpts from the Cercle Harmonique séance registers at Rene Grandjean Collection, Special Collections, Earl K. Long Library, University of New Orleans. Translations completed by Emily Suzanne Clark. Reprinted with the permission of Earl K. Long Library Special Collections.

Chapter 6: Ghost Dance Movement

Excerpt from "The Indian Millennium," *The Wichita Daily Eagle*, October 28, 1890. In public domain.

Excerpt from James Mooney, *The Ghost-Dance Religion and the Sioux Outbreak of 1890*, extract from the Fourteenth Annual Report of the Bureau of Ethnology (Washington, DC: Government Printing Office, 1896), 777–782. In public domain.

Excerpt from Charles Alexander Eastman, *From the Deep Woods to Civilization: Chapters in the Autobiography of an Indian* (Boston, MA: Little Brown & Company, 1916), 92–115. In public domain.

Chapter 7: Ku Klux Klan

Excerpt from Thomas Dixon, Jr., *The Clansman: A Historical Romance of the Ku Klux Klan* (New York: DoubleDay, Page & Company, 1905), 318–326. In public domain.

"Oath of the American Krusaders," undated but marked "Form 103—J.F.H." From the Radicals Collection, Box 11, USA West Archives, Jesuits West, Gonzaga University. Reprinted with permission of Jesuits West Archive.

Excerpt from *The Ku Klux Klan: Hearings Before the Committee on Rules, House of Representatives, Sixty-seventh Congress, First Session* (US Government Printing Office, 1921), 94–95. In public domain.

Excerpt from Hiram Wesley Evans, "The Klan: Defender of Americanism," *The Forum* LXXIV.6 (December 1925): 801–814. Reprinted under "Fair Use," as no contact information can be found for *The Forum*.

Chapter 8: Theosophy

Excerpt from Alfred Percy Sinnett, *Esoteric Buddhism* (New York: Houghton, Mifflin, 1887), 105–113. In public domain.

Excerpt from Helena Petrovna Blavatsky, *The Key to Theosophy* (New York: The Theosophical Publishing Company, Limited, 1889), 39–41. In public domain.

Excerpt from Helena Petrovna Blavatsky, The Secret Doctrine, Volume 2 (Point Loma, CA: Aryan Theosophical Press, 1909), 195–196, 249–250, and 443–445. In public domain.

Chapter 9: Native American Church

Excerpt from United States Congress House Committee on Indian Affairs, "Peyote: Hearings before a subcommittee of the Committee on Indian Affairs of the House of Representatives on H.R. 2614" (Washington, DC: Government Printing Office, 1918), 63, 70–71, and 80–81. In public domain.

Excerpts from Employment Division, *Department of Human Resources of Oregon v. Smith, 494 US 872*, decided 17 April 1990. Government document with no copyright.

Chapter 10: Commandment Keepers

Rabbi Wentworth A. Matthew, "The Truth about Black Jews and Judaism in America: Part I," *New York Age*, May 17, 1958, page 9. W.A. Matthew Collection, 1929–1979. Schomburg Center for Research in Black Culture, New York, New York.

Rabbi Wentworth A. Matthew, "The Truth about the Black Jews and Judaism in America: Part III," *New York Age* (date and page unknown). W.A. Matthew Collection, 1929–1979. Schomburg Center for Research in Black Culture, New York, New York.

Rabbi Wentworth Matthew, "The Anthropology of the Ethiopian Hebrews and their Relationship to the Fairer Jews," in Howard Brotz, *The Black Jews of Harlem: Negro Leadership and the Dilemmas of Negro Leadership* (New York: Schoken Books, 1970), 19–22.

Rabbi Wentworth Matthew, "The Root and Inception of The House of Israel" (Flyer). W.A. Matthew Collection, 1929–1979. Schomburg Center for Research in Black Culture, New York, New York.

Chapter 11: Moorish Science Temple of America

Excerpt from Noble Drew Ali, The Holy Koran of the Moorish Science Temple, Chapter 48. Limited excerpt reprinted under "Fair Use."

Excerpts from the FBI monitoring files of the movement. Available publicly from the FBI's online "vault": https://vault.fbi.gov. Government documents with no copyright.

Chapter 12: International Peace Mission Movement

Excerpt from "FATHER DIVINE Delivers Message to Mighty Throng, Heralding the Glad Tidings of the New Day," *Spoken Word* 2.14 (January 14, 1936). Reprinted with permission of Christopher B. Stewart, Ph.D., Woodmont archivist, Father Divine Peace Mission Movement.

Excerpt from "The Righteous Government Platform is a Foundation on Which Men Can Build Who Have Been Hungering and Thirsting After Righteousness and Finding None," The New Day 2.37 (September 15, 1938). Reprinted with permission of Christopher B. Stewart, Ph.D., Woodmont archivist, Father Divine Peace Mission Movement.

Excerpt from "Those Who Use Segregated Terms are Endorsing Lynch Mob Murders Even if They are Not Conscious of It," The New Day 3.43 (October 26, 1939). Reprinted with permission of Christopher B. Stewart, Ph.D., Woodmont archivist, Father Divine Peace Mission Movement.

Chapter 13: Nation of Islam

Malcolm X, Harvard Law School Forum Speech (March 24, 1961). http://malcolmxfiles. blogspot.com/2013/07/harvard-law-school-forum-december-16.html (accessed March 14, 2019).

Malcolm X, The Race Problem Speech (January 23, 1963). http://ccnmtl.columbia.edu/ projects/mmt/mxp/speeches/mxt17.html (accessed March 14, 2019).

Excerpts from Elijah Muhammad, *Message to the Blackman in America* (Chicago, IL: Muhammad Mosque of Islam No. 2, 1965).

Chapter 14: Peoples Temple

"A True Follower of This Activist Christian Ministry." Flyer distributed by The Peoples Temple sometime between 1965 and 1974. Reprinted with permission of the California Historical Society.

Evangelist S. D. Peter, "Thy Kingdom Come," *The Living Word: An Apostolic Monthly* (1 July 1972): 4. Reprinted with permission of the California Historical Society.

Sermon by Jim Jones (1973), The Jonestown Institute, Annotated Transcript Q957.

"Five Sundays at the Peoples Temple," *Le Nouvel Observatoire* (1978): 51–54.

Chapter 15: Aryan Nations

Excerpt from "Who What Why When Where: Aryan Nations," 1990s-era Aryan Nations tri-fold pamphlet, distributed publicly in northern Idaho. Reprinted under "Fair Use," as the group lost a major lawsuit and disbanded, and no contact information can be found for Richard Butler's descendants.

Excerpt from "Where to Look in the Bible: Jews," 1990s-era Aryan Nations pamphlet, distributed publicly in northern Idaho. Reprinted under "Fair Use," as the group lost a major lawsuit and disbanded, and no contact information can be found for Richard Butler's descendants.

Excerpt from "Where to Look in the Bible: On Negroes," 1990s-era Aryan Nations pamphlet, distributed publicly in northern Idaho. Reprinted under "Fair Use," as the group lost a major lawsuit and disbanded, and no contact information can be found for Richard Butler's descendants.

Excerpts from Pastor Richard G. Butler, *The Aryan Warrior*, booklet distributed publicly in the 1990s in northern Idaho. Reprinted under "Fair Use," as the group lost a major lawsuit and disbanded, and no contact information can be found for Richard Butler's descendants.

"The Death of the White Race," flyer publicly disseminated in northern Idaho in the 1980s. Reprinted under "Fair Use," as the group lost a major lawsuit and disbanded, and no contact information can be found for Richard Butler's descendants.

Chapter 16: The Nation of Yahweh

Excerpts from God of Gods, *You are not a Nigger! Our True History, The World's Best Kept Secret* (Seguin, TX: PEESS Foundation, 1981).

Chapter 17: Odinism

Alexander Rud Mills, "The Odinist Religion Overcoming Jewish Christianity" (Melbourne, Australia: Mills), 1933.

"Overview," *The Odinist* 113 (1988): 1–4.

"Anarchism," *The Odinist* 125 (1989): 1–2.

David Lane, "88 Precepts." https://ia800303.us.archive.org/3/items/88Precepts_937/88Precepts.pdf (accessed March 14, 2019).

David Eden Lane, "To: 'Christian Rightwing American Patriots,'" *Wotansvolk* (The WAU Sisterhood), 2017: 59–60.

1

Introduction

In 1919, an immigrant in New York named Wentworth Arthur Matthew created the Commandment Keepers of the Living God, where he taught his fellow black Americans that they were the Biblical Hebrews. The other people who called themselves Hebrews or Jews, he argued, stole their true identity, and in the process, alienated them from their past. Several years later, a self-proclaimed prophet calling himself Noble Drew Ali told black Americans in Chicago a different story. Like Matthew, he claimed to bring black Americans knowledge of their forgotten identity, but where Matthew taught that black Americans were Hebrews, Ali taught that they were Islamic Moors from Africa. Less than a decade later, one of his followers, a door-to-door peddler named W.D. Fard, told his black American customers a different message. Fard agreed that Islam was the true religion of all black people, but where Ali taught that they were Moors, Fard claimed that black people are descendants of the lost Tribe of Shabazz.

These few examples from the interbellum period offer a cursory glimpse into a much larger history of innovative social groups in America that blended religious and racial identities and discourses. These movements are not unique to black Americans; rather, they are associated with various racial and ethnic groups including Native Americans, Asian Americans, white Americans, and of course, black Americans, among others. Though this blending of racial and religious discourses occurred in other countries as well, the unique combination of race-based slavery, immigration, a legal system sympathetic to religion, pervasive Protestantism, and the social construction of whiteness as a hegemonic discourse in the United States combined to create a particularly ripe environment for such *bricolage*.[1] These groups peaked in the 1900s, but the larger trend to blend religious and racial identities is a story that is as old as America itself.

---

[1] *Bricolage* here refers to the use of ideas and practices in existence to create new identities or cultural traditions and comes from the work of French anthropologist Claude Lévi-Strauss and his book *The Savage Mind*. For use of Lévi-Strauss's understanding of *bricolage* in the study of new religious movements, see Jacob S. Dorman, "'I Saw You Disappear with My Own Eyes': Hidden Transcripts of New York Black Israelite Bricolage," *Nova Religio: The Journal of Alternative and Emergent Religions* 11.1 (August 2007): 61–83.

Despite the pervasive presence of such groups throughout American history, the earliest scholars of American religious history ignored these groups in their comprehensive histories of American religion, where they offered sympathetic analyses of the Anglo Protestants who were their primary objects of study. Religious minorities, particularly those who blended religious and racial identities, were largely absent from their histories.[2] More recently, however, scholars inspired by racial, ethnic, and gender studies—and by sociocultural studies more broadly—have questioned the alleged Anglo-Protestant-centric model of American religious history. Instead, they argue that so-called new or minority religions are important or even mainstream elements of the complex tapestry that is American religious history.[3] Instead of a history dominated by a hegemonic Protestantism, their histories highlighted contestation, dialogue, and innovation where numerous marginal and new religious movements either influence or occupy the "center" of American religious history.

Today, scholars are prone to add racialized religions to this evolving story, yet to date, no one has offered a comprehensive and focused analysis of innovative social groups that combined religious and racial language to create unique identities. This book fills the resulting void. Through a variety of primary sources, this volume explores various intersections of racial and religious discourses and identities as manifest in a variety of new social groups (commonly termed "new" or "emergent" religious traditions).

Key terminology

This anthology primarily documents the blending of racial and religious rhetoric and identities in US history. Some eras in this history proved more fertile for this blending than others, but from the colonial period to the present, various leaders, preachers, rabbis, and self-proclaimed prophets often invoked religious and racial rhetoric to create what scholars have often called "new" or "emergent" religious movements. Elijah Mohammad, for example—the leader for roughly forty years of the Nation of Islam— only called upon black people to embrace his form of Islam. Leaders of the Ku Klux Klan only asked white people to embrace their form of Protestant Christianity. Where traditional forms of Islam and Protestantism claimed to be universal religions, the Nation of Islam and the Klan added racial elements to their evolving identities, thereby limiting group membership. The Nation of Islam and the Klan appealed to people on the alleged opposite ends of the racial spectrums as they called their followers to embrace

---

[2] Despite the immense size of Sydney Ahlstrom's classic tome *A Religious History of the American People* (over 1000 pages), the movements covered here are not more than mentioned in his narrative. Sydney Ahlstrom, *A Religious History of the American People* (New Haven, CT: Yale University Press, 1972). Also see, William Warren Sweet, *The Story of Religion in America* (New York: Harper & Row, 1983); and Edwin Scott Gaustad, *A Religious History of America* (New York: Harper & Row, 1990).

[3] For example, R. Laurence Moore argued that "outsider groups" belong "at the center" of American religious history. See R. Laurence Moore, *Religious Outsiders and the Making of Americans* (Oxford: Oxford University Press, 1987), xiv.

different religions, but despite their theological, racial, and religious differences, they shared a similar vocabulary as they constructed what historian Judith Weisenfeld called religio-racial identities.[4] These identities, predicated as they were on the blending of religious and racial rhetoric, would have been unthinkable for most of human history, as modern notions of race and religion are relatively recent historical inventions.

Modern notions of race, for example, contend that humans are classified into one of the several major races, with skin color or phenotype the primary indicator of one's race and racial heritage. This taxonomy—or ordering of racial differences—is neither a neutral nor a historical constant. Understandings of racial difference and racial identities began in American history at moments of first encounter between Native Americans, Europeans, and Africans. Race provided a system for ordering and categorizing human groups, and America's racial "order of things" was predicated on a racial hierarchy.[5] These encounters of difference took on loaded meaning based on prejudiced understandings of "the other" that preceded ideas about race itself.

As award-winning American writer Ta-Neshi Coates argued, "race is the child of racism, not the father."[6] When arguing a similar point, sociologist Jacqueline Battalora outlined how the racial category of whiteness emerged in the English colony of Virginia as a violent and destructive means of discrimination.[7] Laws that used the term "white" to demarcate a specific identity codified the already existent hierarchy of white over non-white into law. Euro-Americans attributed the cultural differences they observed to differences of phenotype they noted between themselves and Native Americans and Africans. These variations in phenotype were understood to be the cause of racial difference. In this way, the presumed superior civilization and religion of Europeans became a part of their racial identity, and, likewise, the presumed heathen cultures and primitive religions of Africans and Native Americans were inseparable from their racial identities. Through this process these imagined racial categories were perceived to be *real*, biological facts.

In the United States, notions of property, competition for economic and political power, and contests for social domination shaped understandings of racial identity and racial difference. Race remains intertwined with the issues of politics, economics, power, and property. As argued by legal scholar and critical race theorist Cheryl Harris, "it was the interaction between conceptions of race and property that played a critical role in establishing and maintaining racial and economic subordination."[8] Harris argued that whiteness is a form of property in American history and culture. It is legally, socially, culturally, and politically protected and maintained. Non-whites not only lack

---

[4] Judith Weisenfeld, *New World A-Coming: Black Religion and Racial Identity during the Great Migration* (New York: New York University Press, 2016).

[5] In *The Order of Things: An Archaeology of the Human Sciences* (1966; New York: Pantheon Books, 1970), Michel Foucault notes the human propensity for imposing order on things that are the "Same."

[6] Ta-Neshi Coates, *Between the World and Me* (New York: Speigel & Grau, 2015), 7.

[7] Jacqueline Battalora, "White People Did Not Exist Until 1681," http://www.jacquelinebattalora.com/white-people-did-not-exist-until-1681/.

[8] Cheryl Harris, "Whiteness as Property," *Harvard Law Review* 106.8 (1993): 1716.

that property but that absence of whiteness has allowed them to be seen as property. Part of what enables the protection and power of whiteness is settler colonialism. Since the US "was created as an Anglo-American republic of White-only citizens," it is a racial state.[9] To fulfill its manifest destiny, the nation-state needed economic power, which was achieved with slavery, and western expansion, which required the defeat and/or relocation of Native Americans. Thus, notions of "race" are major forces in American culture broadly and certainly in American religious history specifically.

Collectively, this analysis suggests that the modern category of race is neither a natural nor timeless category. Instead, it emerged at particular moments in history and served the interests of the people who developed and deployed it. We can also apply these insights to the modern category of religion, which has a similar yet distinct history. Religion, we are often taught, is a universal and transhistorical aspect of humanity. People may or may not be religious, we learn, but religion is always present in some form, either forced on people by the state, or in free societies, something individuals choose to embrace or reject. We also learn that religion is a sphere of life that might overlap with the state if the state enforces some degree of religious practice or belief, but a sphere ideally relegated to the private, personal, or apolitical. In short, we learn that religion is potentially—and ideally—separate from politics.

Scholars have repeatedly demonstrated, however, that this understanding of religion has a distinct history that extends back to the early 1600s, specifically to England, where scholars, philosophers, and theologians experimented with traditional understandings of the term "religion."[10] The word "religion" comes from the Latin *religio*. According to historian Brent Nongbri, "the word [*religio*] had a variety of meanings in antiquity and that none of those corresponds to the modern notions of religion."[11] As Christianity spread throughout the Roman Empire in the early centuries of the common era, Christianity adopted the word *religio* and modified its meaning in multiple times and contexts, but these modifications never resembled modern notions of religion. Additionally, *religio* remained a proprietary category that Christians used primarily to talk about themselves and other Christians.

The older and more traditional notions of "religion" began to change in the 1600s within the larger contexts of religious wars, the Enlightenment, and European colonialism. According to prominent anthropologist Talal Asad, the Enlightenment and its emphasis on rationality effectively motivated European thinkers to reconceive of "religion" as a private and interior matter separate from politics. Additionally, in the context of colonialism, European explorers and missionaries encountered a variety of new societies and cultures. When confronted with the previously unknown, they

---

[9] Sylvester Johnson, "What is 'American' in American Religion?," an online forum with Kathryn Gin Lum and Rhys H. Williams (February 2014), Center for the Study of Religion and American Culture, http://raac.iupui.edu/forum/what-american-american-religion-february-2014/

[10] See Peter Harrison, *"Religion" and the Religions in the English Enlightenment* (New York: Cambridge University Press, 1990).

[11] Brent Nongbri, *Before Religion* (New Haven, CT: Yale University Press, 2012), 26.

abandoned their old notions of "religion" as they decided that other groups "had religion" as well.[12] For their part, native cultures either rejected or appropriated the term "religion" to suit their interests, often inventing native words or modifying existing words to reflect their understandings of the category of "religion."[13]

Simultaneously, Europeans not only classified native cultures as "religions," they also ranked them in a religious hierarchy with "Christianity" at the top and "heathenism" or "paganism" at the bottom.[14] "Heathenism" and "paganism" were also racial categories, as Europeans classified non-European "races" under the pejorative categories of "heathen" and "pagan." In these religio-racial taxonomies, white Christians thought themselves the most advanced and sophisticated, while "native heathens" or "pagans" were considered the least advanced or sophisticated. The so-called "heathens" and "pagans" rejected this taxonomy, but their objections often fell on deaf ears as European colonizers exported their novel notions of "religion" and "race" all around the globe, including North America, where the founders of the United States embraced them unequivocally. As history subsequently demonstrated, the categories of "religion" and "race" proved some of the more pervasive and potent categories in American history.

In light of religion's slippery and historically contingent meanings, the term "new religious movements" is similarly problematic. The academic study of so-called "new religious movements" emerged in the wake of the Second World War when scholars developed various methods and methodologies to study the groups they called "new religious movements."[15] This branch of study became popular in the field of sociology, although scholars in religious studies departments became the dominant voices in this subfield in the 1970s and 1980s. Today, the study of "new religious movements" is a staple in the academic study of religion.

In the past seventy or so years, scholars have disagreed over the terminology they use to study these groups ("cults," "sects," "new religious movements," and "emergent religions" are some of the more common terms in the academic study of the groups that scholars commonly reference in these discussions), they have debated which groups belong in the preferred category, and they have disagreed over the manner in which scholars should approach these groups. Furthermore, the study of new religious

---

[12] David Chidester, "Anchoring Religion in the World: A Southern African History of Comparative Religion," *Religion* 26 (1996): 141–160.

[13] See Talal Asad, *Genealogies of Religion: Discipline and Reasons of Power in Christianity and Islam* (Baltimore, MD: Johns Hopkins University Press, 1993); and Tisa Wenger, *We Have a Religion: The 1920s Pueblo Indian Dance Controversy and American Religious Freedom* (Chapel Hill, NC: University of North Carolina Press, 2009).

[14] For a discussion of the relationship between the categories race and religion, see Sylvester Johnson, *African American Religions, 1500–2000: Colonialism, Democracy, and Freedom* (New York: Cambridge University Press, 2015); and Malory Nye, "Race and Religion: Postcolonial Formations of Power and Whiteness," *Method & Theory in the Study of Religion* (2018): 28 pages, DOI: https://doi.org/10.1163/15700682-12341444.

[15] For a brief history of the study of new religions movements, see W. Michael Ashcraft, "A History of the Study of New Religious Movements," *Nova Religio: The Journal of Alternative and Emergent Religions* 9.1 (August 2005): 93–105.

movements (or whatever term the scholar prefers) tends to examine smaller and recently conceived social groups, particularly those outside the Christian traditions. These studies typically omit some of the groups that we include in this volume. Without naturalizing or reinforcing any notion of "authentic" new religious movements, the editors of this volume include a variety of social groups that offer innovative blending of religious and racial discourses, focusing specifically on groups commonly labeled "new religious movements."

We are not arguing that these are racialized new religious movements; rather, we seek to identify and highlight that the blending of religious and racial discourses is a persistent theme in American history. The movements and documents included here prompt a number of questions about American history and culture: How do we as scholars account for this persistent theme? To what extent is this a uniquely American phenomenon? Does this trend seem to have peaked in the past or is it just as prevalent today? What historical forces help account for this trend's popularity?

How to use this book

The following chapters of *Race and New Religious Movements in the USA* each focus on a particular social group that blended religious and racial rhetoric or that situated racial discourses as important or even essential aspects of their theologies. One could rightfully argue that perhaps all religions have addressed the issue of race, so any attempt to document the blending of religious and racial rhetoric is necessarily incomplete. The editors of this volume would agree. This book specifically addresses the larger, more influential, or more innovative social groups who taught and who believed that religio-racial theologies are essential aspects of their identities, paying particular attention to groups commonly designated new religious movements or emergent religions. We organized these chapters chronologically, typically by the group's founding date.[16]

Each chapter begins with an Editors' Introduction that offers historical and cultural context and background. These introductions include brief biographical information about the founder (when relevant) and cursory information about the group's history. The introductions also discuss the primary sources that follow the introductions. Primary sources comprise the majority of the chapters, followed by recommendations for additional reading. Rather than indicate spelling in context, with either the Latin [*sic*] or square brackets around a correction to note what may read as a misspelling or grammatical error, all documents here are transcribed as in their original rendering. Unless preceded by "Editors' Note" and an explanation, what appears in brackets is original to the text.

---

[16] Some of these groups do not have founding dates *per se*.

2

The Code of Handsome Lake

Editors' Introduction: Born around 1735 in present-day New York, Handsome Lake was a Native American who in the early 1800s became a religious leader and prophet of the Iroquois people. His teachings blended native Haudenosaunee traditions with Protestant Christianity (more specifically, Quakerism) to revive the culture and religion of the beleaguered Iroquois. Handsome Lake was born during a period of relative abundance for the Seneca, but the era of relative peace and prosperity that accompanied Handsome Lake's youth came to an abrupt end after the American Revolution, when his people lost most of their land and were forced to live on reservations. A period of rapid cultural decay soon followed as dislocation, disease, poverty, wars, and alcoholism combined to almost destroy their traditions, including their religion and the family unit itself that formed the basis of their society. Handsome Lake was not immune to these problems, as he drank excessively for many years.

Things began to change for Handsome Lake in 1799 when he alleged that the Creator and four messengers appeared in a series of visions and gave Handsome Lake information and teachings that formed the basis of a revitalization movement designed to provide the Iroquois people with a path forward in an otherwise rapidly changing and deleterious environment. Handsome Lake subsequently taught this message and encouraged his followers to learn English, to honor the sanctity of marriage, to avoid divorce, not to have abortions, and to respect and nurture their children and the elderly. He also cautioned against gossip, stealing, and witchcraft; and he repeatedly told his followers to avoid "strong drink," or alcohol, entirely. These teachings formed the basis of the Gaiwiio (or the "Good Word") that Handsome Lake taught the remainder of his life.

Handsome Lake gained a modest audience, but he also had many critics. Chief among them were "traditionalists," who argued that Handsome Lake's teachings resembled the Quakers' moral and social proscriptions and were little more than blatant appropriations of Christianity. That Handsome Lake invoked terms and concepts long associated with Christianity (such as sin, evil, concerns with the end times, the devil, and the reality of heaven and hell) only added to their argument. Other would-be followers simply converted to Christianity and rejected Handsome Lake's teachings as mired in his native "paganism." For these reasons, Handsome Lake was only modestly successful during his lifetime as he gained some Iroquois followers, although he did gain the attention of some white admirers, including President Thomas Jefferson, who in 1803 wrote a letter to Handsome Lake supporting his work.

After his death in 1815, however, some followers began to gather his teachings, the majority of which were recited and later written down. Led primarily by his grandson James Johnson, these teachings, in addition to writings and teachings provided by people considered "minor prophets" in this new religion, were compiled into *The Code of Handsome Lake*, which provided the canonical text for his followers. Handsome Lake's followers recited *The Code of Handsome Lake* either in part or full, particularly at the annual "Six Nation meetings."

The writings below are excerpted from *The Code of Handsome Lake*, beginning with a story that describes how the devil tricked white people into coming to America to harm the natives. The subsequent writings elaborate on many of the previously mentioned moral and sociocultural proscriptions. They also describe how the Great Creator displays a sincere desire to protect and restore Handsome Lake's followers, either in this world or the next.

Documents

Document One: *The Code of Handsome Lake, the Seneca Prophet*, by Arthur C. Parker (1913)

[*Editors' Note*: Many of the following writings from *The Code of Handsome Lake* are divided into "Sections." These "Sections" typically begin with "Now another message" and end with "So they said. Eniaiehuk." We have omitted these lines, or similar introductions and conclusions, from the text below.]

How the White Race Came to America and Why the Gaiwiio Became a Necessity
Related by So-Son-Do-Wa

Now this happened a long time ago and across the great salt sea, odji'ke'dāgi'ga, that stretches east. There is, so it seems, a world there and soil like ours. There in the great queen's country where swarmed many people—so many that they crowded upon one another and had no place for hunting—there lived a great queen. Among her servants was a young preacher of the queen's religion, so, it is said.

Now this happened. The great queen requested the preacher to clean some old volumes which she had concealed in a hidden chest. So he obeyed and when he had cleaned the last book, which was at the bottom of the chest, he opened it and looked about and listened, for truly he had no right to read the book and wanted no one to detect him. He read. It was a great book and told him many things which he never knew before. Therefore he was greatly worried. He read of a great man who had been a prophet and the son of the Great Ruler. He had been born on the earth and the white men to whom he preached killed him. Now moreover the prophet had promised to return and become the King. In three days he was to come and then in forty to start his kingdom. This did not happen as his followers had expected and so they despaired. Then said one chief follower, "Surely he will come again sometime, we must watch for him."

Then the young preacher became worried for he had discovered that his god was not on earth to see. He was angry moreover because his teachers had deceived him. So then he went to the chief of preachers and asked him how it was that he had deceived him. Then the chief preacher said, "Seek him out and you will find him for indeed we think he does live on earth." Even so, his heart was angry but he resolved to seek.

On the morning of the next day he looked out from the opening of his room and saw out in the river a beautiful island and he marveled that he had never seen it before. He continued to gaze and as he did he saw among the trees a castle of gold and he marveled that he had not seen the castle of gold before. Then he said, "So beautiful a castle on so beautiful an isle must indeed be the abode of him whom I seek." Immediately he put on his clothes and went to the men who had taught him and they wondered and said, "Indeed it must be as you say." So then together they went to the river and when they came to the shore they saw that it was spanned by a bridge of shining gold. Then one of the great preachers fell down and read from his book a long prayer and arising he turned his back upon the island and fled for he was afraid to meet the lord. Then with the young man the other crossed the bridge and he knelt on the grass and he cried loud and groaned his prayer but when he arose to his feet he too fled and would not look again at the house-the castle of gold.

Then was the young man disgusted, and boldly he strode toward the house to attend to the business which he had in mind. He did not cry or pray and neither did he fall to his knees for he was not afraid. He knocked at the door and a handsome smiling man welcomed him in and said, "Do not be afraid of me." Then the smiling man in the castle of gold said, "I have wanted a young man such as you for some time. You are wise and afraid of nobody. Those older men were fools and would not have listened to me (direct) though they might listen to some one whom I had instructed. Listen to me and most truly you shall be rich. Across the ocean that lies toward the sunset is another world and a great country and a people whom you have never seen. Those people are virtuous, they have no unnatural evil habits and they are honest. A great reward is yours if you will help me. Here are five things that men and women enjoy; take them to these people and make them as white men are. Then shall you be rich and powerful and you may become the chief of all great preachers here."

So then the young man took the bundle containing the five things and made the bargain. He left the island and looking back saw that the bridge had disappeared and before he had turned his head the castle had gone and then as he looked the island itself vanished.

Now then the young man wondered if indeed he had seen his lord for his mind had been so full of business that he had forgotten to ask. So he opened his bundle of five things and found a flask of rum, a pack of playing cards, a handful of coins, a violin and a decayed leg bone. Then be thought the things very strange and he wondered if indeed his lord would send such gifts to the people across the water of the salt lake; but he remembered his promise,

The young man looked about for a suitable man in whom to confide his secret and after some searching he found a man named Columbus and to him he confided the story. Then did Columbus secure some big canoes and raise up wings and he sailed away. He sailed many days and his warriors became angry and cried that the chief who led them was a deceiver. They planned to behead him but he heard of the plan and promised that on the next day he would discover the new country. The next morning came and then did Columbus discover America. Then the boats turned back and reported their find to the whole world. Then did great ships come, a good many. Then did they bring many bundles of the five things and spread the gifts to all the men of the great earth island.

Then did the invisible man of the river island laugh and then did he say, "These cards will make them gamble away their wealth and idle their time; this money wilt make them dishonest and covetous and they will forget their old laws; this fiddle will make them dance with their arms about their wives and bring about a time of tattling and idle gossip; this rum will turn their minds to foolishness and they will barter their country for baubles; then will this secret poison eat the life from their blood and crumble their bones." So said the invisible man and be was Hanīsse'ono, the evil one.

Now all this was done and when afterward he saw the havoc and the misery his work had done he said, "I think I have made an enormous mistake for I did not dream that these people would suffer so." Then did even the devil himself lament that his evil had been so great.

So after the swarms of white men came and misery was thrust upon the Ongwe-oweh the Creator was sorry for his own people whom he had molded from the soil of the earth of this Great Island, and he spoke to his four messengers and many times they tried to tell right men the revelations of the Creator but none would listen. Then they found our head man sick. Then they heard him speak to the sun and to the moon and they saw his sickness. Then they knew that he suffered because of the cunning evils that Hanīsse'ono had given the Ongwe-oweh. So then they knew that he was the one. He was the one who should hear and tell Gai'wiio'. But when Ganio'dai'io' spoke the evil being ceased his lament and sought to obstruct Gai'wiio', for he claimed to be master.

The Gai'wiio' came from Hodiänok'doo Hĕd'iohe', the Great Ruler, to the Hadiöyǎ'geono, the four messengers. From them it was transmitted to Ganio'dai'io', Handsome Lake who taught it to Skandyo'gwadī (Owen Blacksnake) and to his own grandson, Sos'heowǎ (James Johnson). Blacksnake taught it to Henry Stevens (Ganishando), who taught it to Soson'dowa, Edward Cornplanter. "So I know that I have the true words and I preach them," adds Cornplanter.

Section 1

"Now the beings spoke saying, 'We must now relate our message. We will uncover the evil upon the earth and show how men spoil the laws the Great Ruler has made and thereby made him angry.'

"'The Creator made man a living creature.'

"'Four words tell a great story of wrong and the Creator is sad because of the trouble they bring, so go and tell your people.'

"'The first word is One'ga'. It seems that you never have known that this word stands for a great and monstrous evil and has reared a high mound of bones. Ga'nigoĕntdo'tha, you lose your minds and one'ga' causes it all. Alas, many are fond of it and are too fond of it. So now all must now say, "I will use it nevermore. As long as I live, as long as the number of my days is I will never use it again. I now stop." So must all say when they hear this message.' Now the beings, the servants of the Great Ruler, the messengers of him who created us, said this. Furthermore they said that the Creator made one'ga' and gave it to our younger brethren, the white man, as a medicine but they use it for evil for they drink it for other purposes than medicine and drink instead of work and idlers drink one'ga'. No, the Creator did not make it for you."

Section 2

"Now spoke the beings and said, 'We now speak of the second word. This makes the Creator angry. The word is Got'go.

Witches are people without their right minds. They make disease and spread sickness to make the living die. They cut short the numbered days, for the Creator has given each person a certain number of days in which to live in this world.

"'Now this must you do: When you have told this message and the witches hear it they will confess before all the people and will say, "I am doing this evil thing but now I cease it, forever, as long as I live." Some witches are more evil and can not speak in public so these must come privately and confess to you, Handsome Lake, or a preacher of this Gai'wiio'. Now some are most evil and they must go far out upon an abandoned trail and there they must confess before the Creator alone. This course may be taken by witches of whom no one knows.

Now when they go they must say:

"Our Creator, O listen to me!
I am a miserable creature.
I think that way
So now I cease.
Now this is appointed
For all of my days,
As long as I live here
In this earth-world.
I have spoken."

"'In this manner all must say and say truly, then the prayer will be sufficient.'"

Section 3

"Now the beings spoke again saying, 'This is the third word. It is a sad one and the Creator is very sad because of this third word. It seems that you have never known that a great pile of human bodies lies dead because of this word, Ono'ityi'yende, the nigâ'hos'sää', the secret poisons in little bundles named Gawênnodûs'hä (compelling charms). Now the Creator who made us commands that they who do this evil, when they hear this message, must stop it immediately and do it nevermore while they live upon this earth-world. It matters not how much destruction they have wrought—let them repent and not fail for fear the Creator will not accept them as his own.'"

Section 4

"'Now another word. It is sad. It is the fourth word. It is the way Yondwi'nias swa'yas.

"'Now the Creator ordained that women should bear children.

"'Now a certain young married woman had children and suffered much. Now she is with child again and her mother wishing to prevent further sufferings designs to administer a medicine to cut off the child and to prevent forever other children from coming. So the mother makes the medicine and gives it. Now when she does this she forever cuts away her daughter's string of children. Now it is because of such things that the Creator is sad. He created life to live and he wishes such evils to cease. He wishes those who employ such medicines to cease such practices forevermore. Now they must stop when they hear this message. Go and tell your people.'"

Section 16

"'Now another message.

"'Tell your people that the Creator is sad because of what they are doing.

"'Some people live together well as man and wife and family, but the man of the family uses strong drink. Then when he comes home he lifts up his child to fondle it and he is drunk. Now we, the messengers of the Creator, say that this is not right for if a man filled with strong drink touches his child he burns its blood. Tell your people to heed this warning.'"

Section 19

"'Now another message.

"'Now the Creator of mankind ordained that people should live to an old age. He appointed that when a woman becomes old she should be without strength and unable to work. Now the Creator says that it is a great wrong to be unkind to our grandmothers. The Creator forbids unkindness to the old. We, the messengers, say it. The Creator appointed this way: he designed that an old woman should be as a child again and when she becomes so the Creator wishes the grandchildren to help her, for only because she is, they are. Whosoever does right to the aged does right in the sight of the Creator.'"

Section 25

"'Three things that our younger brethren (the white people) do are right to follow.

"'Now, the first. The white man works on a tract of cultivated ground and harvests food for his family. So if he should die they still have the ground for help. If any of your people have cultivated ground let them not be proud on that account. If one is proud there is sin within him but if there be no pride there is no sin.

"'Now, the second thing. It is the way a white man builds a house. He builds one warm and fine appearing so if he dies the family has the house for help. Whoso among you does this does right, always providing there is no pride. If there is pride it is evil but if there is none, it is well.

"'Now the third. The white man keeps horses and cattle. Now there is no evil in this for they are a help to his family. So if he dies his family has the stock for help. Now all this is right if there is no pride. No evil will follow this practice if the animals are well fed, treated kindly and not overworked. Tell this to your people.'"

Section 26
"'Now another message to tell your relatives.

"'This concerns education. It is concerning studying in English schools.

"'Now let the Council appoint twelve people to study, two from each nation of the six. So many white people are about you that you must study to know their ways.'"

Section 38
"'Now another message for your people.

"'If all the world would repent the earth would become as new again. Because of sin the under-world is crumbling with decay. The world is full of sin. Truly, this is so.'"

Section: 40
"'Now another message to tell your people.

"'The religious leaders and the chiefs must enforce obedience to the teachings of Gai'wiio'.'"

Section 41
"'This thing will happen when it is new.

"'Truly men will repent and reform but it will happen that three certain ones will neither confess nor reform. Nothing will induce them to confess.

"'There are grades of sin: the sins of Hasan'owa:n'ê', the sins of Honon'diont and the sins of the ordinary people.

"'Now when you are preaching repentance, Gaiänt'wakâ will say that these men when they pass from this world are most vile. He will say, "Let us cast them into the water for they are not worthy to be dressed for the grave. The Creator will not receive them." Now no one will object to what Gaiänt'wakâ says.'"

Now this thing did happen as predicted and when the messenger arose the first thing that he did was to spread the news and give the command that it must not be done. "Now they said, 'The Creator will not give up hope of them until they pass from the earth. It is only then that they can lose their souls if they have not repented. So the Creator always hopes for repentance.'"

Section 43
"'Now another message to tell your people.

"'Good food is turned into evil drink. Now some have said that there is no harm in partaking of fermented liquids.

"'Then let this plan be followed: let men gather in two parties, one having a feast of food, apples and corn, and the other have cider and whiskey. Let the parties be equally divided and matched and let them commence their feasting at the same time. When the feast is finished you will see those who drank the fermented juices murder one of their own party but not so with those who ate food only.'"

Section 44

"'You have had the constant fear that the white race would exterminate you. The Creator will care for his Oñgwe'owe (real people).'"

Section 45

"'Now another message for your people.

"'Some of your relatives and descendants will say, "We lack an understanding of this religion," and this will be the cry of the people. But even we, the servants of the Creator, do not understand all things. Now some when they are turned to the right way will say, "I will continue so for all of my days," but this will not be so for they surely will fall short in some things. This is why even we can not understand all things.'"

Section 49

"'There is a dispute in the heaven-world between two parties. It is a controversy about you, the children of earth. Two great beings are disputing—one is the Great Ruler, the Creator, and the other is the evil-minded spirit.

"'You who are on earth do not know the things of heaven.

"'Now the evil one said, "I am the ruler of the earth because when I command I speak but once and man obeys."

"'Then answered the Great Ruler, "The earth is mine for I have created it and you have helped me in no part."

"'Now the evil one answered, "I do not acknowledge that you have created the earth and that I helped in no part, but I say that when I say to men, 'Obey me,' they straightway obey, but they do not hear your voice."

"'Then the Great Ruler replied, "Truly the children are my own for they have never done evil."

"'And the evil one answering said, "Nay, the children are mine for when I bid one saying, 'Pick up that stick and strike your fellow,' they obey me quickly. Aye, the children are mine."

"'Then was the Great Ruler very sad and he said, "Once more will I send my messengers and tell them my heart and they will tell my people and thus I will redeem my own."

"'Then the evil one replied, "Even so it will not be long before men transgress your commands. I can destroy it with a word for they will do my bidding. Verily I delight in the name Hanîsse'ono. It is very true that they who love my name, though they be on the other side of the earth, will find me at their backs the moment they pronounce my name."

"'Now at that time the Great Ruler spoke to the four messengers saying, "Go tell mankind that at present they must not call me Hawi'n'io', the Great Ruler, until a later time, for the Evil One calls himself the Ruler of Mankind. So now whosoever is turned into my way must say when he calls upon my name, Hodiänok'doo Hêd'iohe' our Creator. So also whosoever speaks the name of the evil one must say, Segoewa'tha, The Tormentor. Then will the evil one know that you have discovered who he is, for it is he who will punish the wicked when they depart from this world.'"

Section 62

"'Now there are some who have boasted that they could drink all the strong drink in the world. Now we, the messengers, say that they who thus idly boast will never live to accomplish what they boast. White men will ever distil the evil liquor.'"

Section 70

"Now we say that you must tell your friends and relatives that there will be a time when all the earth will withhold its sustaining foods. Then will come the end of the world and those who refuse to believe in Gai'wiio' will suffer great hardships."

Section 71

"Now we think that a time will come when a great plague will kill many people and no one will know its cause. Then will you know that the end is near and those who do not believe will suffer great hardships."

Section 72

"Now we think that a time will come when a woman will be seen performing her witch spells in the daylight. Then will you know that the end is near. She will run through the neighborhood boasting how many she has slain by her sorcery. Then will you see how she who refused to believe in Gai'wiio' will suffer punishment."

Section 73

"In that time you will hear many rumors of men who say, 'I have spoken with the Creator.' So also will you see many wonders but they will not endure for they will be the work of the evil spirit.

"Verily we say that there will be none other than you who will receive a message from the Creator through us. This truth will be proclaimed when the end comes."

Section 76

"Now we think that the Creator will stop the earth and heavens. All the powers of nature will he suspend. Now they will see this who refuse to believe in Gai'wiio'."

Section 77

"Now we think that when the end comes the earth will be destroyed by fire and not one upon it will escape for all the earth will be enveloped in flames and all those who refuse to believe in Gai'wiio' will be in it."

Section 101

"Now as they looked they saw a being walking about as if he were the master of the lodge. He seemed continually distorting himself. At times horns shot out from his forehead, at times a cloven foot appeared and at times a tail was visible.

"Then said the four messengers to Ganiodai'io', 'That being is the punisher. It is he who torments those who have refused the words of Gai'wiio' when they heard them on the earth.'"

Section 102
"In a loud voice the punisher cried to a certain person saying, 'Come hither.' The punisher held a drinking vessel in his hand and within it was molten metal and thrusting it in the hands of the man he had called he said, 'Now warm yourself again as was your custom while on the earth for you loved hot drink.' Now the man pleaded but the punisher compelled him to swallow the molten metal. Then the man screamed in a loud voice and fell prone upon the ground with vapor steaming from his throat. Now he cried no more."

"Then said the four messengers, 'You have seen the manner of punishing those who persist in taking the fiery drink.'"

Additional reading

Dennis, Matthew. *Seneca Possessed: Indians, Witchcraft, and Power in the Early American Republic* (Philadelphia, PA: University of Pennsylvania Press, 2010).
Irwin, Lee. *Coming Down From Above: Prophecy, Resistance, and Renewal in Native American Religions* (Norman, OK: University of Oklahoma Press, 2008).
Tooker, Elizabeth. "On the Development of the Handsome Lake Religion," *Proceedings of the American Philosophical Society* 133.1 (March 1989): 35–50.
Wallace, Anthony. *The Death and Rebirth of the Seneca* (New York: Vintage Books, 1972).

3

Conjure

Editors' Introduction: Conjure, sometimes called Hoodoo or rootwork, brought together various West African ritual practices and healing rites within the contextual frame of slavery in the South. A simple definition of Conjure is the use of natural things to achieve supernatural ends. The aims of Conjure typically centered on healing, helping, or harming. While processes of helping, healing, and harming might not initially seem supernatural, Conjure theorized that the particular use of natural items could bring about these changes. Additionally, many West and Central African traditions viewed medicine as a religious phenomenon, which connected the healing aspect of Conjure to African Americans' African roots. To achieve these goals, a conjure man or conjure woman (those with this knowledge) would use roots, water (particularly river water), herbs, auspicious dirts (such as graveyard dirt), and additional organic substances (ranging from hair to blood) and inorganic items (such as perfume or ribbon) to create powerful objects, poultices, amulets, drinks, and more. Typically, conjure men and conjure women passed on their knowledge through means of oral tradition, and when they did so, emphasizing the power of Africa or Africa as a place of knowledge's origin was not uncommon. This placed Conjure outside the power of whites and squarely within the religious worlds of black Americans.

   While much of the early historiography renders the relationship between Christianity and Conjure as "inimical," Religious Studies scholar Yvonne Chireau has argued that none of the justifications for that statement do "complete justice to describing the relationships of accommodation and assimilation that allowed practitioners of Conjure and Christianity to reconcile their beliefs." She continues, "as religious traditions, both Conjure and Christianity provided unique resources that addressed diverse cultural needs and interests within African American life."[1] Chireau encourages scholars to see the ways in which Conjure and Christianity asked and answered different theological and religious questions; whereas one focused on the transcendent and

---

[1] Yvonne Chireau, "Conjure and Christianity in the Nineteenth Century: Religious Elements in African American Magic," *Religion and American Culture: A Journal of Interpretation* 7.2 (Summer 1997): 226–227.

life after death, the other offered explanations for what happened in this world and offered a means of power over this world. In this way, the religions of Christianity and Hoodoo were not necessarily at odds; instead, practitioners could ascribe to both concurrently.

Although some white folkways also offered alternative forms of medicine, black Americans, especially southern blacks, practiced Conjure. (Though there is evidence of southern whites having concerns about the power—real or perceived—of Conjure.) The power that Conjure offered was very significant. Slavery was a system that denied black Americans their political and social personhood; Conjure offered alternative means of power and control. Though practitioners had limited control over their everyday lives, Hoodoo opened up mediums of religious power outside of the purview of whites. Additionally, the healing component of Conjure offered medical treatment in a societal context that refused such treatment to southern blacks, first during slavery and then afterwards in the era of Jim Crow.

Though scholars typically emphasize the late eighteenth century and the nineteenth century when discussing Conjure, the tradition continues today. In the first half of the twentieth century, many conjure men and conjure women offered their products and advice through mail-order catalogs, which got some in trouble with federal law on charges of mail fraud (with courts viewing Conjure as akin to snake oil). While this practice of mail-order Hoodoo lost popularity in the later part of the twentieth century, some still sell products, books, and consultations over the internet.

Document One is an excerpt from Jacob Stroyer's *Sketches of My Life in the South*. Stroyer was born in South Carolina, the son of a "salt-water" slave from Sierra Leone. After the Civil War, Stroyer became a preacher in the northeast and published his autobiography. This section of *Sketches of My Life in the South* discusses the "custom of witches among slaves." The use of the term "witches" echoes how many of the nineteenth century viewed Conjure and similar African practices like Obeah. Document Two is also an excerpt from a slave narrative. It comes from William Wells Brown's slave narrative *My Southern Home*. Brown was an escaped slave and outspoken abolitionist. This segment of *My Southern Home* recounts "Uncle Dinkie," a conjure man living on the same plantation as he in Missouri. Document Three is a newspaper article from the 1880s that discusses Conjure, namely a Florida woman who was victim to a supposed hoodooing. This report illustrates how those who utilized the power of Conjure understood themselves to be in larger networks. Additionally, the newspaper likely sensationalized the story to some extent, as was common in the general media. Finally, Document Four is an excerpt from anthropologist, folklorist, and novelist Zora Neale Hurston's 1931 study "Hoodoo in America." This particular excerpt focuses on the power and stories of Marie Laveau (spelled Leveau by Hurston), a powerful New Orleans Voudou priestess and famous "voodoo queen." New Orleans Voudou was distinctive from southern Conjure but also overlapped with it, especially in regards to the use of natural objects to achieve supernatural ends. Some of these documents used slave dialect, which is retained here.

Documents

Document One: Jacob Stroyer, *Sketches of My Life in the South, Part I* (Salem, MA: The Salem Press, 1879), 42–45.

Custom of Witches among Slaves

The witches among slaves were supposed to have been persons who worked with them every day, and were called old hags or jack lanterns. Those, both men and women, who, when they grew old looked odd, were supposed to be witches. Sometimes after eating supper the negroes would gather in each other's cabins which looked over the large openings on the plantation, and when they would see a light at a great distance and saw it open and shut they would say "there is an old hag," and if it came from a certain direction where those lived whom they called witches, one would say "dat looks like old Aunt Susan," another said "no, dat look like man hag," still another "I tink dat look like ole Uncle Renty."

When the light disappeared they said that the witch had got into the plantation and changed itself into a person, and went around on the place talking with the people like others until those whom it wanted to bewitch went to bed, then it would change itself to a witch again. They claimed that they rode human beings like horses, and the spittle that run on the side of the cheek when one slept was the bridle that the witch rode with. Sometimes a baby would be smothered by its mother and they would charge it to a witch. If they went out hunting at night and were lost it was believed that a witch led them off, especially if they fell into a pond or creek. I was very much troubled with witches when a little boy and am now sometimes, but it is only when I eat a hearty supper and then go to bed. It was said by some of the slaves that the witches would sometimes go into the rooms of the cabins and hide themselves until the family went to bed, and when any one claimed that they went into the apartment before bed time and thought he saw a witch, if they had an old bible in the cabin that would be taken into the room and the person who carried the bible would say as he went in "In de name of de Fader and of de Son and de Hole Gos wat you want?" then the bible would be put in the corner where the person thought he saw the witch as it was generally believed that if this were done the witch could not stay. When they could not get the bible they used red pepper and salt pounded together and scattered in the room, but in this case they generally felt the effects of it more than the witch, for when they went to bed it made them cough all night. When I was a little boy my mother sent me into the cabin room for something, and as I got in I saw something black and white, but did not stop to see what it was, and running out said there was a witch in the room, but father having been born in Africa did not believe in such things, so he called me a fool and whipped me and the witch got scared and ran out of the door; it turned out to be our own black and white cat that we children played with every day. Although it proved to be the cat, and father did not believe in witches, still I held the idea that there were such things, for I thought as the majority of the people believed it that they ought to know more than one man. Sometime after I was free, in traveling from Columbia to Camden, a distance of about thirty-two miles; night overtook me when about half way there, it was very dark and rainy, and as I approached a creek I saw a great number of lights of those witches opening and shutting, I did not know what to do and thought of turning back, but when I looked behind I saw some witches in the distance, so I said if I turn back those will meet me and I will be in as much danger as if I go on, and I thought of what some of my fellow negroes had said about their leading men into ponds and creeks; there was a creek just ahead, so I concluded that I should be drowned that night, however I went on, as I saw no chance of turning back. When I came near the creek one of the witches flew into my face; I jumped back and grasped it, but it proved to be one of those little lightning bugs, and I thought if all the witches were like that one I should not be in any great danger from them.

Document Two: William Wells Brown, *My Southern Home: or, The South and Its People* (Boston, MA: A. G. Brown & Co., 1880), 72–81.

Nearly every large plantation, with any considerable number of negroes, had at least one, who laid claim to be a fortune-teller, and who was regarded with more than common respect by his fellow-slaves. Dinkie, a full-blooded African, large in frame, coarse featured, and claiming to be a descendant of a king in his native land, was the oracle on the "Poplar Farm." At the time of which I write, Dinkie was about fifty years of age, and had lost an eye, and was, to say the least, a very ugly-looking man.

No one in that section was considered so deeply immersed in voudooism, goopherism, and fortune-telling, as he . . .

A new overseer was employed, by Dr. Gaines, to take charge of "Poplar Farm." His name was Grove Cook, and he was widely known as a man of ability in managing plantations, and in raising a large quantity of produce from a given number of hands. Cook was called a "hard overseer." The negroes dreaded his coming, and, for weeks before his arrival, the overseer's name was on every slave's tongue.

Cook came, he called the negroes up, men and women; counted them, looked them over as a purchaser would a drove of cattle that he intended to buy. As he was about to dismiss them he saw Dinkie come out of his cabin. The sharp eye of the overseer was at once on him.

"Who is that n—?" inquired Cook.

"That is Dinkie," replied Dr. Gaines.

"What is his place?" continued the overseer.

"Oh, Dinkie is a gentleman at large!" was the response.

"Have you any objection to his working?"

"None, whatever."

"Well, sir," said Cook, "I'll put him to work to-morrow morning."

Dinkie was called up and counted in.

At the roll call, the following morning, all answered except the conjurer; he was not there.

The overseer inquired for Dinkie, and was informed that he was still asleep.

"I will bring him out of his bed in a hurry," said Cook, as he started towards the negro's cabin. Dinkie appeared at his door, just as the overseer was approaching.

"Follow me to the barn," said the impatient driver to the negro. "I make it a point always to whip a n—, the first day that I take charge of a farm, so as to let the hands know who I am. And, now, Mr. Dinkie, they tell me that you have not had your back tanned for many years; and, that being the case, I shall give you a flogging that you will never forget. Follow me to the barn." Cook started for the barn, but turned and went into his house to get his whip.

At this juncture, Dinkie gave a knowing look to the other slaves, who were standing by, and said, "Ef he lays the weight ob his finger on me, you'll see de top of dat barn come off."

The reappearance of the overseer, with the large negro whip in one hand, and a club in the other, with the significant demand of "follow me," caused a deep feeling in the breast of every negro present.

Dr. Gaines, expecting a difficulty between his new driver and the conjurer, had arisen early, and was standing at his bedroom window looking on.

The news that Dinkie was to be whipped, spread far and near over the place, and had called forth men, women, and children. Even Uncle Ned, the old negro of ninety years, had crawled out of his straw, and was at his cabin door. As the barn doors closed behind the overseer and Dinkie, a death-like silence pervaded the entire group, who, instead of going to their labor, as ordered by the driver, were standing as if paralyzed, gazing intently at the barn, expecting every moment to see the roof lifted.

Not a word was spoken by anyone, except Uncle Ned, who smiled, shook his head, put on a knowing countenance, and said, "My word fer it, de oberseer ain't agwine to whip Dinkie.

Five minutes, ten minutes, fifteen minutes passed, and the usual sound of "Oh, pray, massa! Oh, pray, massa!" heard on the occasion of a slave being punished, had not yet proceeded from the barn.

Many of the older negroes gathered around Uncle Ned, for he and Dinkie occupied the same cabin, and the old, superannuated slave knew more about the affairs of the conjurer, than anyone else. Ned told of how, on the previous night, Dinkie had slept but little, had closely inspected the snake's skin around his neck, the petrified frog and dried lizard, in his pockets, and had rubbed himself all over with goopher; and when he had finished, he knelt, and exclaimed, —

"Now, good and lovely devil, for more than twenty years, I have served you faithfully. Before I got into your service, de white folks bought an' sold me an' my old wife an' chillen, an' whip me, and half starve me. Dey did treat me mighty bad, dat you knows. Den I use to pray to de Lord, but dat did no good, kase de white folks don't fear de Lord. But dey fears you, an' ever since I got into your service, I is able to do as I please. No white dares to la his hand on me; and dis is all owing to de power dat you give me.

Oh, good and lovely devil! please to continer dat power. A new oberseer is to come here to-morrow, an' he wants to get me in his hands. But, dear devil, I axe you to stand by me in dis my trial hour, an' I will neber desert you as long as I live. Continer dis power; make me strong in your cause, make me to be more faithful to you, an' let me still be able to conquer my enemies, an' I will give 'you all de glory, and will try to deserve a seat at your right hand."

With bated breath, everyone listened to Uncle Ned. All had the utmost confidence in Dinkie's "power." None believed that he would be punished, while a large number expected to see the roof of the barn burst off at any moment. At last the suspence was broken. The barn door flew open; the overseer and the conjurer came out together, walking side by side, and separated when half-way up the walk. As they parted, Cook went to the field, and Dinkie to his cabin.

The slaves all shook their heads significantly. The fact that the old negro had received no punishment, was evidence of his victory over the slave driver. But how the feat had been accomplished, was a mystery. No one dared to ask Dinkie, for he was always silent, except when he had something to communicate. Everyone was afraid to inquire of the overseer.

There was, however, one faint chance of getting an inkling of what had occurred in the barn, and that was through Uncle Ned. This fact made the old, superannuated slave the hero and centre of attraction, for several days. Many were the applications made to Ned for information, but the old man did not know, or wished to exaggerate the importance of what he had learned.

"I tell you,["] said Dolly, "Dinkie is a power."

"He's nobody's fool," responded Hannah.

"I would not make him mad wid me, fer dis whole world," ejaculated Jim.

Just then, Nancy, the cook, came in brim full of news. She had given Uncle Ned some "cracklin bread," which had pleased the old man so much that he had opened his bosom, and told her all that he got from Dinkie. This piece of information flew quickly from cabin to cabin, and brought the slaves hastily into the kitchen.

It was night. Nancy sat down, looked around, and told Billy to shut the door. This heightened the interest, so that the fall of a pin could have been heard. All eyes were upon Nancy, and she felt keenly the importance of her position. Her voice was generally loud, with a sharp ring, which could be heard for a long distance, especially in the stillness of the night. But now, Nancy spoke in a whisper, occasionally putting her finger to her mouth, indicating a desire for silence, even when the breathing of those present could be distinctly heard.

"When dey got in de barn, de oberseer said to Dinkie, 'Strip yourself; I don't want to tear your clothes with my whip. I'm going to tear your black skin.'

"Den, you see, Dinkie tole de oberseer to look in de east corner ob de barn. He looked, an' he saw hell, wid all de torments, an' de debble, 'wid his cloven foot, a-struttin' about dar, jes as ef he was cock ob de walk. An' Dinkie tole Cook, dat ef he lay his finger on him, he'd call de debble up to take him away."

"An' what did Cook say to dat?" asked Jim.

"Let me 'lone; I didn't tell you all," said Nancy. "Den you see de oberseer turn pale in de face, an' he say to Dinkie, 'Let me go dis time, an' I'll nebber trouble you any more.'"

This concluded Nancy's story, as related to her by old Ned, and religiously believed by all present.

Document Three: "The 'Hoodoo' Superstition," *Rocky Mountain News* (Denver, CO), Sunday, December 11, 1887, page 18.

The "Hoodoo" Superstition
Its Existence Among the Colored Citizens of a Florida
Town—Knocking Out a "Hoodoo."

To be "conjured" or "hoodooed" is the negro's bane. Even now there are hundreds who as implicitly believe in it as in the older days of slave regime. A very amusing case came to the attention of the correspondent there this week. A respectable colored woman, who is keeping a boarding house for colored people, and who is comparatively speaking, intelligent and energetic, and quite well to do, is the subject of a spell, and she is in great tribulation over it. About a fortnight ago she began treating herself for rheumatism in one of her legs. Her home treatment didn't seem to be very effective, so she became worried and spoke to her neighbors about it. One of them suggested a "conjure." This met ready affirmation, and the woman was urged to see if such was the case. To do this required her to rise up as early, as soon as she heard the first crow of a cock and with one shoe on and one stocking on the other foot, fully dressed otherwise and with a red cap on to visit the front gate and see if there were any signs of a "hoodoo." This is deemed an infallible. So the next morning the woman, fully equipped, rose early after hearing a cock crow and investigated.

On her front porch she found scattered bunches of hen's feathers, and in the center of the gateway a medium-sized vial with large mouth, with several feathers sticking out of it, and lying beside it a rag baby, which she had, she avers, a pin thrust through one of its legs. This was enough, and the next day that home was thronged by dozens of negro women, all anxious to see the "conjure" or "hoodoo." The woman called in three or four of her intimate friends, and they proceeded to get up an "anti-conjure." This was done very secretly, and was only ascertained by the babblings and gossip of a home girl in the writer's employ, who confided the story partially to her mistress as a great secret.

These four women began their work early in the evening, as soon as the house was clear of all intruders. A round barrel hoop was hung up at the front and rear doors, and the windows closely curtained. A big fire was kindled and four kettles full of water put on, no two of the kettles being the same size. Going out into the garden as soon as it became dark, two of the women, in bare feet, gathered certain herbs from each of the four corners. These were bruised up and thrown into a kettle. A rooster was killed and his head, right food, and wing were put into another, and in the other was thrown about two handfuls of the cock's feathers, all plucked from the right side, and several ounces of red pepper. While these were boiling the women sat around the stove, holding hands and as close to it as possible.

After watching it intently one would cry out: "Go away from her," another "I throw you back to her," and others would address it as if speaking to a person, asking why it troubled their friend, etc. this was kept up for an hour, and then the contents of all the smaller kettles were turned into the larger. After some more of the incantations they took off the big kettle, and each with a bundle of feathers in her right hand, as the clock struck 12, went out in single file, each woman barefooted and with a red cap on. The foremost one had a stick with a red flannel top. The two following carried the kettle, and the one in the rear had in her hands the left leg and the other wing of the dead cock the spur being cut off the foot. Going to the house of the woman who was suspected of "conjuring," the water and contents of the big kettle were emptied into her yard at three different points, and the feathers and remains of the cock were buried under the gate. As this was an effectual barrier to further evil work of the "conjurer," and left her at the mercy of her would-be victim, they all retired satisfied. The next day the woman said she began to feel better at once, and now claims to be fully recovered. The funniest part is that the other woman has suspicioned something from the mysterious hints thrown out by the parties interested, and she now threatens to "church 'em" or to get up a counter "hoodoo." Colored circles are worked up over the matter, but are divided greatly over the merits of the case.

Document Four: Zora Neale Hurston, "Hoodoo in America," *The Journal of American Folklore* 44.174 (1931): 326–327.

Hoodoo in the Southern States
Marie Leveau

Marie Leveau is the great name of Negro conjure in America. There were three Marie Leveaux, of whom the last, the daughter and granddaughter of the other two, was the most renowned.

The first one is said to have been a small black Congo woman. The daughter was a mulatto of very handsome body and face. The granddaughter was an octoroon of great beauty. Her curly head is described as bandeaued with bright tignons clasped with expensive jewels.

This granddaughter became the greatest hoodoo queen of America. She was born February 2, 1827, according to the birth records in St. Louis Cathedral, New Orleans and studied hoodoo with one Alexander. She was the natural daughter of Marie Leveau and Christophe Glapion. She lived on St. Anne Street, between North Rampart and Burgundy, in the French Quarter, but also kept a home on Bayou St. John near Lake Pontchartrain. There is very little contemporary record of her, but her glory has not suffered with the passing of time. She is traditionally said to have been consulted by Queen Victoria, who was so pleased with the results that she sent her a shawl and a large sum of money. An oil painting of her hangs in the Cabildo, the Museum of the State of Louisiana, and her fame extends far beyond the borders of hoodoo. She is supposed to have been attended by a huge rattlesnake. The morning after her death he was seen crawling away to the woods about Lake Pontchartrain and was never seen again.

There is the story of the storm when she was at her home on the shore of Lake Pontchartrain. She refused to flee, in spite of urging. Finally the storm swept the cabin into the lake. She resisted rescue, saying that she wished to die there in the lake in the storm. She was always the magnificent savage, and she perhaps felt that, being old, her end was near. She preferred an exit with nature itself playing its most magnificent music than dry rotting in a bed. She was forcibly rescued, but it is said that neither wind, water nor thunder ceased until she had set foot on land.

She held a dance the first Friday night in each month and a grand annual dance on the eve of St. John's, June 24. The dance drums were made by stretching cow-hide over a halfbarrel.

They were beaten with the jaw-bone or leg-bone of a jackass or some other large animal. Some people called the dance the can-can. It is said that when she held her dances on the shore of Lake Pontchartrain, every St. John's Eve she used to rise out of the lake with a huge communion candle burning on top of her head and one in each hand, all lighted and burning brightly as she rose from the bosom of the lake and walked to the shore upon the water. When the ceremony was over, she would go back upon the waters as she had come and disappear in the lake.

People feared hoodoo in general and Marie Leveau in particular to such an extent that one day some one saw a sizeable cloth package lying in the mud in the street. No one would touch it. It lay there so long that the cloth rotted and a buggy driving over it tore it open and revealed gold coins.

When she lived in St. Anne Street the police tried to raid her place. One came and she confounded him. Two were sent and she put them to running and barking like dogs. Four came and she put them to beating each other over the head with their night sticks. The whole station force came at last. They knocked at her door. She knew who they were before she even went to the door. So she did some work at her altar and put the whole force to sleep on her steps.

It is difficult to say how much of hoodoo in Louisiana today stems from Marie Leveau. Both Samuel Thompson and Albert Frechard told me in all seriousness that they were her grandnephews, which, however unlikely in a physical sense indicates that they count themselves spiritually affiliated with her "works." It is probable that she sums up traditionally a whole era of hoodoo; she was the great name in its Golden Age.

Additional reading

Chireau, Yvonne. *Black Magic: Religion and the African American Conjuring Tradition* (Berkeley, CA: University of California Press, 2006).

Fett, Carla. *Working Cures: Healing, Health, and Power on Southern Slave Plantations* (Chapel Hill, NC: University of North Carolina Press, 2002).

Gordon, Michelle Y. "'Midnight Scenes and Orgies': Public Narratives of Voodoo in New Orleans and Nineteenth-Century Discourses of White Supremacy," *American Quarterly* 64.4 (December 2012): 767–786.

Mitchem, Stephanie. *African American Folk Healing* (New York: New York University Press, 2007).

4

The Church of Jesus Christ of Latter-day Saints

Editors' Introduction: The Church of Jesus Christ of Latter-day Saints (historically also known as Mormonism) was the most successful group from what historian Jon Butler termed "the antebellum spiritual hothouse."[1] The early American republic was a space of religious innovation and diversity. Prophet Joseph Smith founded The Church of Jesus Christ of Latter-day Saints in the 1830s after receiving a number of visions from God, Jesus, and others, like the angel Moroni. The Book of Mormon, a text that Moroni supposedly led Smith to find, contained a narrative that detailed America's biblical past, including Jesus's appearance to Native Americans, who were the descendants of a lost tribe of Israel. According to the Book of Mormon, this Native American community divided into separate righteous and unrighteous communities, and the darker-skinned community who fell away from Jesus's teachings slaughtered the righteous. The Church of Jesus Christ of Latter-day Saints understands those ancient inhabitants of the Americas to be among the ancestors of modern-day Native Americans.

Under Smith's leadership, the early church emphasized the second coming of Christ, and Smith and his followers believed they were restoring the past in order to bring forth the millennium. Through his revelations and with the Book of Mormon Smith restored ancient practices and the priesthoods of the Old Testament. In search of a freer place to practice their unorthodox Christianity, Smith moved his followers to the Midwest where Smith received new revelations from God that further marked the community as outsiders. These included the secretive temple work of the early church and the relationship between these temple ordinances (or eternal seals) and the levels of heaven. Citing revelation from God and the practice of polygamy by many of the Old Testament patriarchs, Smith introduced polygamy in 1843, which about thirty percent of the community practiced. An angry mob of non-Mormon men dressed up as Native Americans murdered Smith and his brother on June 27, 1844.

---

[1] Jon Butler, *Awash in a Sea of Faith: Christianizing the American People* (Cambridge: Harvard University Press, 1992).

All men in good standing with the church were admitted into the priesthood, which grants the ability to perform certain rituals and affords a level of respectability and authority. Though some Native Americans out West converted to The Church of Jesus Christ of Latter-day Saints as well as some African Americans, men of color were denied full church membership and the priesthood until the 1970s. It was not until after this rule was lifted that famous Jane Manning James, a black member of the church who lived as a servant of Smith's family for a time, was fully endowed posthumously. Outsiders too looked at the movement through a racial lens. They saw The Church of Jesus Christ of Latter-day Saints as a dangerous threat to America. Their newly revealed scripture and seemingly abnormal practices, like polygamy in the nineteenth century, labeled them as suspect. Outsiders and the press regularly associated polygamy with slavery and referred to "Mormon harems." Outsiders even saw members of The Church of Jesus Christ of Latter-day Saints as akin to another race, since they treated women as "Africans" and "Asiatics" did. Others referenced "the Mormon race," arguing that through polygamous inbreeding the Mormons had become something other than white.

When Jesus, God, Moroni, and others appeared to Smith, they did so in luminous, white bodies. In many ways, The Church of Jesus Christ of Latter-day Saints followed suit with many other white Protestants of the antebellum period and their theology reflected the contemporary white supremacy of the day. This could be seen in their regard for Native Americans and African Americans. In the twentieth century the church has become more outspoken about race challenges, diversity within the church, and the importance of inclusion. Many scholars associate the opening of the priesthood to men of color with the twentieth-century civil rights movement and the church's growing international significance.

Document One is an excerpt from the Book of Mormon that describes how Israelite patriarch Lehi brought his people to the new world hundreds of years before the birth of Christ. After Jesus's resurrection, he appeared to them and all was peaceful until inner turmoil developed among the ancient Israelite-turned Native Americans. They divided into the light-skinned Nephites who continued to worship God and the Lamanites who began to ignore God. The Lamanites turned on the Nephites, and for this behavior their skin was darkened, making them appear like the Native Americans who, centuries later, met European settlers. Document Two is a report published by US Army assistant-surgeon Roberts Bartholow following his assignment in Utah Territory. This report reflects the racialized anti-Mormon sentiment of the nineteenth century. Document Three is a description of Joseph Smith given by Jane Manning James, who worked as a free black servant in his household. James and her family had to walk from Buffalo, New York to Nauvoo, Illinois, and when they arrived she met Smith and his first wife Emma at their home. The final document is "Official Declaration 2" and focuses on the church's official acceptance of African Americans as full church members in the late 1970s. From the leadership of Brigham Young to this declaration, the church excluded African American men from the priesthood, which is now open to all men who meet standards of spiritual worthiness.

Documents

Document One: 2 Nephi 5:1–34, Book of Mormon.

1. Behold, it came to pass that I, Nephi, did cry much unto the Lord my God, because of the anger of my brethren.

2. But behold, their anger did increase against me, insomuch that they did seek to take away my life.

3. Yea, they did murmur against me, saying: Our younger brother thinks to rule over us; and we have had much trial because of him; wherefore, now let us slay him, that we may not be afflicted more because of his words. For behold, we will not have him to be our ruler; for it belongs unto us, who are the elder brethren, to rule over this people.

4. Now I do not write upon these plates all the words which they murmured against me. But it sufficeth me to say, that they did seek to take away my life.

5. And it came to pass that the Lord did warn me, that I, Nephi, should depart from them and flee into the wilderness, and all those who would go with me.

6. Wherefore, it came to pass that I, Nephi, did take my family, and also Zoram and his family, and Sam, mine elder brother and his family, and Jacob and Joseph, my younger brethren, and also my sisters, and all those who would go with me. And all those who would go with me were those who believed in the warnings and the revelations of God; wherefore, they did hearken unto my words.

7. And we did take our tents and whatsoever things were possible for us, and did journey in the wilderness for the space of many days. And after we had journeyed for the space of many days we did pitch our tents.

8. And my people would that we should call the name of the place Nephi; wherefore, we did call it Nephi.

9. And all those who were with me did take upon them to call themselves the people of Nephi.

10. And we did observe to keep the judgments, and the statutes, and the commandments of the Lord in all things, according to the law of Moses.

11. And the Lord was with us; and we did prosper exceedingly; for we did sow seed, and we did reap again in abundance. And we began to raise flocks, and herds, and animals of every kind.

12. And I, Nephi, had also brought the records which were engraven upon the plates of brass; and also the ball, or compass, which was prepared for my father by the hand of the Lord, according to that which is written.

13.   And it came to pass that we began to prosper exceedingly, and to multiply in the land.

14.   And I, Nephi, did take the sword of Laban, and after the manner of it did make many swords, lest by any means the people who were now called Lamanites should come upon us and destroy us; for I knew their hatred towards me and my children and those who were called my people.

15.   And I did teach my people to build buildings, and to work in all manner of wood, and of iron, and of copper, and of brass, and of steel, and of gold, and of silver, and of precious ores, which were in great abundance.

16.   And I, Nephi, did build a temple; and I did construct it after the manner of the temple of Solomon save it were not built of so many precious things; for they were not to be found upon the land, wherefore, it could not be built like unto Solomon's temple. But the manner of the construction was like unto the temple of Solomon; and the workmanship thereof was exceedingly fine.

17.   And it came to pass that I, Nephi, did cause my people to be industrious, and to labor with their hands.

18.   And it came to pass that they would that I should be their king. But I, Nephi, was desirous that they should have no king; nevertheless, I did for them according to that which was in my power.

19.   And behold, the words of the Lord had been fulfilled unto my brethren, which he spake concerning them, that I should be their ruler and their teacher. Wherefore, I had been their ruler and their teacher, according to the commandments of the Lord, until the time they sought to take away my life.

20.   Wherefore, the word of the Lord was fulfilled which he spake unto me, saying that: Inasmuch as they will not hearken unto thy words they shall be cut off from the presence of the Lord. And behold, they were cut off from his presence.

21.   And he had caused the cursing to come upon them, yea, even a sore cursing, because of their iniquity. For behold, they had hardened their hearts against him, that they had become like unto a flint; wherefore, as they were white, and exceedingly fair and delightsome, that they might not be enticing unto my people the Lord God did cause a skin of blackness to come upon them.

22.   And thus saith the Lord God: I will cause that they shall be loathsome unto thy people, save they shall repent of their iniquities.

23.   And cursed shall be the seed of him that mixeth with their seed; for they shall be cursed even with the same cursing. And the Lord spake it, and it was done.

24.   And because of their cursing which was upon them they did become an idle people, full of mischief and subtlety, and did seek in the wilderness for beasts of prey.

25. And the Lord God said unto me: They shall be a scourge unto thy seed, to stir them up in remembrance of me; and inasmuch as they will not remember me, and hearken unto my words, they shall scourge them even unto destruction.

26. And it came to pass that I, Nephi, did consecrate Jacob and Joseph, that they should be priests and teachers over the land of my people.

27. And it came to pass that we lived after the manner of happiness.

28. And thirty years had passed away from the time we left Jerusalem.

29. And I, Nephi, had kept the records upon my plates, which I had made, of my people thus far.

30. And it came to pass that the Lord God said unto me: Make other plates; and thou shalt engraven many things upon them which are good in my sight, for the profit of thy people.

31. Wherefore, I, Nephi, to be obedient to the commandments of the Lord, went and made these plates upon which I have engraven these things.

32. And I engraved that which is pleasing unto God. And if my people are pleased with the things of God they will be pleased with mine engravings which are upon these plates.

33. And if my people desire to know the more particular part of the history of my people they must search mine other plates.

34. And it sufficeth me to say that forty years had passed away, and we had already had wars and contentions with our brethren.

Document Two: "Sanitary Report—Utah Territory," *Statistical Report on the Sickness and Mortality in the Army of the United States* (Washington, DC: George W. Bowman, 1860), 300–304.

Sanitary Report—Utah Territory
Assistant Surgeon Roberts Bartholow: September, 1858

During the past quarter having, in the course of duty, passed over the most important part of the Territory of Utah, I have thought it not improper to speak somewhat upon its medical topography, productions, and upon the social customs of its inhabitants. This report will exhibit one fact with especial prominence—the salubrity of the climate. How far this quality redeems the general barrenness and dearth of interest, is differently estimated according to the temperaments of individuals. It is generally conceded in the army, however, that Utah is a very proper "Zion" for the Mormon community, but for other sentient beings not particularly suitable.

. . .

Whatever of value is produced in this territory, comes by the labor of man. Nature has accomplished little towards enriching the country in the varied productions of the vegetable world. In the spring and summer, the valleys are clothed in a luxuriant herbage, but as the season advances, the grasses quickly grow cere and yellow, and the whole country becomes arid and dusty. Along the streams occasional groves of cottonwood (*Populus angustifolia*) and a thick growth of herbaceous willow are seen, but on the table-lands no vegetation lives, except the wide-spread Artemisia. In the mountain ranges, several varieties of the pinus (*Pinus palustris* and *P. abies*) grow, but not abundantly, except in a few situations. Mineral springs, hot, cold, and all intermediate temperatures, abound. In a geological point of view, the whole Territory is full of interest; not, at present, in an economic view; not until extended researches shall develop the mineral resources. Judging by the formations usually connected with mineral wealth, the indications are not without certainty. A rigid concealment of these indications, has been a measure of policy with the Mormon people, who, wisely enough, foresee how injurious an influence of discovery of mineral wealth would exert over their peculiar social, religious, and political institutions.

. . .

The most important animal here as elsewhere is that of the order *Bimana*, and genus *homo sapiens*. The Mormon, of all the human animals now walking this globe, is the most curious in every relation. It would be quite beyond the scope of this report to say anything of the political and religious aspects of Mormonism; but as a great social solecism, seriously affecting the physical stamina and mental health, it is full of interest to the medical philosopher. Isolated in the narrow valleys of Utah, and practicing the rites of a religion grossly material, of which polygamy is the main element and cohesive force, the Mormon people have arrived at a physical and mental condition, in a few years of growth, such as densely-populated communities in the older parts of the world, hereditary victims of all the vices of civilization, have been ages in reaching. This condition is shown by the preponderance of female births, by the mortality in infantine life, by the large proportion of the albuminous and gelatinous types of constitution, and by the striking uniformity in facial expression and in physical conformation of the younger portion of the community. The "peculiar institution," is practically upheld by the older men, the elders, bishops, apostles, and prophets; and so eager is the search for young virgins, that notwithstanding the preponderance of the female population, a large percentage of the younger men remain unmarried. To sustain the system, girls are "sealed" at the earliest manifestations of puberty, and I am credibly informed, that means are not infrequently made use of to hasten the period. The activity of the reproductive function, as a rule, is not diminished by polygamy; on the contrary, the women are remarkable for fecundity; but in the harems the proportion of children arriving at maturity, is much less than in the rural districts of our country. An illustration of this fact is afforded by the results in that chief of polygamists, Brigham Young's case. He has, at least, forty wives. A large number of children have been born to him, a majority of whom died in infancy, leaving twenty-four, according to the most reliable accounts. These forty women in monogamous society, married, would have borne, probably, one hundred and sixty children, two thirds of whom under hygienic circumstances equally favorable, would have been reared. In Brigham and his wives, we have presented the most favorable conditions for successful polygamy possible in Mormon society, yet, in this instance, the violation of a natural law, has been speedily evinced. One of the most deplorable effects of polygamy, is shown in the genital weakness of the boys and young men, the progeny of the "peculiar institution." The most observant Mormons, cannot hide from themselves the evidence of these sad effects. One of their saints, Heber C. Kimball, in recent sermons, has adverted to this sexual debility, but, with a singular blindness, attributed it to a vicious style of dressing. The sexual desires are stimulated to an unnatural degree at a very young age, and as female virtue is easy, opportunities are not wanting for their gratification. It is a curious fact, that Mormonism makes its impress upon the countenance. Whether owing to the practice of a purely sensual and material religion, to the premature development of the passions, or to isolation, there is, nevertheless, an expression of countenance and a style of feature, which may be styled the Mormon expression and style; an expression compounded of sensuality, cunning suspicion, and a smirking self-conceit. The yellow, sunken, cadaverous visage; the greenish-colored eyes; the thick, protuberant lips; the low forehead; the light, yellowish hair; and the lank, angular person, constitute an appearance so characteristic of a new race, the production of polygamy, as to distinguish them at a glance. The older men and women, present all the physical peculiarities of the nationalities to which they belong; but these peculiarities are not propagated and continued in the new race; they are lost in the prevailing Mormon type.

If Mormonism received no additions from outside sources, these influences continuing, it is not difficult to foresee that it would eventually die out. The increase of population, independently of large annual accessions from abroad, has not been coequal with the increase in other portions of our country. The results of polygamy here are not to be compared, without some limitations, to the results of the same institution elsewhere: its decadence must follow more speedily. In eastern life, where it has been a recognized domestic institution for ages, women are prepared for its continuance, and do not feel degraded by their association with it. The women of this Territory, how fanatical and ignorant soever, recognize their wide departure from the normal standard in all Christian countries; and from the degradation of the mother follows of the child, and physical degeneracy is not a remote consequence of moral depravity.

Mormonism, considered in a relation purely sanitary, presents some interesting features. The Mormon theology, contemplates the cure of disease by miraculous interposition; hence, the disciples of the healing art are not held in much estimation. The church authorities are exceedingly jealous at an attempt to cure by ordinary therapeutics, and denounce from the pulpit any invasion of their special province. Though they claim for the "laying on of hands" (*cheirapsia*) wonderful efficacy, the number of deformities, the result of malpractice, to be seen in any of the populous towns, rather indicates a necessity for the use of carnal means. The art of surgery is at a low ebb. Epidemic erysipelas of a virulent form is reported to prevail in this Territory, but, thus far, no cases of the disease have fallen under the observation of the medical officers serving with this army. I have reason to believe that "erysipelas," is a conventional term applied to various dissimilar affections, as rheumatism, erythema, anthrax, &c.

Document Three: "Joseph Smith, the Prophet," *Young Woman's Journal* 16.12 (December 1905): 551–553.

[*Editors' Note*: All of the published descriptions of Smith in this article begin by identifying the woman giving them. James is the only name with a title given (in quotation marks or otherwise) or a note of clarification about how she knew the founder.]

"Aunt" Jane James
(Colored Servant in the Prophet's House)

Yes, indeed, I guess I did know the Prophet Joseph. That lovely hand! He used to put it out to me. Never passed me without shaking hands with me wherever he was. Oh, he was the finest man I ever saw on earth. I did not get much of a chance to talk with him. He'd always smile, always just like he did to his children. He used to be just like I was his child. O yes, my, I used to read the Bible so much and in the Book of Mormon and Revelations, and now I have to sit and can't see to read, and I think over them things, and I tell you I do wake up in the middle of the night, and I just think about Brother Joseph and Sister Emma and how good they were to me. When I went there I only had two things on me, no shoes nor stockings, wore them all out on the road. I had a trunk full of beautiful clothes, which I had sent around by water, and I was thinking of having them when I got to Nauvoo, and they stole them at St. Louis, and I did not have a rag of them. They was looking for us because I wrote them a letter. There was eight of us, my mother and two sisters and a brother and sister-in-law, and we had two children, one they had to carry all the way there, and we traveled a thousand miles. Sister Emma she come to the door first and she says, "Walk in, come in all of you," and she went up stairs, and down he comes and goes into the sitting room and told the girls that they had there, he wanted to have the room this evening, for we have got company come. I knew it was Brother Joseph because I had seen him in a dream. He went and brought Dr. Bernhisel down and Sister Emma, and introduced him to everyone of us, and said "Now, I want you to tell me about some of your hard trials. I want to hear of some of those hard trials." And we told him. He slapped his hands.

"Dr. Bernhisel," he said, "what do you think of that?" And he said, "I think if I had had it to do I should have not come; would not have had faith enough."

I was the head leader. I had been in the Church a year and a little over. That is sixty-nine years ago. [She was at the time about twenty years of age.] So then our folks got places. He kept them a whole week until they got homes, and I was left. He came in every morning to see us and shake hands and know how we all were. One morning, before he came in, I had been up to the landing and found all my clothes were gone. Well, I sat there crying. He came in and looked around.

"Why where's all the folks?"

"Why Brother," I says, "they have all got themselves places; but," I says, "I haint got any place," and I burst out a-crying.

"We won't have tears here," he says.

"Well you've got a home here," he says, "Have you seen Sister Emma this morning."

"No, sir," I says.

So he started out and went upstairs and brought Sister Emma down and says, "Here's a girl who says she's got no home. Don't you think she's got a home here?"

And she says, "If she wants to stay here."

And he says, "do you want to stay here?"

"Yes, sir," says I. "Well, now," he says, "Sister Emma you just talk to her and see how she is." He says, "Good morning," and he went.

We had come afoot, a thousand miles. We lay in bushes, and in barns and outdoors, and traveled until there was a frost just like a snow, and we had to walk on that frost. I could not tell you, but I wanted to go to Brother Joseph.

I did not talk much to him, but every time he saw me he would say, "God bless you," and pat me on the shoulder. To Sister Emma, he said, "go and clothe her up, go down to the store and clothe her up." Sister Emma did. She got me clothes by the bolt. I had everything.

The folks that come to me think I ought to talk and tell what Brother Joseph said, but he was hid up (his enemies were seeking his life) and I cannot remember now. I could not begin to tell you what he was, only this way, he was tall, over six feet; he was a fine, big, noble, beautiful man! He had blue eyes and light hair, and very fine white skin.

When he was killed, I liked to have a died myself, if it had not been for the teachers, I felt so bad. I could have died, just laid down and died; and I was sick abed, and the teachers told me,

"You don't want to die because he did. He died for us, and now we all want to live and do all the good we can."

Things came to pass what he prophesized about the colored race being freed. Things that he said has come to pass. I did not hear that, but I knew of it.

After I saw him plain, I was certain he was a prophet because I knew it. I was willing to come and gather, and when he came in with Dr. Bernhisel I knew him. Did not have to tell me because I knew him. I knew him when I saw him back in old Connecticut in a vision, saw him plain and knew he was a prophet.

This is the Gospel of Jesus Christ and there will never be any other on earth. It has come to stay.

Document Four: Official Declaration 2, Doctrine and Covenants, The Church of Jesus Christ of Latter-day Saints.

June 8, 1978

To all general and local priesthood officers of The Church of Jesus Christ of Latter-day Saints throughout the world:

Dear Brethren:

As we have witnessed the expansion of the work of the Lord over the earth, we have been grateful that people of many nations have responded to the message of the restored gospel, and have joined the Church in ever-increasing numbers. This, in turn, has inspired us with a desire to extend to every worthy member of the Church all of the privileges and blessings which the gospel affords.

Aware of the promises made by the prophets and presidents of the Church who have preceded us that at some time, in God's eternal plan, all of our brethren who are worthy may receive the priesthood, and witnessing the faithfulness of those from whom the priesthood has been withheld, we have pleaded long and earnestly in behalf of these, our faithful brethren, spending many hours in the Upper Room of the Temple supplicating the Lord for divine guidance.

He has heard our prayers, and by revelation has confirmed that the long-promised day has come when every faithful, worthy man in the Church may receive the holy priesthood, with power to exercise its divine authority, and enjoy with his loved ones every blessing that flows therefrom, including the blessings of the temple. Accordingly, all worthy male members of the Church may be ordained to the priesthood without regard for race or color. Priesthood leaders are instructed to follow the policy of carefully interviewing all candidates for ordination to either the Aaronic or the Melchizedek Priesthood to insure that they meet the established standards for worthiness.

We declare with soberness that the Lord has now made known his will for the blessing of all his children throughout the earth who will hearken to the voice of his authorized servants, and prepare themselves to receive every blessing of the gospel.

Sincerely yours,
Spencer W. Kimball
N. Eldon Tanner
Marion G. Romney
The First Presidency

Recognizing Spencer W. Kimball as the prophet, seer, and revelator, and president of The Church of Jesus Christ of Latter-day Saints, it is proposed that we as a constituent assembly accept this revelation as the word and will of the Lord. All in favor please signify by raising your right hand. Any opposed by the same sign.

The vote to sustain the foregoing motion was unanimous in the affirmative.

Salt Lake City, Utah, September 30, 1978.

Additional reading

Bennett, James B. "'Until This Curse of Polygamy Is Wiped Out': Black Methodists, White Mormons, and Constructions of Racial Identity in the Late Nineteenth Century,"

Religion and American Culture: A Journal of Interpretation 21.2 (Summer 2011): 167–194.

Farmer, Jared. *On Zion's Mount: Mormons, Indians, and the American Landscape* (Cambridge, MA: Harvard University Press, 2008).

Mueller, Max Perry. *Race and the Making of the Mormon People* (Chapel Hill, NC: University of North Carolina Press, 2017).

Newell, Quincy D. "The Autobiography and Interview of Jane Elizabeth Manning James," *Journal of Africana Religions* 1.2 (2013): 251–291.

5

Spiritualism

Editors' Introduction: American Spiritualism was not the first religious movement to center on communication with the worlds of the afterlife, but it was perhaps the most successful movement of its kind in the United States. To put it succinctly, American Spiritualism centered on the possibility of communication with the spirit world beyond the material world. Most often this took the form of séances, though Spiritualists also used photography and magnetism to communicate with the dead. American Spiritualism began to rise in popularity in the late 1840s and would remain somewhat popular through the early twentieth century. It developed out of liberal Christianity, along with the ideas of Anton Franz Mesmer (who focused on an invisible force he called animal magnetism, which flowed throughout the world and all living people) and Emanuel Swedenborg (who claimed to visit the Heaven and Hell beyond this world and see the afterlives of spirits). It is estimated that around six million Americans experimented with Spiritualism. Spiritualism was most popular among white liberals on the east coast, whose version brought together reform movements with nineteenth-century practices of mourning for the dead.

Spiritualism was not without complexities and controversies. Mediums claimed their authority beyond any institutional church, which made Spiritualism suspect to those with traditional authority and made it appealing to those without it. Those who were politically marginalized in society, especially women and racial minorities, no longer needed the intervening command of the traditional church. The authority of mediumship provided direct, spiritual power to those without public power and equal rights. As such, conversations about gender and race were not uncommon around certain séance tables.

Spiritualists of all races discussed issues of racial power, racial difference, and racial identity. White liberal Spiritualists often channeled the spirits of Native Americans. The "ambivalent affiliations" Anglo-American Spiritualists developed with the Native American spirits they channeled reflected their "romantic attachments to an ideal or imagined Indian."[1] In her work on the politics of Spiritualism, Molly McGarry illustrates

---

[1] Molly McGarry, *Ghosts of Futures Past: Spiritualism and the Cultural Politics of Nineteenth-Century America* (Berkeley, CA: University of California Press, 2008), 67.

how, for Anglo-Spiritualists already in possession of racial privilege, racial difference continued on in the spiritual world. In their communications with Native American spirits, they acknowledged but also reaffirmed Native dispossession of land and identity. The spirits who appeared often fit with the stereotypical, mystical Indian trope that was developing in the nineteenth century, akin to another form of what Philip Deloria termed "playing Indian." It was another example of white Americans benefitting from Native Americans (and not the other way around).

African Americans also practiced Spiritualism. One particularly active, yet small, group was composed of Afro-Creole men in New Orleans. Calling themselves the Cercle Harmonique, these men received political, social, and spiritual advice from the spirits of a diverse pantheon that included Abraham Lincoln, Montesquieu, Jesus, John Brown, and Saint Vincent de Paul. The group's peak years overlapped with Reconstruction, and the messages they recorded often centered on the cause of human rights and achieving equality. The Cercle Harmonique practiced in the wake of the Civil War during Reconstruction when African Americans finally received full political and civil personhood in law but not in actuality. It made it a powerful time to receive advice from the dead.

The documents included here are excerpts from séance records and Spiritualist writings. Document One is a series of excerpts from the 1843 volume of *The Spiritual Telegraph*. Published in its pages were dispatches and reports from Spiritualists around the country. None of the included excerpts came from the same Spiritualist communities. The first excerpt features a woman who channeled the spirit of Pocahontas. Readers should note the physical reaction reported by the witnesses and the claim to an "Indian" song, despite not having backgrounds in identifying various Native American languages (which leaves a question of how they knew it was "Indian"). The second excerpt focuses on a woman who channeled the spirit of a Native American man and the third excerpt also involved speaking in a "turned" language. Document Two is short but demonstrative. It comes from the writings of Robert Hare, a scientist and chemistry professor at the University of Pennslyvania turned Spiritualist. He invented a number of devices meant to prove scientifically Spiritualism's veracity and he wrote about the movement. Included here is one point of evidence for the morality of Spiritualism, and it is based on white supremacy.

Document Three is excerpts from famous American Spiritualist Emma Hardinge Britten's extensive history of the movement published in 1870. In it, she included dispatches from around the country. The first excerpt compares the Spiritualism commonly practiced by white Spiritualists with a Native American. It is followed by a longer analysis of "Indian Spiritualism" by Britten in which she continues that comparison.

Finally, Document Four is a series of excerpts from the records of the Cercle Harmonique. As already mentioned, they emphasized equal human rights; in addition, their records reflect a denial of the ontology of race. Rather than seeing race as a helpful or even a real identity marker, their records describe race as an oppressive system and seeks to place people in hierarchies. The excerpts cover topics such as: the insignificance of race, a poem delivered by a spirit about being black, the importance of doing good (despite one's immediate context), the racial identity of Jesus, the horrors of slavery, and, finally, a message from Abraham Lincoln on black civil rights. The dates of the messages' receipt and the spirits who sent them are noted.

Documents

Document One: *The Spiritual Telegraph*, vol. 3, edited by S.B. Brittan (New York: Partridge & Brittan, 1843), 202, 492, and 571.

. . .

Some time after these occurrences took place, a medium (Miss Sarah Mason, daughter of Rev. Almon Mason, now of Michigan) came to the house of Mr. Briggs, and while there was subjected to a variety of strange experiences which claimed to be Spiritual. She was first controlled by an influence which purported to be of the spirit of Pocahontas, during which she combed her hair down upon her shoulders, and assumed the actions and even the physiognomy of an Indian woman, and sang what appeared to be an Indian song. Coming out of this state, another influence suddenly came upon her. . .

. . .

We have another lady medium whose guardian spirit represents himself to have been an Indian chief, who left the American hunting-grounds before the advent of the pale faces. He speaks Indian through her organs with great fluency; but no one here in the normal state can understand a word of it. Sometimes the Spirit attempts an English translation of what he utters in his native tongue, but he succeeds poorly. At the last meeting of the circle, when this lady was present, Miss B. being in the magnetic state, the chief addressed some remarks to her, which it was evident that she understood. Sentences uttered by the chief, closing with the rising inflection, were responded to by Miss B. with an affirmative nod or a negative shake of the head. We asked Miss B. to tell us what the chief said, and she instantly spelled his questions with her fingers. He seems to be an elevated Spirit by the copiousness of his knowledge; but still he indulges in facetious repartee, which, though entirely innocent, seems to be wanting in gravity suitable to the high importance of these developments. For instance, some of the circle jocosely observed to Mrs.—, the medium, "This chief seems to have taken a great fancy to you—does he take you for a squaw?" The chief immediately replied through her to Miss B., and Miss B. to the circle, by giving several ludicrous occurrences in the courtship of several members who joined in joking the medium. The most recent of these occurrences happened more than twenty years ago, and had entirely passed from the memory of the parties. Perhaps you can explain how the Spirit of this savage came by this information, of which he availed himself so readily. Remember that the lady medium has not been an acquaintance of any member of the circle more than four months, and that Miss B. was born long after the occurrences had been forgotten.

. . .

A skeptical lady, who belonged to another circle, said that if the powers influencing her would prove to her that what she was controlled to utter really was a *language* she would believe it to be Spirits. A few days afterward, a gentleman who had for the last seventeen years been trafficking with the Indians attended one of the meetings of the circle and two or three of the mediums addressed him in what appeared to be different Indian tongues, one of which he thought was a dialect with which he had a slight acquaintance. The next day he and the skeptical lady met at a neighboring town. She was moved to go to him and speak in a language which she did not understand. The gentleman seemed astounded. The earnestness of the medium increased, until she thought the Spirit controlling her was getting excited. The gentleman understood what she was saying, and she urged him to give her an interpretation of the communication, which he refused to do. A communication was subsequently given through the mediumship of the same clairvoyant, stating this gentlemen had defrauded the Indian that addressed him of a deerskin before his death. The speaker himself had been made to speak that which was not English, and what was supposed to be a language.

Document Two: Robert Hare, *Experimental Investigation of the Spirit Manifestations* (New York: Partridge & Brittan, 1856), 138.

. . .

727. In this book [*Editors' Note*: of nature] we read, as matters of fact, that there is an infinite series of gradation in the rank of animals, as well as variety in their dispositions and propensities. This may be seen, from the half-animal, half-vegetable known as the polypus, up to man, there being gradations not of genera, but of species and varieties. Thus amid men there are various races, rising one above the other in development, from the Bushmen, Hottentot [*Editors' Note*: this is a reference to indigenous South African], or lowest Negro, up to the most highly-developed race of white men. But when we have passed through the gradation of the races, we have to enter upon that of individuals, who in the same race are by diversity of organization or education, or of both, made extremely different as to intellectual, moral, and scientific pre-eminence.

. . .

Document Three: Emma Hardinge Britten, *Modern American Spiritualism* (New York: The Author, 1870), 401, 481–482, and 485.

. . .

Spiritualism has ever been rife amongst the North American Indians; but its manifestations generally differ so widely from that which prevails amongst the whites, and the source by the Indians themselves is claimed to be so different to that of their civilized neighbors, that we have deemed it fitting to devote a special chapter to the subject. We shall, however, notice the experience of a very distinguished Sioux warrior, whose "mediumship," as we may term it, so closely resembles the phases familiar amongst ourselves that we may justly rank them in the same category.

An eminent traveller, writing to the Banner of Light, thus describes the spiritual endowments of the son of the forest, Spotted Tail:

"Spotted Tail, chief of the Brute Sioux, recently enunciated his views of the spirit land to a party of whites at North Platte, Nebraska. After death he had an idea that the spirit always moved about.

"He had frequently heard voices, in the stillness of the forest, from friends that had departed.

"He once went to the war with the Pawnees. He heard a voice calling to him from the top of a high hill. He went up to the top of the hill, and the voice continued calling to him from the timber. He looked about and found no one there. It was a spirit. The voice told him what to do; he believed it, and, following the advice, went into the fight and came out victorious.

"Thrillingly interesting was our conversation with this great Sioux chief, through the interpreter, relative to the religious views of his people.

"They believe in one great spirit, infinite, changeless; that smiles in the sun, whispers in the winds, and dances unseen in the shimmering waters of seas and rivers. They believe the soul is immortal and pursues occupations in the future life something similar to what employs it here. Bad Indians go to poor hunting grounds; good and brave ones ascend to glorious lands, seas, and forests, where fish, game, and every earthly delight, await them; where streams are crystal, flowers deathless; where dusky maidens meet their lovers, sport to the rhythm of the winds and waves, and never Christian robbers enter. This chief told us distinctly that many of his tribe saw blanketed ghosts; and spirits returned from their heavenly hunting grounds to counsel their mortal brothers.

"When the Indian is about to die, he said, spirits came for them, and were often so clearly visible that their relatives and friends, seeing them around the lodge, would shoot arrows at them in the air, in the hope of preventing their carrying their loved ones away. They have set seasons for talking with and making presents to the dead, and they constantly send messages by the dying to those who have gone before."

. . .

Indian spirits play a prominent and most noble part in the Spiritualism of America. Nearly every medium is attended by one of these beneficent beings, guiding, counselling, protecting them, and using their peculiar knowledge of herbs, plants, and earthly productions, to suggest rare and invaluable medicaments for the cure of disease. What a comment on the principles and practices of Christianity does this phase of Spiritualism present! Hapless ignorant beings, nay, whole tribes, that have been despoiled and cheated by Christian cupidity, out of land, home, and life itself, now seem to be the most prominent of all the returning spirits, in practically illustrating the lesson which the Christians so glibly teach and so wantonly falsify by their deeds, namely, to "overcome evil with good," and forgive those who know not what they do.

It is one of the strangest and most instructive of lessons—this relation between the white man and the spirit of his" savage victim."

The Indian mocks the Christian missionary by scornfully repudiating the gentle theories of Christianity, and urges the teachings of his forefathers, which deem vengeance for injuries the virtue of the brave; but no sooner does he become a spirit, than he practically adopts the neglected duties of true Christianity, and by deeds of love and mercy shows the white man how to prove the truth of his creed. Death is in his case the angel of transfiguration. We have denied him all rights and privileges in his and our father's heritage on earth: what mortal hand can bar him out of the kingdom of heaven, to which we may not unduly affirm he has pressed in before us? We repeat, that among the healing mediums, Indian spirits are ever deemed the most successful of operators. Doubtless the nomadic and simply natural life which these poor children of the forest lived on earth, has instructed them in the peculiar virtues and manifold forms of healing balm that the earth generates in her bosom.

Besides these healing spirits, it appears that many of the once powerful and renowned chiefs amongst the redmen, delight to work out a new and beautiful mission for themselves, in guarding and protecting the toiling mediums through whom the truths of Spiritualism are disseminated. They attend the circles also, and perform vast feats of physical strength, for which it is alleged their strong magnetic spiritual bodies are eminently fitted.

Thus "Black Hawk," "Osceola," "King Philip," "Red Jacket," "Logan," and other renowned "braves" are familiarly known as the leaders of spirit bands at circles, where the most wonderful phenomena and shrewd intelligence have been exhibited under their influence. The services rendered by those spirits to their media, would in many instances form a touching and remarkable history of occult power and beneficence.

To the warnings, guidance, and protection of a mighty war spirit calling himself "Arrow-head the terrible," the author has been indebted for services only to be comprehended by those who have experienced a similar spiritual guardianship.

Amongst our future records of phenomena, mediumship, and spirit healing, several instances of Indian Spiritualism will be found, but the tithe of this truly Christian ministry cannot be told. Many noble and distinguished Indians, both male and female, claim to see and hold converse with the spirits of departed friends and kindred; and the faith in immortality, and the presence and ministry of ancestral spirits as guardians to mortals, might well put to shame the cold and unfaithful materialism, even of many professing churchmen.

But there is another view of Indian Spiritualism, and a darker side to the picture, which it is equally instructive and necessary to consider; and this we shall now present to the reader, with all the candor the subject requires. Whilst it is admitted that individuals, no less than whole tribes of this aboriginal people, profess to hold communion with the spirits of the departed, there is a still wider field of Indian Spiritualism occupied by beings of an unknown and doubtful character, and mixed up with rites and phenomena of a strange, occult, and repulsive character.

The red Indian invokes other spirits than the souls of ancestors, and his history bears witness of phenomena which find no parallel or analogy amongst the records of modern Spiritualism. The poems of Bryant, Whittier, and Longfellow, contain vivid descriptions of the spiritual faith of the red Indian, and the "Hiawatha" of the latter especially, abounds with elaborate descriptions of the belief and practices of the Indian in reference to Spiritualism.

. . .

The following interesting account of the famous "Wau-chus-co," is given by Mr. Johnson, the talented author of many valuable works on American Indian life and customs, described from his own personal observations. The article here quoted was written for the *Detroit Daily Tribune*, of which Mr. Johnson was an esteemed correspondent:

"In my previous letter I enumerated the different powers exercised by the Indian, 'Ches-a-kees.' In addition to those named, is the power of influencing the mind of an Indian at a distance for good or evil. This power was frequently exercised to the destruction of wealth, also in cases of rivalship between warriors, hunters, and lovers. They claimed that the influence of the mind or will, could be put upon material things, such as guns, traps, etc., and it was only through counter spiritual influences that the charm or spell could be dissipated.

"The charm they used upon women was also very powerful. No young warrior was without his love-sack, consisting of a weasel-skin containing the love-powders prepared by great medicine-men. A pinch of this powder placed upon the clothes or hair of any girl they loved, could not be resisted. They would pine, and follow the enchanter, as gentle as a lamb.

"Wau-chus-co was a noted Ches-a-kee, a clairvoyant, who died in the year 1840, on Round Island, near Macinac. He had for ten years previous to his death led a most exemplary Christian life, and was a communicant of the Presbyterian church then on this island, up to the time of his death . . .

The first time I ever Ches-a-keed, was on a war expedition. We had gone towards Chicago. The occasion was urgent, and our chief was afraid that our foes would attack us unawares, and we were also destitute of provisions.

"'Our chief incessantly urged me, and finally I consented. Having prepared myself, I entered the Ches-a-kee lodge, and the instant presence of the spirit was proved by the violent rocking to and fro of the lodge. "Tell us; tell us! where are our enemies?" cried the chief and warriors.

"'Soon the vision of my thinking mind, or spirit, embraced a large extent of country which I had never seen before. Every object was plainly before me. Our enemies were there in their villages, unsuspicious of danger. Their acts and conversation were made known to me. Game abounded in another direction. All this I told. Next day we procured food in abundance, and a few days afterwards a dozen scalps graced our return to the cross village. I exerted my powers frequently amongst my tribe, and to satisfy the doubtful, permitted them to tie me as they thought proper.

They would sometimes place men in the Ches-a-kee lodge, which would then commence shaking, indicating the presence of the spirit. The cords with which I was tied would then drop from my limbs. Frequently I have seen a bright light at the opening at the top of the lodge, and strange faces were Invisible to me. The words of the spirits were audible to the spectators outside, but none could understand them but me . . .

William M. Johnson. August 6, 1859."

Such are some of the phases in which spirit communion exhibits itself amongst the people whom we call "savage," and whom, in comparison to our more advanced civilization, we may justly call so; and yet, does our knowledge of the occult and invisible forces in nature furnish us with any clue to the mystery of these astounding manifestations or the power by which the unlettered "savage" can avail himself of a knowledge which all our control over the elements fails to compete with? In a word, the red Indian can do what we can neither explain nor imitate.

Document Four: Excerpts from the séance registers; Rene Grandjean Collection, Special Collections, Earl K. Long Library, University of New Orleans. Translations completed by volume editor.

26 October 1870

> Black in the land of America,
> But my hands pure in the spirit-land.
> I look with joy that from Africa
> No Americans, to spirit-land.
> Are sent.
> I went
> Forgiving
> And Helping,
> For I was right
> From darkness, light
> I received.
> Never deceived
> Are men in the spirit-land.
> Oh, Come and join our band
> White men of America
> Join the sons of Africa.
> In love we live
> In love forgive
> White men
> Black men.
> — A black man, once

24 April 1872

How many human beings have passed over to the spiritual world leaving their relatives in tears, while they were able, if those same relatives had not been fastened to tradition, to reveal to them the glorious existence which is theirs, and to make shine in their mind the comprehension of equality of all beings, here, where each one appears with his works, where the remembrance of the former position occupied while on Earth with the material envelope often is a very aggravating souvenir; for, the one who is placed in a more advantageous position, ought not to crush his fellow Being, on the contrary, to elevate him!

Lessons are met, here, which cause many to shed very bitter tears, at the remembrance of the past injustice which made them to regard a brother, or a sister, as being of a low extraction. Oh! my God!

There is the Soul which comes from God and which is all. The body is a mere envelope to be used for the transient time of the Mission; but, before God, there are equal beings only. Jesus with a black envelope capped with wooly or crisped hair, would be disowned by many! But, have you any knowledge what complexion was his? In a high degree he was charitable by his soul; but, his envelope, was it black, yellow, or white, has none the less been the prey of vermin as well as yours will be. Old age which, with a fresh and smooth face, makes it parchment-like, shows the decrepitude of all what belongs to Earth. You meet lessons at each one of your steps: sickness, accidents, pains, everything is common. Although you have placed the body of your relatives in a magnificent mausoleum, decomposition will take place the same; a skeleton will appear, and, from your cherished mother, some dust and a skull, a few bones will show the hideous proof how of an ephemeral nature is this covering which causes you condemn and reject from your society the virginal maid, and to entertain with respect the prostitute who defiles herself with art, and who, by the doubt of her actions hidden by a certain amount of pomp, frolics in your midst. A salute full of disdain and pride, testifies of your presumption at the sight of her to whom you make a crime of her ancestors. But, here, when both of you shall come, you will be judged according to your deeds; and, then, where will be the envelope of each?—the prey of worms, two skeletons, a few bones, some dust, nothing more!

. . .

—Annette Bouligny

6 May 1872

. . .

Understand that there are no different races, but there are brothers!
Flags must give way to the universal flag that comes with the Purity of Beings.
There is only one God.
Children of the same father.
There is death of the material envelope, that is to say his disappearance into the Great Whole.

This is the great lesson of equality, of solidarity and of common, fraternal, and charitable Thought that must establish the love of each other.

—Confucius

16 June 1872

My name was Jean Pierre on your Earth; I had a black envelope. Someone called himself my master! I was his property. He plowed my body with blows! A bloody whip dried in the sun . . . my blood that made it wet. I suffered! Poor martyr! It was forbidden for me to state that my thinking.

I saw before my footsteps, their rise! I was shaking sometimes . . . I shuddered when the road I went to see the woman I loved, that was the price of my miserable material existence and I risked the renewal of that barbarous scene which tied me down at four stakes, of the virulent and barbarous language of the pitiless one who called himself the master of his black brother. I was sweet though! And yet . . . I dreamed of hatred and vengeance at the door of my hut or filtered the north wind. And, a hundred times, I had to leave, despite wind and storm expected loved one who suffered like me further . . . These hours of delight were mixed with our tears.

The whip lay me dead on the spot one day.

That is to say, my body remained as the memory of hatred and prejudice.

I saw another myself, Bright! A bright and shiny Being approached me and said: I'm one of those lights that once shone with you; are you afraid of me today, my brother?

His language was beautiful, gorgeous. It was such a pure and holy melody off. I was transported.

You're free, he continued, and forever!

I was enlightened and radiant, I followed my guide.

I was always called Jean Pierre, but this is no longer the slave Jean Pierre; I was Jean Pierre, the Sublime One.

My master often called me dull and silent!

He is rising from the Past! He is a slave to his prejudices and his Passions the material world.

I am the Sublime One! the spiritual world!

I call him my cruel brother, and soon he will come, I will instruct you and I will show him how much I am noble and sublime!

—Jean Pierre

4 September 1874

The shedding of the blood belonging to the unfortunate ones who have lost their lives under the blows of the monstrous oligarchy who wanted and still wants to crush out the germ of civil rights for the dark skinned children—this blood belonging to unfortunate ones, is a shame for the infuriated ones inhabiting your section and who, one day, will come here to mediate on their horrible crimes and their depravity of manners.

I have qualified these brother-victims, unfortunate ones, for, they do suffer in quitting as soon their material envelope, thus leaving their family helpless and unsheltered, and, moreover, with their knowledge so limited of their existence out of the Flesh, they come over here unprepared, but are granted; however, the sympathy of their luminous brothers.

Oh! You who have participated in the shedding of this blood, either your oral and quiescent approval, or by the sophisms you have preached, Retribution will give you it heart-rending lessons.

The genealogy of your ancestors will be there to surprise nearly every one of you; and your silly vanities will be lost in this exposition of what will render you very humble, believe me!

Oh! This blood shed will have served to create the elect army who are recruited here by the progress of beings out of the body, and they will be your guides who will show you the way toward which they will lead you, as the one which will cleanse you from your defilement and infamies!

There will be triumph for the martyrs, and there will be shame for the oppressors!

You cannot delay the triumph of justice. There will be, for the downtrodden their rights proclaimed and upheld in spite of all!

You may gnash your teeth, oppressors; but you will be compliant and yielding. . .
—Lincoln

Additional reading

Bennett, Bridget. "Sacred Theatres: Shakers, Spiritualists, Theatricality, and the Indian in the 1830s and 1840s," *The Drama Review* 49.3 (2005): 114–134.

Clark, Emily Suzanne. *A Luminous Brotherhood: Afro-Creole Spiritualism in Nineteenth-Century New Orleans* (Chapel Hill, NC: University of North Carolina Press, 2016).

McGarry, Molly. *Ghosts of Futures Past: Spiritualism and the Cultural Politics of Nineteenth-Century America* (Berkeley, CA: University of California Press, 2008).

Troy, Kathryn. *The Specter of the Indian: Race, Gender, and Ghosts in American Séances, 1848–1890* (Albany, NY: State University of New York Press, 2017).

6

Ghost Dance Movement

Editors' Introduction: In the late 1880s, the Ghost Dance movement spread quickly across the American West and Great Plains. As evidenced by Handsome Lake, revitalization movements were not a new phenomenon among Native American communities, though the Ghost Dance seemed to spread more quickly than previous ones. On January 1, 1889 during an eclipse of the sun, Paiute prophet Wovoka (also known as Jack Wilson) experienced a vision. During this vision he saw a utopian future for Native Americans and the way to make this vision a reality. In his vision Wovoka saw a Native paradise on earth: Indians dead and alive were reunited, whites vanished, and the world was restored to its pre-European-arrival state. Wovoka taught that if certain ethical rules were followed and if the Ghost Dance, a group round dance, was performed, this prophetic vision would come true. Many of those ethical rules were reminiscent of Wovoka's Christian upbringing and adoptive white family, the Wilsons. Thus, a reunion with the ancestors would take place in heaven if the Native Americans on earth lived moral lives consistent with traditional Indian worldviews and select Christian teachings; then the prophesy declared, the dead would return and the old way of life would be revived on earth.

As the message of the Ghost Dance spread from Nevada throughout the West and Great Plains, it took on differences with each group. Some Native communities believed that whites would simply return to Europe when the world was restored, while others believed that whites would perish in fire. What was clear was that whites and Native Americans had different fates in this new world. Many regarded Wovoka as the Indian messiah, and the scratches and scars on his head and hands seemed to resemble the wounds of Christ from the crucifixion. The main response from whites was disgust. Christian missionaries saw the spread of the Ghost Dance prophecy and ritual as a sign of their failure to "civilize" Native communities, and the military viewed it as a war dance. With these disparaging views came tragedy. On December 29, 1890, while the US Army forcibly disarmed a group of Lakota who followed the Ghost Dance, a gun discharged and the Army opened fire on the entire community. The massacre at Wounded Knee ended with over two hundred Lakota men, women, and children dead. Some of their bodies lay two miles from camp.

The Lakota living at Pine Ridge who met with anthropologist James Mooney in 1891 told him the following about the Ghost Dance: "The dance was our religion, but the government sent soldiers to kill us on account of it. We will not talk more about it." However, 1890 was not the last time the Ghost Dance was danced there. A seventy-one-day occupation of the town of Wounded Knee began on February 27, 1973. Some participants in the American Indian Movement and members of the Ogala Lakota tribe took control of the city in protest against what they identified as local and national corruption and mistreatment of Native people. The occupiers and US Marshals and the Federal Bureau of Investigation exchanged nightly gunfire that would claim the lives of two protestors and wound thirteen others, along with wounding two US government agents. During the occupation, the protestors engaged in an emotionally charged and pan-Indian performance of the Ghost Dance.

The first two documents that follow catalog the Ghost Dance from the view of whites who witnessed it. First is a newspaper story from *The Wichita Daily Eagle* that reflects the biased view on the movement held by many white Americans of the day. It heavily quotes Bureau of Indian Affairs Agent James McLaughlin, who uses language typical of most non-natives. Seeing Native Americans as "savages," most white Americans could not see the Ghost Dance as anything but a dangerous movement. Next comes excerpts from anthropologist James Mooney's extensive tome *The Ghost-Dance Religion and the Sioux Outbreak of 1890*. This 1896 book was the result of years of ethnographic work among numerous communities who followed the Ghost Dance movement. While Mooney was not innocent of ethnocentrism in his depictions of the Ghost Dance, his work and the newspaper account make for an interesting comparison. The third document comes from Dr. Charles Eastman (Ohiyesa), a Santee Sioux. After attending a nearby mission school, Eastman received a BA from Dartmouth College and an MD from Boston University. He later became employed by the US Government and was sent to serve as the physician at the Pine Ridge Agency not long before the Massacre at Wounded Knee. Document Three comes from his 1916 autobiography, *From the Deep Woods to Civilization: Chapters in the Autobiography of an Indian*.

Documents

Document One: "The Indian Millennium," *The Wichita Daily Eagle*, October 28, 1890.

The Indian Millennium
An Agent's Report on the Craze Now Taking Possession of the Sioux

Washington, Oct. 27.—The Indian bureau has received from Agent McLaughlin at the Standing Rock Indian agency, a report upon the prospective outbreak among the Sioux in consequence of the promised coming of the "New Messiah." The agent says:

"I trust that I may not be considered an alarmist, and I do not wish to be misunderstood as considering the present state of excitement so alarming as to apprehend any immediate uprising or serious outcome; but I do feel it my duty to report the present craze and the nature of the excitement existing among the Sitting Bull faction of Indians over the expected "Indian millennium"—the annihilation of the white man and supremacy of the Indians, which is looked for not later than next spring. They are promised by some members of the Sioux tribe, who have lately developed into medicine men, that the Great Spirit has promised them that their punishment by the white demi-nation has ended, and that their numbers having become so decimated, will be reinforced by all the Indians who are dead, that the dead are returning to re-inhabit this earth, which belongs to the Indians; that they are driving back with them, as they return, immense herds of buffalo and elegant wild horses, to have for the catching; that the Great Spirit promises them that the white men will be unable to make gunpowder in the future, and that all attempts at such will be a failure, and that the gunpowder now on hand will be useless against Indians, as it will not throw bullets with sufficient force to pass through the skin of an Indian; that the Great Spirit has deserted the Indians for a long time, but is now with them, and against the whites, and will cover the earth over with thirty feet of soil, well sodded and timbered, under which the whites will all be smothered; and any whites who may escape this great phenomena will become fishes in the rivers of the country; but in order to bring about this happy result, the Indians must do their part, and become believers and thoroughly organize.

Sitting Bull is high priest and leading apostle of this latest Indian absurdity; in a word, he is the chief mischief-maker at this agency, and if he were not here this craze, so general among the Sioux, would never have gotten a foothold at this agency. He has been a disturbing element here since his return from confinement as a military prisoner in the spring of 1883, but has been growing gradually worse the past year . . .

On the 9th instant, upon an invitation from Sitting Bull, and Indian named Kicking Bear, belonging to the Cheyenne river agency, the chief medicine man of the ghost dance among the Sioux, arrived at Sitting Bull's camp on Grand river, to inaugurate a ghost dance and initiate the members. Upon learning of his arrival there, I sent a detachment of thirteen policemen, including the captain and second lieutenant, to arrest and escort him from the reservation; but they returned without executing the order, both officers in a dazed condition, and fearing the powers of the medicine man.

Sitting Bull was very insolent to the officers, and made threats against certain members of the force; but said that the visitors would leave the following day. On the 14th I sent the lieutenant and one man back to see whether the party had left, and to notify Sitting Bull that his insolence and bad behavior would not be tolerated longer, and that the ghost dance must not be continued. The lieutenant returned yesterday, and reported that the party had not started back to Cheyenne before his arrival there, on the morning of the 15, but left immediately upon his ordering them to do so. Sitting Bull told him that he was determined to continue the ghost dance. The Great Spirit had sent a direct message to Kicking Bear that to live they must do so, but he would not have any more dancing until after he had come to the agency and talked the matter over with me; but the news came in this morning that they are dancing again. Desiring to exhaust all reasonable means before resorting to the extreme, I have sent a message to Sitting Bull by his nephew, One Bull, that I want to see him at the agency; and I feel confident that I shall succeed in allaying the present excitement and put a stop to this absurd craze for the present."

Document Two: James Mooney, *The Ghost-Dance Religion and the Sioux Outbreak of 1890*, extract from the Fourteenth Annual Report of the Bureau of Ethnology (Washington, DC: Government Printing Office, 1896), 777–782.

Chapter X
The Doctrine of the Ghost Dance

The great underlying principle of the Ghost dance doctrine is that the time will come when the whole Indian race, living and dead, will be reunited upon a regenerated earth, to live a life of aboriginal happiness, forever free from death, disease, and misery. On this foundation, each tribe has built a structure from its own mythology, and each apostle and believer has filled in the details according to his own mental capacity or ideas of happiness, with such additions as come to him from the trance. Some changes, also, have undoubted resulted from the transmission of the doctrine through the imperfect medium of sign language. The differences of interpretation are precisely such as we find in Christianity, with its hundreds of sects and innumerable shades of individual opinion. The white race, being alien and secondary and hardly real, has no part in this scheme of aboriginal regeneration, and will be left behind with the other things of earth that have served their temporary purpose, or else will cease entirely to exist.

All of this is to be brought about by an overruling spiritual power that needs no assistance from human creatures; and though certain medicine men were disposed to anticipate the Indian millennium by preaching resistance to the further encroachment of the whites, such teachings form no part of the true doctrine, and it was only when chronic dissatisfaction was aggravated by recent grievances, as among the Sioux, that the movement assumed a hostile expression. On the contrary, all believers were exhorted to make themselves worthy of the predicted happiness by discarding all things warlike and practicing honesty, peace, and good will, not only among themselves, but also toward the whites, so long as they were together. Some apostles have even thought that all race distinctions are to be obliterated and that the whites are to participate with the Indians in the coming felicity; but it seems unquestionable that this is equally contrary to the doctrine as originally preached.

. . . [*Editors' Note*: There is then a section on the mythology of Wovoka as the Indian messiah, including a letter from an Arapaho Indian. That letter is reproduced a number of different ways and different iterations, including the one here.] . . .

The Messiah Letter
(free Rendering)

When you get home you must make a dance to continue for five days. Dance four successive nights, and the last night keep up the dance until the morning of the fifth day, when all must bathe in the river and then disperse to their homes. You must all do in the same way.

I, Jack Wilson, love you all, and my heart is full of gladness for the gifts you have brought me. When you get home I shall give you a good cloud [rain?] which will make you feel good. I give you a good spirit and give you all good paint. I want you to come again in three months, some from each tribe there [the Indian Territory].

There will be a good deal of snow this year and some rain. In the fall there will be such a rain as I have never given you before.

Grandfather [a universal title of reverence among Indians and here meaning the messiah] says, when your friends die you must not cry. You must not hurt anybody or do harm to anyone. You must not fight. Do right always. It will give you satisfaction in life. This young man has a good father and mother. [Possibly this refers to Casper Edson, the young Arapaho who wrote down this message of Wovoka for the delegation.]

Do not tell white people about this. Jesus is now upon the earth. He appears like a cloud. The dead are alive again. I do not know when they will be here; maybe this fall or in the spring. When the time comes there will be no more sickness and everyone will be young again.

Do not refuse to work for the whites and do not make any trouble with them until you leave them. When the earth shakes [at the coming of the new world] do not be afraid. It will not hurt you.

I want you to dance every six weeks. Make a feast at the dance and have food that everybody may eat. Then bathe in the water. That is all. You will receive good words again from me some time. Do not tell lies.

Every organized religion has a system of ethics, a system of mythology, and a system of ritual observance. In this message from the high priest of the Ghost dance we have a synopsis of all three. With regard to the ritual part, ceremonial purification and bathing have formed a part of some form or other of every great religion from the beginning of history, while the religious dance dates back far beyond the day when the daughter of Saul "looked through a window and saw King David leaping and dancing before the Lord." The feasting enjoined is a part of every Indian ceremonial gathering, religious, political, or social. The dance is to continue four successive nights, in accord with the regular Indian system, in which *four* is the sacred number, as *three* is in Christianity. In obedience to this message the southern prairie tribes, after the return of the delegation in August, 1891, ceased to hold frequent one-night dances at irregular intervals as formerly without the ceremonial bathing, and adopted instead a system of four-night dances at regular periods of six weeks, followed by ceremonial bathing on the morning of the fifth day.

The mythology of the doctrine is only briefly indicated, but the principal articles are given. The dead are all arisen and the spirit hosts are advancing and have already arrived at the boundaries of this earth, led forward by the regenerator in the shape of cloud-like indistinctness. The spirit captain of the dead is always represented under this shadowy semblance. The great change will be ushered in by a trembling of the earth, at which the faithful are exhorted to feel no alarm. The hope held out is the same that has inspired the Christian for nineteen centuries—a happy immortality in perpetual youth. As to fixing a date, the messiah is as cautious as his predecessor in prophecy, who declares that "no man knoweth the time, not even the angels of God." His weather predictions also are about as definite as the inspired utterances of the Delphian oracle.

The moral code inculcated is as pure and comprehensive in its simplicity as anything found in religious systems from the days of Gautama Buddha to the time of Jesus Christ. *"Do no harm to any one. Do right always."* Could anything be more simple, and yet more exact and exacting? It inculcates honesty—*"Do not tell lies."* It preaches good will—*"Do no harm to any one."* It forbids the extravagant mourning customs formerly common among tribes—*"When your friends die, you must not cry,"* which is interpreted by the prairie tribes as forbidding the killing of horses, the burning of tipis and destruction of property, the cutting off of hair and gashing of the body with knives, all of which were formerly the sickening rule at every death until forbidden by the new doctrine. As an Arapaho said to me when his little boy died, "I shall not shoot any ponies, and my wife will not gash her arms. We used to do this when our friends died, because we thought we would never see them again, and it made us feel bad. But now we know we shall be united again."

Document Three: Charles Alexander Eastman, *From the Deep Woods to Civilization: Chapters in the Autobiography of an Indian* (Boston, MA: Little Brown & Company, 1916), 92–115.

Chapter VII
The Ghost Dance War

A religious craze such as that of 1890–91 was a thing foreign to the Indian philosophy. I recalled that a hundred years before, on the overthrow of the Algonquin nations, a somewhat similar faith was evolved by the astute Delaware prophet, brother to Tecumseh. It meant that the last hope of race entity had departed, and my people were groping blindly after spiritual relief in their bewilderment and misery. I believe that the first prophets of the "Red Christ" were innocent enough and that the people generally were sincere, but there were doubtless some who went into it for self-advertisement, and who introduced new and fantastic features to attract the crowd.

The ghost dancers had gradually concentrated on the Medicine Root creek and the edge of the "Bad Lands," and they were still further isolated by a new order from the agent, calling in all those who had not adhered to the new religion. Several thousand of these "friendlies" were soon encamped on the White Clay creek, close by the agency. It was near the middle of December, with weather unusually mild for that season. The dancers held that there would be no snow so long as their rites continued.

. . . [*Editors' Note*: Eastman comments about a divide among Sioux between Ghost Dancers and "friendlies," those who were more inclined to work with the US Government and Indian police. This divide included a supposed conspiracy to kill a "friendly" chief named American Horse who is threatened by a Ghost Dancer Sioux.] . . .

After the others had withdrawn, Sword informed me confidentially that certain young men had threatened to kill American Horse while asleep in his tent, and that his friends had prevailed upon him and his wife to ask my hospitality for a few days. I showed Mrs. American Horse to a small room that I had vacant, and soon afterward came three strokes of the office bell—the sign for me to report at the agent's office.

I found there the agent, his chief clerk, and a visiting inspector, all of whom regarded the situation as serious. "You see, doctor," said the agent, "the occurrence of to-day was planned with remarkable accuracy, so that even our alert police were taken entirely by surprise and readily overpowered, what will be the sequel we can not tell, but we must be prepared for anything. I shall be glad to have your views," he added.

I told him that I still did not believe there was any widespread plot, or deliberate intention to make war upon the whites. In my own mind, I felt sure that the arrival of troops would be construed by the ghost dancers as a threat or a challenge, and would put them at once on the defensive. I was not in favor of that step; neither was Mr. Cook, who was called into conference; but the officials evidently feared a general uprising and argued that it was their duty to safeguard the lives of the employees and others by calling for the soldiers without more delay. Sword, Thunder Bear, and American Horse were sent for and their opinions appeared to be fully in accord with those of the agent and inspector, so the matter was given out as settled. As a matter of fact, the agent had telephoned to Fort Robinson for troops before he made a pretense of consulting us Indians, and they were already on their way to Pine Ridge.

I scarcely knew at the time, but gradually learned afterward, that the Sioux had many grievances and causes for profound discontent, which lay back of and were more or less closely related to the ghost dance craze and the prevailing restlessness and excitement. Rations had been cut from time to time; the people were insufficiently fed, and their protests and appeals were disregarded. Never was more ruthless fraud and graft practiced upon a defenseless people than upon these poor natives by the politicians! Never were there more worthless "scraps of paper" anywhere in the world than many of the Indian treaties and Government documents! Sickness was prevalent and the death rate alarming, especially among the children. Trouble from all these causes had for some time been developing, but might have been checked by humane and conciliatory measures. The "Messiah craze" in itself was scarcely a source of danger, and one might almost as well call upon the army to suppress Billy Sunday and his hysterical followers. Other tribes than the Sioux who adopted the new religion were left alone, and the craze died a natural death in the course of a few months.

. . . [*Editors' Note*: Eastman provides a lay of the land and which leaders were the "malcontents" and which were "friendly" to the US. The additional troops arrive and terrify many "friendly" Sioux who feared being attacked by mistake. The soldiers make their camp, and Eastman and other Sioux try to go about their daily lives, despite high tension and anxiety.] . . .

Three days later, we learned that Big Foot's band of ghost dancers from the Cheyenne river reservation north of us was approaching the agency, and that Major Whiteside was in command of troops with orders to intercept them.

Later that afternoon, the Seventh Calvary under Colonel Forsythe was called to the saddle and rode off toward Wounded Knee creek, eighteen miles away. Father Craft, a Catholic priest with some Indian blood, who knew Sitting bull and his people, followed an hour or so later, and I was inclined to go too, but my fiancée pointed out that my duty lay rather at home with our Indians, and I stayed.

The morning of December 29th was sunny and pleasant. We were all straining our ears toward Wounded Knee, and about the middle of the forenoon we distinctly heard the reports of the Hotchkiss guns. Two hours later, a rider was seen approaching at full speed, and in a few minutes he had dismounted from his exhausted horse and handed his message to General Brooke's orderly. The Indians were watching their own messenger, who ran on foot along the northern ridges and carried the news to the so-called "hostile" camp. It was said that he delivered his message at almost the same time as the mounted officer.

The resulting confusion and excitement was unmistakable. The white teepees disappeared as if by magic and soon the caravans were in motion, going toward the natural fortress of the "Bad Lands." In the "friendly" camp there was almost as much turmoil, and crowds of frightened women and children poured into the agency. Big Foot's band had been wiped out by the troops, and reprisals were naturally looked for. The enclosure was not barricaded in any way and we had but a small detachment of troops for our protection. Sentinels were placed, and machine guns trained on the various approaches.

A few hot-headed young braves fired on the sentinels and wounded two of them. The Indian police began to answer by shooting at several braves who were apparently about to set fire to some of the outlying buildings. Every married employee was seeking a place of safety for his family, the interpreter among them. Just then General Brooke ran out into the open, shouting at the top of his voice to the police: "Stop, stop! Doctor, tell them they must not fire until ordered!" I did so, as the bullets whistled by us, and the General's coolness perhaps saved all our lives, for we were in no position to repel a large attacking force. Since we did not reply, the scattered shots soon ceased, but the situation remained critical for several days and nights.

My office was full of refugees. I called one of my good friends aside and asked him to saddle my two horses and stay by them. "When general fighting begins, take them to Miss Goodale and see her to the railroad if you can," I told him. Then I went over to the rectory. Mrs. Cook refused to go without her husband, and Miss Goodale would not leave while there was a chance of being in service. The house was crowded with terrified people, most of them Christian Indians, whom our friends were doing their best to pacify.

At dusk, the Seventh Calvary returned with their twenty-five dead and I believe thirty-four wounded, most of them by their own comrades, who had encircled the Indians, while few of the latter had guns. A majority of the thirty or more

Indians wounded were women and children, including babies in arms. As there were not tents enough for all, Mr. Cook offered us the mission chapel, in which the Christmas tree stood still, for a temporary hospital. We tore out the pews and covered the floor with hay and quilts. There we laid out the poor creatures side by side in rows, and the night was devoted to caring for them as best we could. Many were frightfully torn by pieces of shells, and the suffering was terrible. General Brooke placed me in charge and I had to do nearly all the work, for although the army surgeons were more than ready to help as their own men had been cared for, the tortured Indians would not scarcely allow a man in uniform to touch them. Mrs. Cook, Miss Goodale, and several of Mrs. Cook's Indian helpers acted as volunteer nurses. In spite of all our efforts, we lost the greater part of them, but a few recovered, including several children who had lost all their relatives and who were adopted into kind Christian families.

On the day following the Wounded Knee massacre there was a blizzard, in the midst of which I was ordered out with several Indian police, to look for a policeman who was reported to have been wounded and left some two miles from the agency. We did not find him. This was the only time during the whole affair that I carried a weapon; a friend lent me a revolver which I had put in my overcoat pocket, and it was lost in the ride. On the third day it cleared, and the ground was covered with an inch or two of fresh snow. We had feared that some of the Indian wounded might have been left on the field, and a number of us volunteered to go and see. I was placed in charge of the expedition of about a hundred civilians, ten or fifteen of whom were white men. We were supplied with wagons in which to convey any whom we might find still alive. Of course a photographer and several reporters were of the party.

Fully three miles from the scene of the massacre we found the body of a woman completely covered with a blanket of snow, and from this point on we found them scattered along as they had been relentlessly hunted down and slaughtered while fleeing for their lives. Some of our people discovered relatives or friends among the dead, and there was much wailing and mourning. When we reached the spot where the Indian camp had stood, among the fragments of burned tents and other belongings we saw the frozen bodies lying close together or piled on upon another. I counted eighty bodies of men who had been in the council and who were almost as helpless as the women and babes when the deadly fire began, for nearly all their guns had been taken from them. A reckless and desperate young Indian fired the first shot when the search for weapons was well under way, and immediately all the troops opened fire from all sides, killing not only unarmed men, women, and children, but their own comrades who stood opposite them, for the camp was entirely surrounded.

It took all my nerve to keep my composure in the face of this spectacle, and of the excitement and grief of my Indian companions, nearly every one of whom was crying aloud or singing his death song. The white men became very nervous, but I set them to examining and uncovering every body to see if one were living.

Additional reading

DeMallie, Raymond J. "The Lakota Ghost Dance: An Ethnohistorical Account," *Pacific Historical Review* 51.4 (November 1982): 385–405.

Lynch, Don and Michael Hittman, with the Yerington Paiute Tribe, *Wovoka and the Ghost Dance* (Lincoln, NB: University of Nebraska Press, 1990).

Smoak, Gregory. *Ghost Dances and Identity: Prophetic Religion and American Indian Ethnogenesis in the Nineteenth Century* (Berkeley, CA: University of California Press, 2008).

7

Ku Klux Klan

E*ditors' Introduction:* The Ku Klux Klan emerged in 1866 when a small group of Confederate veterans organized a fraternal society in Pulaski, Tennessee. The Civil War not only decimated the region's economy, but it also stifled the spirit of many southerners wholly committed to the southern cause of white supremacy. The members of this new society wanted to restore their lost dignity and pride as they attempted to reclaim their positions as patriarchal leaders of the white-dominated South. To this end, they adopted the name Ku Klux Klan (*kuklos* is the Greek word meaning circle); they wore uniforms that included tall conical hats; and they targeted African Americans, who as a result of the Reconstruction Amendments to the United States Constitution, gained their freedom and other civil liberties. They also targeted northerners who threatened the Klan's version of white-dominated southern society. The organization spread beyond Tennessee into semi-autonomous chapters. As the Klan spread, members became more determined to restore white supremacy as they threatened, intimidated, and even murdered African Americans and their allies. They interfered with local elections, raided their enemies' homes, and destroyed private property. This first manifestation of the Klan either went underground or disappeared after Congress passed the Enforcement Act of 1871 (the so-called Ku Klux Klan Act), which federalized many of the crimes Klan members routinely committed, held state officials liable for depriving African Americans of their civil rights, and gave the federal government more power to enforce the Act in the South.

The Klan resurfaced decades later in 1915 when William Joseph Simmons revived the organization in Atlanta, Georgia. Simmons drew inspiration from the Klan's earlier writings, from the testimonies of surviving Klan members, and from *The Birth of a Nation*, a popular movie that depicted African Americans as sexual and social predators in need of white stewardship and control. The movie was an adaptation of Thomas Dixon, Jr.'s 1905 novel *The Clansman: A Historical Romance of the Ku Klux Klan*. Dixon was a white politician and Baptist minister in North Carolina, and his views reflected the white, post-war South. In the book and movie, the Klan served the important role of safeguarding white America from black predators. As depicted in both renderings, the Klan also wore white costumes and burned crosses. Simmons incorporated both of these into the second manifestation of the Klan.

The second version of the Klan played a more public role, as it officially did not advocate for violence and instead spread its message through newspapers, pamphlets, and magazines. It also marched in parades and hosted picnics and pageants. This version of the Klan not only looked and acted different from its predecessor, but it also adopted a more explicitly religious rhetoric as it presented itself as a Protestant organization comprised of members from various Protestant denominations who safeguarded not only white America, but white Protestant America. The Klan became more nativist as it argued that Jewish and Catholic immigrants (in addition to African Americans) also threatened American politics and culture. The Klan argued with more liberal Protestants, whom they believed perverted the Bible's teachings. These explicitly conservative Protestant ideas and ideals permeated the Klan's writings in this period. This version of the Klan resonated with millions of Americans as it spread throughout all forty-eight of the continental states before its demise in the 1930s.

Various groups later adopted the name Ku Klux Klan in the 1950s and 1960s in opposition to the civil rights movement and desegregation. These versions of the Klan drew inspiration from the previous versions, although they lacked an official organizational structure at the national level and instead reflected the beliefs and ambitions of their local members. The Klan continues to exist today with over two dozen active Klan groups united perhaps only by their desire to protect white, Christian America.

The documents included below capture the Klan's dedication to white supremacy, anti-Catholicism, and anti-Semitism. These documents also all come from the early twentieth century, at the height of the KKK's influence and power. Document One comes from Dixon's 1905 novel *The Clansman*. The scene, which follows the deaths of a young white woman and her mother who jump off a cliff in order to escape a lust-filled black man, is credited as the inspiration for the Klan's fiery cross. The Klan found the women's bodies, unlawfully seized the "dangerous" black man (Gus), and have begun a meeting and ceremony to determine his fate. Document Two is a copy of the "Oath of the American Krusaders," rendered with its original pause breaks (from when it was spoken and repeated aloud). This version of the oath is undated, but as it is stored along with other Klan effects owned by E.B. Quackenbush, lawyer and Grand Dragon of the Spokane, WA Klan in the 1920s, it is likely from the same era. The oath contains much religious language, reflecting the self-proclaimed sacred nature of the Klan's vision and identity.

Document Three is an excerpt from the House of Representatives Committee on Rules hearing regarding the Klan in 1921. Simmons responded to questions about the organization and defended it from what he saw as misinformation, and in this excerpt, he emphasized the role of prayer and importance of God. Document Four is excerpts from a published rebuttal from Hiram Wesley Evans, Imperial Wizard of the Klan, to a negative piece on the Klan that ran in *The Forum* (a well-known public affairs magazine) in 1925. *The Forum* also printed Evans's response (Document Four), in which he expands on the vision laid out in Document Three, while weaving in the importance of the Klan's Protestantism over and against Catholicism and Judaism.

Documents

Document One: Thomas Dixon, Jr., *The Clansman: A Historical Romance of the Ku Klux Klan* (New York: DoubleDay, Page & Company, 1905), 318–326.

Through the narrow crooked entrance they led Gus into the cave which had been the rendezvous of the Piedmont Den of the Klan since its formation. The meeting-place was a grand hall eighty feet deep, fifty feet wide, and more than forty feet in height, which had been carved out of the stone by the swift current of the river in ages past when its waters stood at a higher level.

To-night it was lighted by candles placed on the ledges of the walls. In the centre, on a fallen boulder, sat the Grand Dragon of the Den, the presiding officer of the township, his rank marked by scarlet stripes on the white cloth spike of his cap. Around him stood twenty or more clansmen in their uniform, completely disguised. One of them wore a yellow sash, trimmed in gold, about his waist, and on his breast two yellow circles with red crosses interlapping, denoting his rank to be the Grand Dragon of the Realm, or Commander-in-Chief of the State.

The Cyclops rose from his seat:

"Let the Grand Turk remove his prisoner for a moment and place him in charge of the Grand Sentinel at the door, until summoned."

The officer disappeared with Gus, and the Cyclops continued.

"The Chaplain will open our Council with prayer."

Solemnly every white-shrouded figure knelt on the ground, and the voice of the Rev. Hugh McAlpin, trembling with feeling, echoed through the cave:

"Lord God of our Fathers, as in times past thy children, fleeing from the oppressor, found refuge beneath the earth until once more the sun of righteousness rose, so we are met to-night. As we wrestle with the powers of darkness now strangling our life, give to our souls to endure as seeing the invisible, and to our right arms the strength of the martyred dead of our people. Have mercy on the poor, the weak, the innocent and defenseless and deliver us from the body of the Black Death. In a land of light and beauty and love our women are prisoners of danger and fear. While the heathen walks his native heath unharmed and unafraid, in this fair Christian Southland, our sisters, wives, and daughters dare not stroll at twilight through the streets, or step beyond the highway at noon. The terror of the twilight deepens with the darkness, and the stoutest heart grows sick with fear for the red message the morning bringeth. Forgive our sins—they are many, but hide not they face from us, O God, for thou art our refuge!"

. . .

A sudden inspiration flashed in Doctor Cameron's eyes. Turning to the figure with yellow sash and double cross he said:

"Issue your orders and dispatch your courier tonight with the old Scottish rite of the Fiery Cross. It will send a thrill of inspiration to every clansman in the hills."

"Good—prepare it quickly," was the answer.

Doctor Cameron opened his medicine case, drew the silver drinking-cover from a flask, and passed out of the cave to the dark circle of blood still shining in the sand by the water's edge. He knelt and filled the cup half full of the crimson grains, and dipped it into the river. From a saddle he took the lightwood torch, returned within, and placed the cup on the boulder on which the Grand Cyclops had sat. He loosed the bundle of lightwood, took two pieces, tied them in the form of a cross, and laid it beside a lighted candle near the silver cup.

The silent figures watched his every movement. he lifted the cup and said:

"Brethren, I hold in my hand the water of your river bearing the red stain of the life of a Southern woman, a priceless sacrifice on the altar of outraged civilization. Hear the message of your chief."

The tall figure with the yellow sash and double cross stepped before the strange altar, while the white forms of the clansmen gathered about him in a circle. He lifted his cap, and laid it on the boulder, and his men gazed on the flushed face of Ben Cameron, the Grand Dragon of the Realm.

He stood for a moment silent, erect, a smoldering fierceness in his eyes, something cruel and yet magnetic in his alert bearing.

He looked on the prostrate negro lying in his uniform at his feet, seized the cross, lighted the three upper ends and held it blazing in his hand, while, in a voice full of feeling, he said:

"Men of the South, the time for words has passed, the hour for action has struck. The Grand Turk will execute this negro to-night and fling his body on the lawn of the black Lieutenant-Governor of the state."

The Grand Turk bowed.

"I ask for the swiftest messenger of this Den who can ride till dawn."

The man whom Doctor Cameron had already chosen stepped forward."

"Carry my summons to the Grand Titan of the adjoining province in North Carolina whom you will find at Hambright. Tell him the story of this crime and what you have seen and heard. Ask him to report to me here the second night from this, at eleven o'clock, with six Grand Giants from his adjoining counties, each accompanied by two hundred picked men. In olden times when the Chieftain of our people summoned the clan on an errand of life and death, the Fiery Cross, extinguished in sacrificial blood, was sent by swift courier from village to village. This call was never made in vain, nor will it be to-night in the new world. Here, on this spot made holy ground by the blood of those we hold dearer than life, I raise the ancient symbol of an unconquered race of men—"

High above his head in the darkness of the cave he lifted the blazing emblem—

"The Fiery Cross of old Scotland hills! I quench its flames in the sweetest blood that ever stained the sands of Time."

He dipped its ends in the silver cup, extinguished the fire, and handed the charred symbol to the courier, who quickly disappeared.

Document Two: Oath of the American Krusaders, undated but marked Form 103—J.F.H. From the Radicals Collection, Box 11, USA West Archives, Jesuits West, Gonzaga University.

Oath of the American Krusaders

You will place your left hand over your heart and raise your right hand to heaven.

Section I

(You will say) "I" — — (Pronounce your full name — and repeat after me) "Before God — and in the presence of — these mysterious Krusaders — on my sacred honor — do most solemnly and sincerely pledge — promise and swear — that I will forever — keep sacredly secret — the signs, words and grip — and any and all other — matters and knowledge — of the American Krusaders — regarding which a most rigid secrecy — must be maintained — which may at any time — be communicated to me — and will never — divulge same nor even cause same to be divulged — to any person in the whole world — unless I know positively — that such person is a member of this Order — in good and regular standing — and not even then — unless it be — for the best interest of this Order.

"I most sacredly vow — and most positively swear — that I will never yield to bribe — flattery — threats — passion — punishment — persecution — persuasion — nor any enticements whatever — coming from or offered by — any person or persons — male or female — for the purpose of — obtaining from me — a secret or secret information — of the American Krusaders — I will die rather than divulge the same — so help me God.

Section II

"I — most solemnly pledge, promise and swear — unconditionally — that I will faithfully obey — the constitution and laws — and will willingly conform to — all regulations, usages and requirements — of the American Krusaders — which do now exist — or which may be hereafter enacted — and will render at all times — loyal respect and steadfast support — to the Authority of same — and will heartily heed — all official mandates — decrees — edicts — rulings and instructions — of the Supreme Regent thereof. — I will yield prompt response — to all summonses — I having knowledge of same — Providence along preventing.

Section III

"I most solemnly and sincerely pledge — promise and swear — that I will diligently guard and faithfully foster — every interest of the American Krusaders — and will maintain — its social cast and dignity.

"I swear that I will never recommend — any person for membership in this Order — whose mind is unsound — or whose reputation I know to be bad — or whose character is doubtful or whose loyalty to our country — is in any way questionable.

"I swear that I will pay promptly — all just and legal demands — made upon me to defray the expenses — of my Kamps and this Order — when same are due or called for.

"I swear that I will protect the property — of the American Krusaders — of any nature whatsoever — and if any should be entrusted to my keeping — I will promptly keep — or rightly use same — and will freely and promptly surrender same — on official demand — or if ever I am banished from — or voluntarily discontinue — my membership in the Order.

"I swear that I will most determinedly — maintain peace and harmony — in all the deliberations — of the gatherings or assemblies — of the American Krusaders — and of any subordinate jurisdiction — or Kamp thereof.

"I swear that I will most strenuously — discourage selfishness — and selfish political ambition — on the part of myself or any Krusader — and I furthermore pledge, promise and swear — that if it should ever become my duty to preside over a Krusader Kamp — I will not allow personal or partisan political discussions to arise.

"I swear that I will never allow — personal friendship — blood or family relationship — nor personal — political — or professional prejudice — malice nor ill will — to influence me in casting my vote — for the election or rejection — of an applicant — for membership in this Order — God being my helper.

Section IV
"I most solemnly pledge, promise and swear — that I will never slander — defraud — deceive — or in any manner wrong — the American Krusaders — a Krusader — nor a Krusader's family — nor will I suffer the same to be done — if I can prevent it.

"I swear that I will be faithful — in defending and protecting — the home — reputation — and physical and business interest — of a Krusader — and that of a Krusader family.

"I swear that I will at any time — without hesitating — go to the assistance or rescue — of a Krusader in any way — at his or her call I will answer — I will be truly — klannish towards Krusaders — in all things honorable.

"I swear that I will never allow — any animosity — friction nor ill will — to arise and remain — between myself and a Krusader — but will be constant in my efforts — to promote real clannishness — among the members of this Order.

"I swear that I will keep secure to myself — a secret of a Krusader — when same is committed to me — in the sacred bond of friendship — the crime of· violating THIS solemn oath — treason against the United States of America — rape — and malicious murder — alone excepted.

"I swear that I will not — aid in the organization — of a clandestine Kamp — or participate in the meeting — of a clandestine Kamp — or permit others to do so — if same lies within my power to prevent.

"I most solemnly assert and affirm — that to the government of the United States of America — and any State thereof, of which I may become a resident — I faithfully swear an unqualified allegiance — above any other and every kind of government — in the whole world — I here and now pledge my life — my property — my vote — and my sacred honor — to uphold its flag — its constitution — and constitutional laws — and will protect — defend — and enforce the same unto death.

"I most solemnly promise and swear — that I will always, at all times and in all places — help, aid and assist — the duly constituted officers of the law — in the proper performance of their legal duties, — and I furthermore promise and swear — to learn to read and write — the English language — intelligibly.

"I swear that I will most zealously — and valiantly — shield and preserve — by any and all — justifiable means and methods — the sacred constitutional rights — and privileges of — free public schools — and support them in preference to every other kind of school whatsoever — free speech — free press — separation of church and state — liberty — white supremacy — just laws — the and pursuit of happiness — against any encroachment — of any nature — by any persons or persons — political party or parties — religious sect or people — native, naturalized or foreign — of any race — color — creed — lineage or tongue whatsoever.

"By this oath I hereby subscribe — to all the foregoing declarations of principles — and pledge my life — hereafter to support same, — and as God is my witness — I will seal this oath with my blood."

You will drop your hands.

Document Three: *The Ku Klux Klan: Hearings Before the Committee on Rules, House of Representatives, Sixty-seventh Congress, First Session* (US Government Printing Office, 1921), 94–95.

[*Editors' Note*: Simmons is in the process of answering questions from Committee Chairman Philip P. Campbell and describing how the organization works.]

A klonklave or meeting of a local organization has, at its opening, a devotional ceremony. I want to state to you, sir, that the opening of a meeting of a local organization, which is known as a klonklave, can not be opened in regular order unless the sacred altar is properly prepared. To properly prepare that sacred altar the flag of our country must be unfurled and placed at the altar. The altar is draped with the Stars and Stripes. Upon the altar is a vessel of water, which is the dedicating fluid, an unsheathed sword, which represents the ability of American citizens to strike in defense of the flag, and upon that altar, sir, is the Holy Bible, opened at the twelfth chapter of Romans. Every oath administered in that meeting is on the Holy Bible. Of course, when we have large classes coming in all can not actually touch it. but the Holy Bible is open upon the altar and the oath is administrated on that sacred book.

I call your attention to the opening song, which breathes every sentiment of fraternity, of honor, love, justice, and sublime patriotism for our common country.

The newspapers published broadcast, with a strain of ridicule, the next to last passage of our opening prayer, where it says:

"We invoke Thy blessings upon our emperor."

They did not publish, sir, in justice to this organization, the paragraph just above it, which I will read:

"God save our nation! And help us to be a Nation worthy of existence on earth. Keep ablaze in each klansman's heart the sacred fire of a devoted patriotism to our country and its Government."

Mr. Chairman, I do not believe there is another organization on earth, of a fraternal nature, that has those words and that sentiment expressed as forcibly as in the prayer of the Ku-Klux Klan. I wish to ask you to review this prayer when you have the time to take it up. It is especially marked.

In the closing ceremony the question is always asked:

"Faithful klaliff, what is the fourfold duty of a klansman?"
He answers:

"To worship God; be patriotic towards our country; be devoted and loyal to our klan and emperor, and to practice clannishness towards his fellow klansmen."
The faithful kludd is asked:

"How speaketh the oracles of our God?
The answer is:

"Thou shalt worship the Lord thy God. Render unto the State the things which are the State's; love the brotherhood; honor the king. Bear ye one another's burdens, and so fulfill the law of Christ."

Those are quotations from the book. I call your attention to the closing klode or the closing song, and it reads:

"God of eternity
Guard, guide our great country,
Our homes and store
Keep our great State to Thee,
Its people right and free;
In us thy glory be
Forevermore."

Document Four: Hiram Wesley Evans, "The Klan: Defender of Americanism," *The Forum* LXXIV.6 (December 1925): 801–814.

... The real value of the Klan, or the real evils, is to be found in the needs, the purposes, and the convictions of the great mass of Americans of the old stock. It is only because the Klan has met these needs and voiced these convictions that it has won strength.

There is no possibility of trying to prove the soundness of the Klan position, or of the controlling instincts and beliefs of the common people of American descent, to any of those who insist on measuring either by the purely theoretic philosophy of cosmopolitanism: of universal equality in character, social value, and current rights. I will not attempt to argue about the doctrine. Science does not support it, and certainly the average American does not believe it. Our attitude toward the Orientals proves this, no matter what our oral professions may be, as well as does our treatment of the Negro.

Mr. Pattangall [*Editors' Note*: Pattangall was the author of the piece that prompted this essay from Evans], on this point, makes an argument for social equality. It is not a matter that will be settled by argument. It will be settled, if ever, by race instinct, personal prejudices, and sentiment. We Americans all deny equality to ten millions of our own citizens; deny it with facts and in fact, if we do not deny it by argument. The idea itself, however it may be glossed over and given theoretic acceptance, is actually abhorrent in practice to the American mind. And in fact, actual social equality between whites and any other race is not practiced to any important extent anywhere on earth. Facts prove the idea unworkable. This beautiful philosophy, therefore, the Klan will not argue about. It merely rejects it, as almost all Americans do.

Neither will we argue at all about the questions of white supremacy. In that case, even, we do not propose to permit any argument to avail. We may be intolerant in this, but we will not delude other races into looking forward to privileges that will, in truth, be forever denied. The Klan looks forward to the day when the union of a white person with one of any other race will be illegal in every State of the Union, and when the question of social supremacy will have been settled on a much safer basis than that of racial mongrelization.

. . .

We believe that the pioneers who built America bequeathed to their own children a priority right to it, the control of it and its future, and that no one on earth can claim any part of this inheritance except through our generosity. We believe, too, that the mission of America under Almighty God is to perpetuate and develop just the kind of nation and just the kind of civilization which our forefathers created. This is said without offense to other civilizations, but we do believe that ours, through all possible growth and expansion, should remain *the same kind* that was "brought forth upon this continent." Also, we believe that races of men are as distinct as breeds of animals; that any mixture between races of any great divergence is evil; that the American stock, which was bred under highly selective surroundings, has proved its value and should not be mongrelized; that it has automatically and instinctively developed the kind of civilization which is best suited to its own healthy life and growth; and that this cannot safely be changed except by ourselves and along the lines of our own character. Finally, we believe that all foreigners were admitted with the idea, and on the basis of at least an implied understanding, that they would become a part of us, adopt our ideas and ideals, and help in fulfilling our destiny along those lines, but never that they should be permitted to force us to change into anything else.

. . .

There can be no doubt about the traditional American spirit, the Americanism of the pioneers, which we are trying to save. It is to be seen in the character and spirit of those pioneers, far more than in formal political documents. Americanism is not wholly lovely, perhaps. It is certainly neither soft nor lax, neither easily ductile nor imitative, neither silken nor oily. It is a thing of rugged steel, tempered and forged in the terrific stress of the task of wresting a continent from savages and from the wilderness. It is welded of convictions, independence, self-reliance, freedom, justice, achievement, courage, acceptance of responsibility, and the guidance of his own conscience by each man personally. If inheritance counts for anything it is to be found in the children of the pioneers far more than in any other group on earth, for only those who have had this spirit survived.

And,—remember we are looking at facts,—it has been bound up from the first with the spirit of Protestantism. This had to be. Only men and women who dared to speak to their God face to face could have the courage and self-reliance necessary to the mighty work of the pioneer. It is true historically; and, in fact, Protestantism has never been able to survive except in the so-called Nordic countries. It is a vital part of all Americanism, of all successful democracy.

. . .

Moreover, since the danger was pointed out to them, instead of helping fight it, the liberals have given out only condemnations of the growing protest, platitudinous comforting's, and bally-hoo stuff about the beauties of alien things and ideas. They give, also, an almost joyous welcome to alien criticism of everything American. The unopposed attack on the Puritan conscience is only one illustration; our liberals today seem ashamed of having any conscience at all. Tolerance is more prized by them than conviction, and is insisted upon even toward people who show no tolerance of us. A Jew may say or write what he pleases against America and American ways, but if an American voices the least criticism of a Jew even the American liberals turn to and hound him as narrow, prejudiced, intolerant, bigoted, and anti-Semitic.

. . .

The real objection to Romanism in America is not that it is a religion,—which is no objection at all,—but that it is a church in politics; an organized, disciplined, powerful rival to every political government. A religion in politics is serious; a church in politics is deadly to free institutions. But the Klan, in calling Protestantism to arms, cannot fairly be accused of mixing church and state, for the Klan is not a church or sect, it represents no ecclesiastic organization or sacerdotal hierarchy. The utmost that can fairly be charged against us is that we have aroused the spirit of Protestantism, from which no church can benefit, for the defense of Americanism of which Protestantism is a part, and without which neither can survive.

. . .

Another ground for our opposition to the Roman Catholic Church is that most of its members in this country are aliens, and that the Church not only makes no effort to help them become assimilated to Americanism, but actually works to prevent this and to keep the Catholics as a group apart. It is notable that few of the evils which so often stamp the Catholic in politic are to be found in Catholics of the English and French stocks who have been in this country for generations. It is notable, too, that these evils seldom appear in Catholics who have attended the public schools. But with most communicants the Roman Church strongly and only too successfully opposes that united, understanding, homogenous "group-mind" which is essential to nationhood, *unless it can control that group-mind*. Just as steadily it denies to those whom it controls that freedom and independence of thought without which Americanism cannot live and which has never been developed except through Protestantism. One of the most amazing situations in all history is that seen today, with the free-thinking liberals joining the Catholics against the Klan.

The Jew, the Klan considers a far smaller problem. For one thing, he is confined to a few cities, and is no problem at all to most of the country. For another thing, his exclusiveness, political activities, and refusal to become assimilated are racial rather than religious, based on centuries of persecution. They cannot last long in the atmosphere of free America, and we may expect that with the passage of time the serious aspects of this problem will fade away . . .

Additional reading

Baker, Kelly J. *Gospel According to the Klan: The KKK's Appeal to Protestant America, 1915–1930* (Lawrence, KS: University of Kansas Press, 2011).
Gordon, Linda. *The Second Coming of the KKK: The Ku Klux Klan of the 1920s and the American Political Tradition* (New York: Liveright, 2017).
Pegram, Thomas. *One Hundred Percent American: The Rebirth and Decline of the Ku Klux Klan in the 1920s* (Lanham, MD: Ivan R. Dee, 2011).

8

Theosophy

Editors' Introduction: While Theosophy is a wide-ranging, hard to define religious movement, here we focus on the Theosophical Society, formed in 1875 by Helena Blavatsky. Blavatsky, a mystic and Russian immigrant, founded the Theosophical Society with Henry Steel Olcott (a lawyer and military officer). Both traveled the world in search of metaphysical truth. For them, that truth was a combination of so-called ancient esoteric knowledge and elements of Buddhism, Hinduism, and Spiritualism. According to Blavatsky's writings and other foundational Theosophical texts, the movement endorsed "a Universal Brotherhood of Humanity without distinction of race, colour, or creed." In *The Key to Theosophy*, Blavatsky explained, "All men have spiritually and physically the same origin, which is the fundamental teaching of Theosophy." After Blavatsky's death, her successor in running the Theosophical Society was Annie Wood Besant, the estranged wife of an Anglican minister and one of the few female speakers at the 1893 World's Parliament of Religions.

Theosophy falls squarely under the category of an American metaphysical religion, which scholarly expert Catherine Albanese has defined as those religions that "stressed mental or spiritual theories about life rather than historical traditions . . . or material elements."[1] Blavatsky and other Theosophists sought the esoteric knowledge of ancient masters in order to better understand the nature of the world and the reality of existence. Theosophy's interpretation of the world included the importance of occult mysteries, a cyclical understanding of time, and a belief in both karma and reincarnation. It was through these cycles that a person developed spiritually.

According to Blavatsky, she had been taught by a community that she called the Mahatmas, a religiously elite brotherhood that had reached a spiritual plane beyond other humans. Blavatsky and other Theosophists claimed to have met with and studied under the Mahatmas during their travels to Asia. Though the Mahatmas lived in the

---

[1] Catherine Albanese, *America: Religions and Religion* (Belomont, CA: Wadsworth Publishing Company, 1981), 165.

mountains of Tibet, they could also appear to Blavatsky for lessons or send messages at speeds faster than the international mail. The study of religion itself, namely early twentieth-century comparative religion, which was orientalist and colonialist, became part of the practice of Theosophy. The "East" with its esoteric and occult power was inherently mystical and mysterious for the Theosophical Society. Blavatsky's authority as a white woman came from claiming access to the spiritual knowledge and authority of foreign, racial others.

Blavatsky and others explained humanity's history as a complicated one. Humanity's evolution included what they called root-races and sub-races. Over the course of human history, there would be seven root-races, each with seven sub-races. The Theosophical Society's views on race also reflected some of the wider views of the day, including scientific racism and white supremacy. Blavatsky's writing identified the current root-race of the day as the fifth root-race, or Aryan race, which could vary in skin color from "dark brown, almost black, red-brown-yellow, down to the whitest creamy color." While this was the current root-race of the turn of the century, earlier forms of humanity also still walked the earth in certain locations; this included "the 'narrow-brained' savage South-Sea Islander, the African, the Australian." By categorizing Africans and others as lower forms of humanity, the movement echoed contemporary white supremacy and the eugenics movement. Additionally, Blavatsky claimed that the next step in the Aryan root-race's evolution would come from the racial mixing in the United States, namely that of Anglo-Americans. She frequently mirrored the racial hierarchy accepted by many of her early twentieth-century peers (European descent above all other identities), with the exception of her reverence for the Indian Mahatmas and their lineages.

Thus, the documents here cover the ways in which the Theosophical Society conceived of race, both in ways similar to other groups in this text and in broader ways about the human race. Document One is from Alfred Percy Sinnett's *Esoteric Buddhism*, which was one of the earliest texts to describe Theosophical ideas. This excerpt explains Theosophy's notion of the root-races of human history and their relationship to time and geography. Discussing the fourth root-race (the Atlanteans) and their lost continent of Lemuria, Sinnett goes on to the fifth and current root-race. Sinnett notes where there are remnants of earlier sub-races or even root-races (various people of color). Document Two comes from Helena Blavatsky's *The Key to Theosophy*, which follows a format of questions and answers. In it she emphasizes the movement's dedication to equality and "Universal Brotherhood," without racial divides. In Document Three, from *The Secret Doctrine*, Blavatsky brings readers back to the root-races, expanding on Sinnett's narration offered in Document One. In *The Secret Doctrine*, she explains how a new sub-race of the fifth root-race was emerging among Anglo-American people. She also makes distinctions between the various sub-races and root-races of the world and world history, making connections to racial identities of "Brown-white," "red Indians," "African negro," and more. Some of her detail appeared in the notes of the text, and so some of the notes are included here in brackets within the text.

Documents

Document One: Alfred Percy Sinnett, *Esoteric Buddhism* (New York: Houghton, Mifflin, 1887), 105–113.

. . . The periods of the great root races are divided from each other by great convulsions of Nature and by great geological changes. Europe was not in existence as a continent at the time the fourth race flourished. The continent on which the fourth race lived was not in existence at the time that the third race flourished, and neither of the continents which were the great vortices of the civilizations of those two races are in existence now. Seven great continental cataclysms occur during the occupation of the earth by the human life-wave for one round period. Each race is cut off in this way at its appointed time, some survivors remaining in parts of the world not the proper home of their race; but these, invariably in such cases, exhibiting a tendency to decay, and relapsing into barbarism with more or less rapidity.

The proper home of the fourth race, which directly preceded our own, was that continent of which some memory has been preserved even in exoteric literature—the lost Atlantis. But the great island, the destruction of which is spoken of by Plato, was really the last remnant of the continent. "In the Eocene age," I am told, "even in its very first part, the great cycle of the fourth race men, the Atlanteans, had already reached its highest point, and the great continent, the father of nearly all the present continents, showed the first symptoms of sinking,—a process that occupied it down to 11,446 years ago, when its last island, that, translating its vernacular name, we may call with propriety Poseidonis, went down with a crash.

"Lemuria" (a former continent stretching southward from India across what is now the Indian Ocean, but connected with Atlantis, for Africa was not then in existence) "should no more be confounded with the Atlantis continent than Europe with America. Both sank and were drowned, with their high civilizations and 'gods,' yet between the two catastrophes a period of about 700,000 years elapsed, Lemuria flourishing and ending her career just about that lapse of time before the early part of the Eocene age, since its race was the third. Behold the relics of that once great nation in some of the flat-headed aborigines of your Australia."

It is a mistake on the part of a recent writer on Atlantis to people India and Egypt with the colonies of that continent, but of that more anon.

"Why should not your geologists," asks my revered Mahatma teacher, "bear in mind that under the continents explored and fathomed by them, in the bowels of which they have found the Eocene age, and forced it to deliver to them its secrets, there may be hidden deep in the fathomless, or rather unfathomed ocean beds, other and far older continents whose strata have never been geologically explored; and that they may some day upset entirely their present theories. Why not admit that our present continents have, like Lemuria and Atlantis, been several times already submerged, and had the time to reappear again, and bear their new groups of mankind and civilization; and that at the first great geological upheaval at the next cataclysm, in the series of periodical cataclysms that occur from the beginning to the end of every round, our already autopsized continents will go down, and the Lemurias and Atlantises come up again.

"Of course the fourth race had its period of the highest civilization." (The letter from which I am now quoting was written in answer to a series of questions I put.) "Greek, and Roman, and even Egyptian civilizations are nothing compared to the civilizations that began with the third race. Those of the second race were not savages, but they could not be called civilized.

"Greeks and Romans were small sub-races, and Egyptians part and parcel of our own Caucasian stock. Look at the latter, and at India. Having reached the highest civilization, and what is more, *learning*, both went down; Egypt, as a distinct sub-race, disappearing entirely (her Copts are but a hybrid remnant); India, as one of the first and most powerful offshoots of the mother race, and composed of a number of sub-races, lasting to these times, and struggling to take once more her place in history some day. That history catches but a few stray, hazy glimpses of Egypt some 12,000 years back, when, having already reached the apex of its cycle thousands of years before, the latter had begun to go down.

"The Chaldees were at the apex of their occult fame before what you term the Bronze Age. We hold—but then what warrant can you give the world that we are right?—that far greater civilizations than our own have risen and decayed. It is not enough to say, as some of your modern writers do, that an extinct period of civilization existed before Rome and Athens were founded. We affirm that a series of civilizations existed before as well as after the glacial period, that they existed upon various points of the globe, reached the apex of glory, and died. Every trace and memory has been lost of the Assyrian and Phoenician civilizations, until discoveries began to be made a few years ago. And now they open a new though not by far one of the earliest pages in the history of mankind. And yet how far back do those civilizations go in comparison with the oldest, and even then history is slow to accept. Archeology has sufficiently demonstrated that the memory of man runs back vastly further than history has been willing to accept, and the sacred records of once mighty nations preserved by their heirs are still more worthy of trust. We speak of civilizations of the ante-glacial period, and not only in the minds of the vulgar and the profane, but even in the opinion of the highly-learned geologist, the claim sounds preposterous. What would you say, then, to our affirmation that the Chinese,—I now speak of the inland, the true Chinaman, not of the hybrid mixture between the fourth and fifth races now occupying the throne,—the aborigines who belong in their unallied nationality wholly to the highest and last branch of the fourth race, reached their highest civilization when the fifth had hardly appeared in Asia? When was it? Calculate. The group of islands discovered by Nordenskiold, of the Vega, was found strewn with fossils of horses, sheep, oxen, etc., among gigantic bones of elephants, mammoths, rhinoceroses, and other monsters belonging to periods when man, says your science, had not yet made his appearance on earth. How came horses and sheep to be found in company with the huge antediluvians?

"The region now locked in the fetters of eternal winter, uninhabited by man, that most fragile of animals, will very soon be proved to have not only a tropical climate, something your science knows and does not dispute, but having been likewise the seat of one of the most ancient civilizations of the fourth race, whose highest relics we now find in the degenerate Chinaman, and whose lowest are hopelessly (for the profane scientist) intermixed with the remnants of the third. I told you before that the highest people now on earth (spiritually) belong to the first sub-race of the fifth root race, and those are the Aryan Asiatics; the highest race (physical intellectuality) is the last sub-race of the fifth,—yourselves, the white conquerors. The majority of mankind belongs to the seventh sub-race of the fourth root race,—the above mentioned Chinamen and their offshoots and branchlets (Malayans, Mongolians, Tibetans, Javanese, etc. etc.),—with remnants of other sub-races of the fourth and the seventh sub-race of the third race. All these fallen semblances of humanity are the direct lineal descendants of highly civilized nations . . .

"A student of occultism ought not to speak of the stagnant condition of the fourth-round people, since history knows next to nothing of that condition, 'up to the beginning of modern progress,' of other nations but the Western. What do you know of America, for instance, before the invasion of that country by the Spaniards? Less than two centuries prior to the arrival of Cortez there was great a rush toward progress among the sub-races of Peru and Mexico as there is now in Europe and the United States. Their sub-race ended in nearly total annihilation through causes generated by itself. We may speak only of the 'stagnant' condition into which, following the law of development, growth maturity, and decline, every race and sub-race falls during the transition periods. It is that latter condition your universal history is acquainted with, while it remains superbly ignorant of the condition even India was in some ten centuries back. Your sub-races are now running toward the apex of their respective cycles, and that history goes no further back than the periods of decline of a few other sub-races belonging most of them to the preceding fourth race."

Document Two: Helena Petrovna Blavatsky, *The Key to Theosophy* (New York: The Theosophical Publishing Company, Limited, 1889), 39–41.

The Objects of the Society

Enquirer: What are the objects of the "Theosophical Society"?

Theosophist: They are three, and have been so from the beginning. (1.) To form the nucleus of a Universal Brotherhood of Humanity without distinction of race, colour, or creed. (2.) To prompt the study of Aryan and other Scriptures, of the World's religion and sciences, and to vindicate the importance of old Asiatic literature, namely, of the Brahmanical, Buddhist, and Zoroastrian philosophies. (3.) To investigate the hidden mysteries of Nature under every aspect possible, and the physic and spiritual powers latent in man especially. These are, broadly stated, the three chief objects of the Theosophical Society.

Enquirer: Can you give me some more detailed information upon these?

Theosophist: We may divide each of the three objects into as many explanatory clauses as may be found necessary.

Enquirer: Then let us begin with the first. What means would you resort to, in order to promote such a feeling of brotherhood among races that are known to be of the most diversified religions, customs, beliefs, and modes of thought?

Theosophist: Allow me to add that which you seem unwilling to express. Of course we know that with the exception of two remnants of races—the Parsees and the Jews—every nation is divided, not merely against all other nations, but even against itself. This is found most prominently among the so-called civilized Christian nations. Hence your wonder, and the reason why our first object appears to you a Utopia. Is it not so?

Enquirer: Well, yes; but what you to say against it?

Theosophist: Nothing against the fact; but much about the necessity of removing the causes which make Universal Brotherhood a Utopia at present.

Enquirer: What are, in your view, these causes?

Theosophist: First and foremost, the natural selfishness of human nature. This selfishness, instead of being eradicated, is daily strengthened and stimulated into a ferocious and irresistible feeling by the present religious education, which tends not only to encourage, but positively to justify it. People's ideas about right and wrong have been entirely perverted by the literal acceptance of the Jewish Bible. All the unselfishness of the altruistic teachings of Jesus has become merely a theoretical subject for pulpit oratory; while the precepts of practical selfishness taught in the Mosaic Bible, against which Christ so vainly preached, have become ingrained into the innermost life of the Western nations. "An eye for an eye and a tooth for a tooth" has come to be the first maxim of your law. Now, I state openly and fearlessly, that the perversity of this doctrine and of so many others *Theosophy alone* can eradicate.

Document Three: Helena Petrovna Blavatsky, *The Secret Doctrine*, Volume 2 (Point Loma, CA: Aryan Theosophical Press, 1909), 195–196, 249–250, and 443–445. Unlike other documents, brackets here are used to set apart the text of two relevant footnotes at where they appear in the text.

. . . A naturalist suggests another difficulty. The human is the only species which, however unequal in its races, can breed together. "There is no question of selection between *human races*," say the anti-Darwinists, and no evolutionist can deny the argument—one which very triumphantly proves *specific unity*. How then can Occultism insist that a portion of the Fourth Race humanity begot young ones from females of another, only *semi-human*, if not quite an animal, race, the hybrids resulting from which union not only bred freely but produced the ancestors of the modern anthropoid apes? Esoteric science replies to this that it was in the very beginnings of physical man.

Since then, Nature has changed her ways, and sterility is the only result of the crime of man's bestiality. But we have to this day proofs of this. The Secret Doctrine teaches that the *specific unity of mankind* is not without exceptions even now. For there are, or rather still were a few years ago, descendants of these half-animal tribes or races, both of remote Lumurian and Lumuro-Atlantean origin. The world knows them as Tasmanians (now extinct), Australians, Andaman Islanders, etc. The descent of the Tasmanians can be almost proved by a fact, which struck Darwin a good deal, without him being able to make anything of it. This fact deserves notice.

Now de Quatrefages and other naturalists, who seek to prove Monogenesis by the very fact of every race of mankind being capable of crossing with every other, have left out of their calculations *exceptions*, which do not in this case confirm the rule. Human crossing may have been a general rule from the time of the separation of sexes and yet that other law may assert itself, viz., sterility between two human races, just as between two animal species of various kinds, in those rare cases when a European, condescending to see in a female of a savage tribe a mate, happens to chose a member of such mixed tribes. [Note 369. Of such semi-annual creatures, the sole remnants known to Ethnology were the Tasmanians, a *portion* of the Australians and a mountain tribe in China, the men and women of which are entirely covered by hair. They were the last descendants in a *direct* line of the semi-animal latter-day Lemurians referred to. There are, however, considerable numbers of the mixed Lemuro-Atlantean peoples produced by various crossings with such semi-human stocks—e.g., the wild men of Borneo, the Veddahs of Ceylon, classed by Prof. Flower among Aryans (!), most of the remaining Australians, Bushmen, Negritos, Andaman Islanders, etc. The Australians of the Gulf of St. Vincent and the neighborhood of Adelaide are *very hairy*, and the brown down on the skin of boys of five or six years of age assumes a *furry appearance*. They are, however, degraded men—not the closest approximation to the "*pithecoid* man," as Haeckel so sweeping affirms. Only a portion of these men are a Lemurian relic.] Darwin notes such a case in a Tasmanian tribe, whose women were suddenly struck with sterility, *en masse*, some time after the arrival among them of the European colonists. The great naturalist tried to explain this fact by change of diet, food, conditions, etc., but finally gave up the solution of the mystery. For the Occultist, it is a very evident one. "Crossing," as it is called, of Europeans with Tasmanian women—*i.e.*, the representatives of a race, whose progenitors were a "soulless" [Note 370. In calling the animal "Soulless," it is not depriving the beast, from the humblest to the highest species, of a "soul," but only of a conscious surviving *Ego-soul, i.e.*, that principle which survives after a man, and reincarnates in a like man. The animal has an astral body, that survives the physical form for a short period; but its (animal) Monad does not re-incarnate in the same, but in a higher species, and has no "Devachan" of course. It has the *seeds* of all the human principles in itself, but they are *latent*.] and mindless monster and a real human, though still a mindless man—brought on sterility. This, not alone as a consequence of a physiological law, but also as a decree of *Karmic* evolution in the question of further survival of an abnormal race. In no one point of the above is Science prepared to believe *as yet*—but it will have to in the long run. Esoteric philosophy, let us remember, only fills the gaps made by science and corrects her false premises.

. . .

Esotericism now classes these seven variations, with their four great divisions, into only *three* distinct primeval races—as it does not take into consideration the First Race, which had neither type nor color, and hardly an objective, though colossal form. The evolution of these races, their formation and development, went *pari passu* and on parallel lines with the evolution, formation, and development of three geological strata, from which the human complexion was as much derived as it was determined by the climates of those zones. It names three great divisions, namely, the RED-YELLOW, the BLACK, and the BROWN-WHITE. The Aryan races, for instance, now varying from dark brown, almost black, red-brown-yellow, down to the whitest creamy color, are yet all of one and the same stock—the Fifth Root-Race—and spring from one single progenitor, called in Hindu *exotericism* by the generic name of Vaivasvata Manu: the latter, remember, being that generic personage, the Sage, who is said to have lived over 18,000,000 years ago, and almost 850,000 years ago—at the same time as the sinking of the last remnants of the great continent of Atlantis, and who is said to live even *now* in his mankind. The light yellow is the color of the first SOLID human race, which appeared after the middle of the Third Root Race (*after its fall* into generation—as just explained), bringing on the final changes. For, it is only at that period that the last transformation took place, which brought forth man as he is now, only on a magnified scale. This Race gave birth to the Fourth Race; "Siva" gradually transforming that portion of Humanity which became "black with sin" into *red-yellow* (the red Indians and the Mongolians being the descendants of these) and finally into Brown-white races—which now, together with the yellow Races, form the great bulk of Humanity. The allegory in *Linga Purana* is curious, as showing the great ethnological knowledge of the ancients.

. . .

The human Races are born one from the other, grow, develop, become old, and die. Their sub-races and nations follow the same rule. If your all-denying modern science and so-called philosophy do not contest that the human family is composed of a variety of well-defined types and races, it is only because the fact is undeniable; no one would say that there was no external difference between an Englishman, an African negro, and a Japanese or Chinaman. on the other hand it is formally denied by most naturalists that *mixed human races, i.e.*, the seeds for entirely new races, are any longer formed in our days. But this last is maintained on good grounds by de Quartrefages and some others.

Nevertheless our general proposition will not be accepted. It will be said that whatever forms man has passed through in the long pre-historic Past there are no new changes for him (save certain variations, as at present) in the future. Hence that our Sixth and Seventh Root Races are fictions.

To this it is again answered: How *do you* know? Your experience is limited to a few thousand years, to less than a day in the whole age of Humanity and to the present types of the actual continents and isles of our Fifth Race. How can you tell what will or will not be? Meanwhile, such is the prophecy of the Secret Books and their no uncertain statements.

Since the beginning of the Atlantean Race many millions years have passed, yet we find the last of the Atlanteans, still mixed up with the Aryan element, 11,000 years ago. This shows the enormous overlapping of one race over the race which succeeds it, though in characters and external type the elder loses its characteristics, and assumes the new features of the younger race. This is proved in all the formations of mixed human races. Now, Occult philosophy teaches that even now, under our very eyes, the new Race and Races are preparing to be formed, and that it is in America that the transformation will take place, and has already silently commenced.

Pure Anglo-Saxons hardly three hundred years ago, the Americans of the United States have already become a nation apart, and, owing to a strong admixture of various nationalities and inter-marriage, almost a race *sui generis*, not only mentally, but also physical. "Every mixed race, when uniform and settled, has been able to play the part of a primary race in fresh crossings," says de Quatrefages. "Mankind, in its present state, has thus been formed, certainly for the greatest part, by the successive crossing of a number of races *at present undetermined*."

Thus the Americans have become in only three centuries a "primary race," *pro tem.*, before becoming a race apart, and strongly separated from all other now existing races. They are, in short, the germs of the *Sixth* sub-race, and in some few hundred years more, will become most decidedly the pioneers of that race which must succeed to the present European or fifth sub-race, in all its new characteristics. After this, in about 25,000 years, they will launch into preparations for the seventh sub-race; until, in consequence of cataclysms—the first series of those which must one day destroy Europe, and still later the whole Aryan race (and thus affect both Americas), as almost most of the lands directly connected with the confines of our continent and isles—the Sixth Root-Race will have appeared on the stage of our Round. When shall this be? Who knows save the great Masters of Wisdom, perchance, and they are as silent upon the subject as the snow-capped peaks that tower above them. All we know is, that it will silently come into existence; so silently, indeed, that for long millenniums shall its pioneers—the peculiar children who will grow into peculiar men and women—be regarded as anomalous *lusus naturae*, abnormal oddities physically and mentally. Then, as they increase, and their numbers become with every age greater, one day they will awake to find themselves in a majority. It is the present men who will then begin to be regarded as exceptional mongrels, until these die out in their turn in civilized lands; surviving only in small groups on islands—the mountain peaks of today—where they will vegetate, degenerate, and finally die out, perhaps millions of years hence, as the Aztecs have, as the Nyam-Nyam and the dwarfish Moola Koorumba of the Nilghirir Hills are dying. All these are the remnants of once mighty races, the recollection of whose existence has entirely died out of the remembrance of the modern generations, just as well shall vanish from the memory of the Sixth Race Humanity. The Fifth will overlap the Sixth Race for many hundreds of millenniums, changing with it slower than its new successor, still changing in stature, general physique, and mentality, just as the Fourth overlapped our Aryan race, and the Third had overlapped the Atlanteans.

Additional reading

Crow, John L. "Lemuria Rising: California in the Place-Making Imagination," Paper presented at the Annual Meeting of the Southeastern Commission for the Study of Religion (March 4–6, 2012).

Santucci, James A. "The Notion of Race in Theosophy," *Nova Religio: The Journal of Alternative and Emergent Religions* 11.3 (February 2008): 37–63.

Versluis, Arthur. *Magic and Mysticism: An Introduction to Western Esoteric Traditions* (Lanham, MD: Rowman & Littlefield Publishers, 2007).

9

Native American Church

Editors' Introduction: Native American communities in the Southwest have used peyote in ceremonial settings for about a thousand years. This practice became more formalized, however, in 1918 with the official founding of the Native American Church. In 1870, Comanche chief Quannah Parker began using peyote more formally in religious ceremonies. Blending indigenous traditions with some elements of Christianity, Parker instituted the "Peyote Way." Peyote Way or Peyote Road is a system of ethics and ceremony. Reflecting Parker's experience with Protestantism, he emphasized self-discipline and encouraged followers to work within the white economy. On the ritual side, Parker and others led ceremonies of song, healings, offerings of peyote, testimonies, and pipe smoking. As a result, ceremonial peyote use became more popular among Southern Plains tribes in particular. Parker and others acted as peyote missionaries, sharing with Native communities the spiritual (which included medicinal) benefits of peyote. Another important early peyote missionary was John Wilson, a Caddo Indian whose version of the Peyote Way reflected his own experience with Catholicism and was more influenced by Christianity than Parker's. Parker died in 1911, before the formalization of Peyote Way in the Native American Church.

When US Congress pushed to make peyote illegal, Native American practitioners decided to formalize their practice in the Native American Church. It is perhaps one of the most doctrinally and ceremonially diverse church movements in the country. Mirroring the differences between Parker and Wilson, many local and tribal communities within the Native American Church vary in their blend of Christianity with indigenous ideas of spiritual power and differ in terms of ceremonial practice. Most communities understand there to be a Creator of the world, who has a son, Jesus Christ. Peyote allows for communication with both the Creator and Jesus. Readings from the Bible, the ceremony of baptism, and the symbol of crosses and crucifixes are used in varying degrees among communities. Peyote ceremonies typically occur once a month and include: the distribution of peyote tea or peyote cactus, numerous songs, a sacred fire, cleansing smoke (similar to a sweat lodge), the offering of prayers, and a communal meal afterwards. Those who lead the ceremonies are known as Road Men, who are often assisted by a Fire Man.

Like the Ghost Dance Movement, the Peyote Way and Native American Church are indigenous revitalization movements. Each blended some Christian ideas and practices with indigenous ideas and practices. Parker also incorporated participation in the white economy, creating a movement that accepted some elements of white culture and society while also remaining firm in an indigenous understanding of the world and how to connect with spiritual power.

Due to peyote as a controlled substance, it provides an interesting lens for studying race, alternative religious movements, and the law. While the law classifies peyote as a hallucinogenic drug, the Native American Church considers peyote as a means of connecting with the sacred. This has led to court cases regarding peyote use and religious freedom, the most famous of which was *Employment Division, Department of Human Resources of Oregon v. Smith, 494 US 872*, decided in 1990. While the Supreme Court ruled that religious freedom did not protect members of the Native American Church who used peyote, Congress passed the Religious Freedom Restoration Act in 1993 and the 1994 amendments to the American Indian Religious Freedom Act, which protected Native American ceremonial use of peyote. The law only permits members of the Native American Church with tribal affiliation to use peyote in religious ceremonies.

Document One is a selection of excerpts from the published proceedings in the US House of Representatives regarding peyote use in 1918 as the Native American Church incorporated. The first section comes from the statement of Gertrude Bonnin, a Sioux graduate of the Carlisle Indian boarding school who spoke against peyote. The published proceedings then move to an interview with James Mooney, a white anthropologist with the Smithsonian Institute who studied Native American religious revitalization movements and then to Francis La Flesche, an Omaha Indian who described a peyote ceremony and emphasized the lack of intoxication associated with the use of peyote. Document Two is an excerpt from the Supreme Court decision *Employment Division, Department of Human Resources of Oregon v. Smith, 494 US 872*. Decisions of jurisprudence are not always easy to read, and so the editors encourage readers to not get swept away by the legalese in Justice Scalia's and Justice Blackmun's writing and rather pay attention to how they articulate whether or not peyote use should be protected by law and the assumptions that their decisions reflect. The editors abbreviated the decisions and removed the references to other law cases for ease of reading.

Documents

Document One: United States Congress House Committee on Indian Affairs, "Peyote: Hearings before a subcommittee of the Committee on Indian Affairs of the House of Representatives on H.R. 2614" (Washington, DC: Government Printing Office, 1918), 63, 70–71, and 80–81.

Indian Woman in Capital to Fight Growing Use of Peyote by Indians—Mrs. Gertrude Bonnin, Carlisle Graduate, Relative of Sitting Bull Describes Effects of Mind Poison

. . .

Description of Feast.

In an account by Mrs. Brabant in 1909, we have a description of a feast of this kind at White Eagle, Okla. She said that the Indians had the peyote bean or button lying on a crescent-shaped altar, and that the worshippers present sang, beat tom-toms, and intoxicated themselves till they imagined that they saw visions of the Saviour. An Arapahoe Indian claimed that he sat gazing at the bean till he saw emerge from it a snake with heads, then a centipede, and that the snake came to him, making his own body feel as if covered with the skin of a snake.

Dr. Havelock Ellis has described his feelings after having eaten three of the peyote beans or "buttons" by way of an experiment. He says his first symptom was that of immense strength and wonderful intellectual power, but that later he felt faint with a very low pulse. A pale shadow seemed to hover over the book he read. Visions came, slowly, then rapidly. First, a vast field of golden jewels studded with red, crimson, and green stones—a wonderful perfume—a dull, rich glow and brilliant points—rare flowers—and iridescent fibrous wings, as of butterflies—then a hollow revolving cylinder lined with marvelous mother-of-pearl—profuse and various images—living in arabesques. Then he saw waves of light, shadows flushed with violet. Once he visioned "floating white drapery" and "feathery forms."

"Thus it is easily to be seen that the use of peyote induces the same mental and physical stimulation that habit-forming drugs generate, and it follows that the same mental and physical evils will result," said Mrs. Bonnin. "My work now is to prevent the destruction of my race by securing legislation forbidding the use of the injurious plant in the same way that alcohol is prohibited. Some have said that as the Indians claim the peyote is used as a sacrament it will prevent any legislation on the ground that such would be interference with religion. But the fact that it is used in a way which outrages decency and induces intoxication and degeneracy precludes any such plea. There is no true friend of the Indian that does not desire this curse to be wiped away. Yet those who profit by this vice, those who are addicted to it, will, of course, plead for its retention."

Mrs. Bonnin is an earnest worker for her people. She is of the opinion that much of the meat supply of the country could be benefited by teaching the Indians to raise cattle on their immense reservations so admirably adapted to grazing.

"White men come in, lease the lands, get money from banks with which they buy cattle," she said, "why can not the Indians, who really own and live on the land, be shown how to do this? Instead he is made to lease and let the white man run the business and make the money. If the tribes now holding vast reservations could be set to raising cattle, the meat problem would be easily solved.

. . . [*Editors' Note*: The published proceedings move to an interview with James Mooney.] . . .

I do not think it [peyote] grows in any part of Oklahoma. I know it grows in Texas, about Laredo, and most of the supply comes from there. It may grow also about the lower Pecos. The Mexican Indians find it on the arid plains eastward from the Sierra Madre. We know it was long used, as far back as we have any connected historical record books refer to it.

The Kiowa story of its origin is that some young men went on the warpath to the south and were gone for so long a time that their friends at home became afraid that they would never return. There was a young woman, a sister of one of the war party, who went out to a hill beyond the camp every evening to watch for her brother, in accordance with Indian custom, to pray for his return. Finally one evening she fell asleep, and a spirit came to her in a dream, telling her that there was something growing out of the ground under her head which would bring her to her brother. When she awoke she looked and found a number of peyotes growing. These she gathered and took back to camp, and then, calling the old men together, told them how to prepare everything for the ceremony as the spirit had directed. They set up the tepee and performed the rite, and in the peyote vision they saw where the young man was lying alone, wounded and starving, and they sent out a party and brought him home to his sister. There is always a religious myth in connection with the peyote rite. That is the story the Kiowa tell of how the rite came to them. Each tribe has its own story. The Kiowa say the Comanche knew of it before they did. Both tribes say they got it from the Mescalero and the Tonkawa, and probably these got it originally from the tribes near the Mexican border, who in turn had it from the tribes in old Mexico. It has come to the more northern tribes only more recently.

You have seen the plant as used. As to their method of using it ceremonially, they have a regular time—Saturday night running into Sunday morning. They set up a special tepee and go into it, after preliminary preparation, about 9 o'clock in the evening. I have seen as many as 30 or more sitting in a circle inside the tepee. They have a drum and a rattle. After an opening prayer the leader hands out four peyotes to each man. Each man chews up one peyote after another, making a pellet of each, which he swallows. Then the singing begins. There is one regular song at the beginning, one song at midnight, one song at daylight, and one song at the close, with other songs all through the night as each man chooses, two men singing at a time, one accompanying with the drum and the other with the rattle. The singing goes on through the night, the drum and rattle passing around the circle repeatedly. There is a fire in the center of the tepee and a large sacred peyote on a little crescent-shaped mound behind it. While two men keep up the songs the others are praying or remain in a state of contemplation, looking toward the fire and the sacred peyote. The ceremony goes on in this way through the night. At intervals the worshippers eat more peyotes. At midnight there is a sort of baptismal ceremony, when one man brings in a bucket of spring water, over which the leader recites a prayer, after which they sprinkle themselves with it. The leader stands up while making the prayer. They pray for all their friends and for themselves, as we pray. If there are any sick in camp, they may be brought in to be prayed for. If a woman is sick, her husband brings her in, and they pray for her and give her some of the peyote to eat. She does not prepare it herself, but it is prepared for her. With the peyote-using tribes that I know best, the Kiowa and Comanche, the only occasion on which a woman is present is when she is there to be prayed for as a member of the family of the man who accompanies her.

. . .

Statement of Mr. Francis La Flesche, Bureau of American Ethnology, an Omaha Indian.

Mr. La Flesche. I have had numerous opportunities to study the use of peyote among the Poncas, the Osage, and my own people, the Omahas. I had heard extraordinary stories told about its effects, about the immorality that it produced, and about the promiscuity of the people who used the peyote at their meetings. I expected to find evidence of the truth of these stories.

When I went among the Osage people, some of the leaders of the peyote religion were anxious for me to attend their meetings, and wishing to know what effect this "medicine," as they called it, had upon each individual, I accepted the invitation. I attended a meeting at which the gentleman who has just spoken to you, Mr. Arthur Bonnicastle, was present, and sat with him. At about 6 o'clock in the evening the people entered their "meeting house" and sat in a circle around a fire kindled over some symbolic figures marked in the center of a shallow excavation in the middle of the room. The peyote was passed around, some of it in pellets of the consistency of dough, and some prepared in liquid form. The drum was ceremonially circulated and accompanied by singing. From all that I had heard of the intoxicating effects of the peyote I had expected to see the people get gloriously drunk and behave as drunken people do. While I saw waiting to see fighting and some excitement the singing went on and on and I noticed that all gazed at the fire or beyond, at a little mound on top of which lay a single peyote. I said to the man sitting next to me, "What do you expect to see?" He said, "We expect to see the face of Jesus and the face of our dead relatives. We are worshipping God and Jesus, the same God that the white people worship." All night long the singing went on and I sat watching the worshipers. It was about 5 o'clock in the morning when suddenly the singing ceased, the drum and ceremonial staff were put away, and the leader, beginning at the right of the door, asked each person: "What did you see?" Some replied, "I saw nothing." Others said, "I saw the face of Jesus and it made me happy." Some answered, "I saw the faces of my relatives, and they made me glad." And so on, around the entire circle. I noticed that there were only a few who had been able to see faces, the greater number of the men and women saw nothing. It was explained to me by the leader that these revelations come quickly to those whose thoughts and deeds are pure. To those who are irreverent, they come slowly, although they may come in time. This meeting, as well as others that I have been permitted to attend, was as orderly as any religious meeting I have seen in this and other cities.

I am thoroughly convinced that these Indians are worshiping God in their own simple way, and if their religion is interfered with by the Government or anybody else, and it is suppressed, the consequences will be very grave.

During the morning the women prepared the food which had been contributed by the members, while the men sat and waited until they were called to the place, where about noon the meal was served. When all were seated, the leader asked a member to offer a prayer. The prayer was such as I have heard among white people. I saw no signs of intoxication.

I do not know about the medicinal qualities of the peyote, whether it can cure consumption or any other disease that the human flesh is subject to, but there is one disease that it has cured—the disease of drunkenness.

Document Two: Excerpts from *Employment Division, Department of Human Resources of Oregon v. Smith, 494 US 872*, decided 17 April 1990.

Syllabus.

Respondents Smith and Black were fired by a private drug rehabilitation organization because they ingested peyote, a hallucinogenic drug, for sacramental purposes at a ceremony of their Native American Church. Their applications for unemployment compensation were denied by the State of Oregon under a state law disqualifying employees discharged for work-related "misconduct." Holding that the denials violated respondents' First Amendment free exercise rights, the State Court of Appeals reversed. The State Supreme Court affirmed, but this Court vacated the judgment and remanded for a determination whether sacramental peyote use is proscribed by the State's controlled substance law, which makes it a felony to knowingly or intentionally possess the drug. Pending that determination, the Court refused to decide whether such use is protected by the Constitution. On remand, the State Supreme Court held that sacramental peyote use violated, and was not excepted from, the state-law prohibition, but concluded that that prohibition was invalid under the Free Exercise Clause.

Held:
The Free Exercise Clause permits the State to prohibit sacramental peyote use and thus to deny unemployment benefits to persons discharged for such use.

(a) Although a State would be "prohibiting the free exercise [of religion]" in violation of the Clause if it sought to ban the performance of (or abstention from) physical acts solely because of their religious motivation, the Clause does not relieve an individual of the obligation to comply with a law that incidentally forbids (or requires) the performance of an act that his religious belief requires (or forbids) if the law is not specifically directed to religious practice and is otherwise constitutional as applied to those who engage in the specified act for nonreligious reasons. The only decisions in which this Court has held that the First Amendment bars application of a neutral, generally applicable law to religiously motivated action are distinguished on the ground that they involved not the Free Exercise Clause alone, but that clause in conjunction with other constitutional protections.

(b) Respondents' claim for a religious exemption from the Oregon law cannot be evaluated under the balancing test set forth in the line of cases following Sherbert v. Verner, whereby governmental actions that substantially burden a religious practice must be justified by a "compelling governmental interest." That test was developed in a context—unemployment compensation eligibility rules—that lent itself to individualized governmental assessment of the reasons for the relevant conduct. The test is inapplicable to an across-the-board criminal prohibition on a particular form of conduct. A holding to the contrary would create an extraordinary right to ignore generally applicable laws that are not supported by "compelling governmental interest" on the basis of religious belief. Nor could such a right be limited to situations in which the conduct prohibited is "central" to the individual's religion, since that would enmesh judges in an impermissible inquiry into the centrality of particular beliefs or practices to a faith. Thus, although it is constitutionally permissible to exempt sacramental peyote use from the operation of drug laws, it is not constitutionally required.

SCALIA, J., delivered the opinion of the Court, in which REHNQUIST, C.J., and WHITE, STEVENS, and KENNEDY, JJ., joined. O'CONNOR, J., filed an opinion concurring in the judgment, in Parts I and II of which BRENNAN, MARSHALL, and BLACKMUN, JJ., joined without concurring in the judgment, post. BLACKMUN, J., filed a dissenting opinion, in which BRENNAN and MARSHALL, JJ., joined.

JUSTICE SCALIA delivered the opinion of the Court.

. . .

The Free Exercise Clause of the First Amendment, which has been made applicable to the States by incorporation into the Fourteenth Amendment, see Cantwell v. Connecticut, 310 US 296, 303 (1940), provides that "Congress shall make no law respecting an establishment of religion, or prohibiting the free exercise thereof. . . ." US Const., Amdt. 1. The free exercise of religion means, first and foremost, the right to believe and profess whatever religious doctrine one desires. Thus, the First Amendment obviously excludes all "governmental regulation of religious beliefs as such." Sherbert v. Verner, supra, at 402. The government may not compel affirmation of religious belief, punish the expression of religious doctrines it believes to be false, impose special disabilities on the basis of religious views or religious status, or lend its power to one or the other side in controversies over religious authority or dogma.

But the "exercise of religion" often involves not only belief and profession but the performance of (or abstention from) physical acts: assembling with others for a worship service, participating in sacramental use of bread and wine, proselytizing, abstaining from certain foods or certain modes of transportation. It would be true, we think (though no case of ours has involved the point), that a State would be "prohibiting the free exercise [of religion]" if it sought to ban such acts or abstentions only when they are engaged in for religious reasons, or only because of the religious belief that they display. It would doubtless be unconstitutional, for example, to ban the casting of "statues that are to be used for worship purposes," or to prohibit bowing down before a golden calf.

Respondents in the present case, however, seek to carry the meaning of "prohibiting the free exercise [of religion]" one large step further. They contend that their religious motivation for using peyote places them beyond the reach of a criminal law that is not specifically directed at their religious practice, and that is concededly constitutional as applied to those who use the drug for other reasons. They assert, in other words, that "prohibiting the free exercise [of religion]" includes requiring any individual to observe a generally applicable law that requires (or forbids) the performance of an act that his religious belief forbids (or requires). As a textual matter, we do not think the words must be given that meaning. It is no more necessary to regard the collection of a general tax, for example, as "prohibiting the free exercise [of religion]" by those citizens who believe support of organized government to be sinful, than it is to regard the same tax as "abridging the freedom . . . of the press" of those publishing companies that must pay the tax as a condition of staying in business. It is a permissible reading of the text, in the one case as in the other, to say that if prohibiting the exercise of religion (or burdening the activity of printing) is not the object of the tax but merely the incidental effect of a generally applicable and otherwise valid provision, the First Amendment has not been offended.

Our decisions reveal that the latter reading is the correct one. We have never held that an individual's religious beliefs excuse him from compliance with an otherwise valid law prohibiting conduct that the State is free to regulate. On the contrary, the record of more than a century of our free exercise jurisprudence contradicts that proposition. As described succinctly by Justice Frankfurter in Minersville School Dist. Bd. of Ed. v. Gobitis (1940): "Conscientious scruples have not, in the course of the long struggle for religious toleration, relieved the individual from obedience to a general law not aimed at the promotion or restriction of religious beliefs. The mere possession of religious convictions which contradict the relevant concerns of a political society does not relieve the citizen from the discharge of political responsibilities (footnote omitted)." We first had occasion to assert that principle in Reynolds v. United States (1879), where we rejected the claim that criminal laws against polygamy could not be constitutionally applied to those whose religion commanded the practice. "Laws," we said, "are made for the government of actions, and while they cannot interfere with mere religious belief and opinions, they may with practices. . . . Can a man excuse his practices to the contrary because of his religious belief? To permit this would be to make the professed doctrines of religious belief superior to the law of the land, and in effect to permit every citizen to become a law unto himself."

. . .

[Justice O'Connor submitted a concurring opinion.]

JUSTICE BLACKMUN, with whom JUSTICE BRENNAN and JUSTICE MARSHALL join, dissenting.

. . .

The State's interest in enforcing its prohibition, in order to be sufficiently compelling to outweigh a free exercise claim, cannot be merely abstract or symbolic. The State cannot plausibly assert that unbending application of a criminal prohibition is essential to fulfill any compelling interest, if it does not, in fact, attempt to enforce that prohibition. In this case, the State actually has not evinced any concrete interest in enforcing its drug laws against religious users of peyote. Oregon has never sought to prosecute respondents, and does not claim that it has made significant enforcement efforts against other religious users of peyote. The State's asserted interest thus amounts only to the symbolic preservation of an unenforced prohibition. But a government interest in "symbolism, even symbolism for so worthy a cause as the abolition of unlawful drugs," cannot suffice to abrogate the constitutional rights of individuals.

Similarly, this Court's prior decisions have not allowed a government to rely on mere speculation about potential harms, but have demanded evidentiary support for a refusal to allow a religious exception. In this case, the State's justification for refusing to recognize an exception to its criminal laws for religious peyote use is entirely speculative.

The State proclaims an interest in protecting the health and safety of its citizens from the dangers of unlawful drugs. It offers, however, no evidence that the religious use of peyote has ever harmed anyone. The factual findings of other courts cast doubt on the State's assumption that religious use of peyote is harmful.

. . .

The carefully circumscribed ritual context in which respondents used peyote is far removed from the irresponsible and unrestricted recreational use of unlawful drugs. The Native American Church's internal restrictions on, and supervision of, its members' use of peyote substantially obviate the State's health and safety concerns.

. . .

Finally, although I agree with JUSTICE O'CONNOR that courts should refrain from delving into questions whether, as a matter of religious doctrine, a particular practice is "central" to the religion, I do not think this means that the courts must turn a blind eye to the severe impact of a State's restrictions on the adherents of a minority religion. (since "education is inseparable from and a part of the basic tenets of their religion . . . [just as] baptism, the confessional, or a sabbath may be for others," enforcement of State's compulsory education law would "gravely endanger if not destroy the free exercise of respondents' religious beliefs").

Respondents believe, and their sincerity has never been at issue, that the peyote plant embodies their deity, and eating it is an act of worship and communion. Without peyote, they could not enact the essential ritual of their religion. See Brief for Association on American Indian Affairs et al. as Amici Curiae 5–6 ("To the members, peyote is consecrated with powers to heal body, mind and spirit. It is a teacher; it teaches the way to spiritual life through living in harmony and balance with the forces of the Creation. The rituals are an integral part of the life process. They embody a form of worship in which the sacrament Peyote is the means for communicating with the Great Spirit").

If Oregon can constitutionally prosecute them for this act of worship, they, like the Amish, may be "forced to migrate to some other and more tolerant region." This potentially devastating impact must be viewed in light of the federal policy—reached in reaction to many years of religious persecution and intolerance—of protecting the religious freedom of Native Americans. See American Indian Religious Freedom Act. ("[I]t shall be the policy of the United States to protect and preserve for American Indians their inherent right of freedom to believe, express, and exercise the traditional religions . . ., including but not limited to access to sites, use and possession of sacred objects, and the freedom to worship through ceremonials and traditional rites"). Congress recognized that certain substances, such as peyote, "have religious significance because they are sacred, they have power, they heal, they are necessary to the exercise of the rites of the religion, they are necessary to the cultural integrity of the tribe, and, therefore, religious survival."

The American Indian Religious Freedom Act, in itself, may not create rights enforceable against government action restricting religious freedom, but this Court must scrupulously apply its free exercise analysis to the religious claims of Native Americans, however unorthodox they may be. Otherwise, both the First Amendment and the stated policy of Congress will offer to Native Americans merely an unfulfilled and hollow promise.

Additional reading

Maroukis, Thomas C. *The Peyote Road: Religious Freedom and the Native American Church* (Norman, OK: University of Oklahoma Press, 2010).
Moore, Steven C. "Reflections on the Elusive Promise of Religious Freedom for the Native American Church," *Wicazo Sa Review* 7.1 (Spring 1991): 42–50.
Stewart, Omer C. *Peyote Religion: A History* (Norman, OK: University of Oklahoma Press, 1987).

10

Commandment Keepers

Editors' Introduction: When Wentworth Arthur Matthew immigrated to New York from the West Indies in 1919, he encountered a vibrant, growing, and religiously diverse black American community centered in Harlem. This community consisted primarily of black Americans who moved north looking for jobs and looking to escape southern racism in the South, but it also included immigrants from the Caribbean and other black Americans born in the North. Matthew found various forms of Christianity in Harlem, including those that resembled the charismatic churches he attended in the West Indies, but he also encountered multiple forms of Ethiopian Hebrews or Black Jews. These groups differed in the minutiae of their respective theologies but they collectively agreed that black people are descendants of Jews and they traced their lineage back to Abraham, Isaac, Moses, and other important Jewish patriarchs. They also taught that colonialism, slavery, and other historical factors combined to conceal their ancestral religion, but that they could now reclaim their authentic religio-racial identity as Black Hebrews or Ethiopian Jews. Unlike many black Americans throughout the United States, Ethiopian Hebrews wrote themselves into a Jewish history that preceded the Christianization, first, of Europeans, and later, of black Americans. By this logic, black Americans were not simply victims of American slavery; they were God's chosen people and heirs to the covenant God made with Abraham millennia earlier. By 1919, several such groups existed in Harlem, and Matthew would soon create his own congregation to add to that number.

Matthew not only encountered black religious diversity in Harlem, but he also joined a growing racial uplift movement centered on black independence, pan-Africanism, and black nationalism. In 1919, the Marcus Garvey's Universal Negro Improvement Association (UNIA) in Harlem was perhaps the center of this larger movement. Matthew promptly joined the UNIA where he learned not only about racial pride, but where he also learned to connect racial pride with black religiosity.

Matthew contributed to this larger movement when he created the Commandment Keepers Church of the Living God, the Pillar and Ground of the Truth. This congregation would eventually become the largest form of Ethiopian Hebrews in America; however, in the group's earlier years it resembled—as its name suggests—a Christian church in the vein of Holiness or Pentecostal Christianity. Matthew also integrated aspects of Freemasonry and New Thought into his teachings, as he claimed that he possessed the power to heal, to read minds, and occasionally control the physical world.

Matthew was an innovator who synthesized various traditions to create a novel form of American religiosity, and Judaism was an important aspect from the beginning. Matthew's church contained Jewish traditions and imagery, including Hebrew inscriptions and the Star of David. Torah and Hebrew studies were also important. Over roughly a decade, Matthew removed most of the Christian imagery and teachings from his congregation as he increasingly highlighted the Jewish elements. By the time Matthew moved his group to Brooklyn in 1930, the Commandment Keepers considered themselves Ethiopian Hebrews or Black Jews.

This new identity was evident in the group's new synagogue, which resembled "traditional" synagogues as it contained an Ark, Torahs, menorahs, the Ten Commandments, and the Hebrew alphabet on the walls. Matthew also separated his congregation by gender, with men in the front. Matthew provided extensive religious education as he taught his black congregation that they are descendants of the Lost Tribes of Israel, specifically the Tribe of Judah, and he encouraged his followers to only marry "within the tribe" (that is, to avoid interreligious and intertribal marriages). He also encouraged his followers to adopt kosher eating practices and "traditional" Jewish attire, and Jewish ceremonies became more common in Commandment Keeper communities. He also advocated for a black migration to the native homeland of Israel.

The Commandment Keepers grew in New York and beyond as they became the largest group of Ethiopian Hebrews in America. To accommodate and encourage this growth, Matthew founded the Israelite Rabbinical Academy, which trained rabbis for new Commandment Keepers synagogues. He also created the Royal Order of Aethiopian Hebrews, an ancillary and fraternal group that supplemented the synagogues' work. Matthew continued to lead the group until his death in 1973. The Commandment Keepers continue to exist, although they have decreased in numbers since his death.

Rabbi Matthew is the author of all four of the following documents. The first two documents appeared in a series of articles where Matthew discussed both the history of black Jews in the United States and their (at times) tense relationship with non-black Jews. The remainder of the documents summarize his understanding of the history of black Jews.

Documents

Document One: Rabbi Wentworth A. Matthew, "The Truth about Black Jews and Judaism in America: Part I," *New York Age*, May 17, 1958, page 9. W.A. Matthew Collection, 1929–1979. Schomburg Center for Research in Black Culture, New York, New York.

That segment of Judaism in the Western Hemisphere which has come to be known as the Black Jews is now universally recognized as not only a part of the Hebrew families and culture, but as a challenge to the authenticity of white Judaism, which is the present-day acknowledged power backing this claim.

Prior to 1919, Judaism was not known to the black man of America or the West indies as it is known today, although, in a measure, it was practiced by black people of almost every island in the Caribbean area.

Blood is Life

These people were among the most enlightened, Biblically, would not eat the flesh of any beast that died of itself, by strangulation, or by storm. Neither would they use flesh without first salting it and allowing it to be drained in order to free it from blood, since it was written, "Flesh with the blood ye shall not eat for the blood is the life of flesh. Ye shall, therefore, pour it out upon the ground that it may be an atonement for you." In other words, if it be poured upon the ground in its original state it would be a compensation to the earth rather than if it were eaten and went through the chemical changes it would naturally go through.

The custom of cooking on three fire stones was an early custom of Israel as a reminder of man's tripartite existence—his spirit, soul, and body, and his past and future.

The fire hearth, which to the people of West Africa and the West Indies and also the South, has been for centuries a significant reminder of the Jewish altar of sacrifice was designed and for the purpose of sacrifice and for the aromatic odors of burning incense.

The command to Moses was, "See that thou do all things according to the pattern shewed thee on the mount" (Ex. 225–40).

Here I am reminded of the Patriarchal plays at Christmas time, also of David and Goliath and the children of Israel, by which the people of islands were reminded from year to year that they were the children of the house of Israel.

In the stories of Joseph in Egypt, Solomon and Sheba, strictly Biblical, are vividly portrayed the same people in American who are "Negroes" and in most parts of the British domain as "darkies."

Document Two: Rabbi Wentworth A. Matthew, "The Truth about the Black Jews and Judaism in America: Part III," *New York Age* (date and page unknown). W.A. Matthew Collection, 1929–1979. Schomburg Center for Research in Black Culture, New York, New York.

Upon the awakening of the black man to self-realization and the glory of his ancient past, my greatest opposition came from the very man I tried to enlighten. He was afraid he would lose the slave master's heaven, with its milk and honey, its golden slippers, and long white robes with flowing wings.

For interfering with this, I was disqualified by my own, and even had bricks thrown at my head from rooftops. Some said I was leading them back to the sacrifices of bull and heifers. But it was not very long before many began to see the light and return to school.

Knowledge of History

They wanted to know about themselves, the Hebrew language, the history of Abraham, Isaac and Jacob, and by what means were the so-called Negro related to the House of Israel.

Our greatest troubles were with the ministers who wanted to know who would stand by them in the Day of Judgment and where would they be when the world is on fire?

They asked again and again, "where will you hide?" These were baby thoughts inherited from the slave masters.

With the coming of the atomic age, everyone soon discovered, no matter what his philosophy of religion, that only the name of the Eternal remains the strong tower of defense, and that only the righteous may run therein and be saved.

Mocked Attire

The next was with some of our Jewish brethren, especially the reporters who wrote all manner of odd things about us. One publication, know at the time as the "American Hebrew" said we were pro-Catholic. They made fun of our prayer shawls and other religious attire.

Even Dr. Jacob Faithlovitch, who has since died, said the American Black Jews were no part of the Ethiopian Jews, for though their skin is dark, they (Ethiopian Jews) are still white. Dr. Faithlovitch was the man who claimed credit for discovering the Falasha Jews of Ethiopia.

His was indeed a strange statement since the whole world knew and still knows that the Ethiopians are as black as any other black people in the world.

Admits Error

No matter what any white man may say about it, the Ethiopian cannot change his skin (Jer. 13:23). The statement by Dr. Faithlovitch was made before the Long Island Chamber of Commerce. He was immediately challenged to meet me, any place suitable to him for an open lecture or debate on the subject. He calmly backed down, and 26 years later in an open public meeting humbly apologized to me and my congregation, admitting he was in error.

However, a majority of the Jews have been in brotherly sympathy with us and without reservation, either.

Seeks United Front

Let me take time here to commend Rabbi Irvin Block for his untiring effort in trying to close the breach. If it can be termed a breach, between white and black Jews, and to present a united front with a mutual understanding and purpose.

However, I think if anything is to be done for the American Black Jews, like all other people or groups, we will have to do it for ourselves.

Document Three: Rabbi Wentworth Matthew, "The Anthropology of the Ethiopian Hebrews and their Relationship to the Fairer Jews," in Howard Brotz, *The Black Jews of Harlem: Negro Leadership and the Dilemmas of Negro Leadership* (New York: Schoken Books, 1970), 19–22.

In order to speed along to a quick understanding, I must treat briefly the history of the sons of men, from Adam, of whom it is only necessary to say that when God decided on the necessity of man's existence; He did not choose to make a black man, or a white man: He simply decided to make man—not white nor black—from the dust of the earth, in whom He encased the reproductive power of all colors, all species, all shades of all races and eventual nationalities. From Adam to Noah, there were only two classes of men, known as the sons of God and the sons of men: a Godly and an ungodly group. In other words, a carnal and a spiritual-minded race of the sons of men, both from Adam.

The two classes eventually met in Noah and his wife: Noah was a son of the Godly (a son of God), he chose a wife form the daughters of men (the carnal-minded), and to the time of the flood he had three sons: Shem, Ham, and Japheth. After the flood Ham took the lead. Nimrod, one of the descendants, created the idea of a tower as the landmark of their capital, that if they became lost upon the face of the earth they might have something to look for as a guide, and also as a security against future floods. They called the name of their tower, or city, Babel. Some have said that Babel means confusion, but this is not so; the word mans "Coming to God."

As Cush rose in power, Africa, the entire continent, including Egypt, became the center of the world's cultural and religious education, and thus Ham secured for himself and his posterity for all time, a name—Pioneers of the World's Civilization.

After the fall of Cush came Egypt, under Mizri the second son of Ham, into power. He and Shem amalgamated by intermarriage and the Mesopotamians were produced, an interrace between Shem and Ham. After this came Abraham, the son of Tera; he married his sister Sarah, who was the daughter of his father but not of his mother. She was barren to him, but after many years she conceived by aid of a Hamitic god (Priest) and brought forth Isaac who, in turn, married Rebecca, his uncle's daughter. When she also, after many years, conceived, she brought forth twins, one red and hairy all over like a hairy garment, while the other was plain and smooth, as the black man invariably is. The first, the red and hairy one, was called Esau; the plain and smooth brother was called Jacob. This same Jacob, by four wives, begot twelve sons. After twenty years his name was changed from Jacob to Israel, and automatically his sons became the sons of Israel.

They went into Egypt and abode there four hundred and thirty years. They mingled greatly with the Egyptians by intermarriage, and thus Shem and Ham were merged into one great people. Of those who left Egypt, there were six hundred thousand footmen, twice as many women, three or four times as many of the half-breed and a host of children. All those who reached maturity before leaving Egypt died in the wilderness except Joshua and Calen; even Moses, the greatest of all legislators, died there. But before coming out of Egypt Moses had fled to Median in Ethiopia, only to become servants to the Ethiopian Priest whose daughter he eventually married and begot two sons.

Those two boys were as much Ethiopians as it was possible to be because they were created out of the soil and born in the land, as they were Israelites of the Tribe of Levi, the Priest, because Moses their father was of the tribe of Levi and of the household of Israel. They of necessity had to be black because their father was black, and so was their mother. They were the first Ethiopian Hebrews of the Tribe of Levi. They were half Hamitic and half Semitic. I could go on endlessly to prove the direct connection all along the ages of the two greatest peoples that ever lived in the earth, but I must hasten along.

This great admixture of two great people left Egypt, tarried in the wilderness forty years, and finally came into the land of Canaan. Eventually David, son of Jesse of the Tribe of Judah, came to the throne of Israel, and in time his son Solomon succeeded him.

When Solomon came to the throng, his fame spread the world over, and to the Queen of Sheba, whose name was Candace Queen of the South, she being also of the children of Rachel, one of the wives of Jacob. She also came to pay her respects and to make her portion of the kingdom subject to King Solomon. Eventually she became the wife of Solomon, the son that was born to them was Menelik the 1st. The line of the Falashas are counted from Menelik 1st to Menelik the great, who was the uncle of his Imperial Majesty, Haile Selassie, the 1st, the Lion of the Tribe of Judah. It is roughly calculated that before the war there were about a million Falasha Jews in Ethiopia (about a tenth of the population of 13 million); however, since the war they have been greatly reduced, and fear is entertained for their continued existence. In Harlem, N.Y., there are about three thousand adherents to the faith and who, with pride, lay claim to this glorious heritage. At the central Congregation, 1 West 123rd Street, N.Y.C., there are about eight hundred registered. At 434 Franklin Ave., Brooklyn are also a goodly number. In Philadelphia, Media, Pittsburgh, and Sharon, Pa., are goodly groups also at Youngstown and Ferrell, Ohio, Chicago, Ill., Cullen, Va., St. Thomas, V.I., and Jamaica, W.I.

It is claimed by these that they are among the oldest families of the Jewish or Hebraic race upon the face of the earth, and that they are the only ones to retain their king to sit upon the Throne of David and, outside of Palestine, to retain the six point star on their money. Our manner and customs are strictly orthodox; we are strictly Koshered. Our children are taught to speak the Hebrew language and to live in keeping with all the commandments of the Almighty.

I am the only rabbi with credentials from Ethiopia, sanctioned by both the Chief Rabbi of the Falashas and the National Coptic Church of St. Michael. The National Church must sanction the existence of all other religious bodies in Ethiopia, but none are ever barred or hindered. Religious practices are as free in Ethiopia as in the USA Thus it is time for the two great people to come together and stand for the true doctrine of the oneness of God.

My prayer is that peace may soon come to the earth, and good will to all men, and an eternal victory for Israel, the elect of the Eternal.

Document Four: Rabbi Wentworth Matthew, "The Root and Inception of The House of Israel" (Flyer). W.A. Matthew Collection, 1929–1979. Schomburg Center for Research in Black Culture, New York, New York.

The root and inception of the house of Israel are to be found in Syria. This country is the original fatherland of Abraham whose father was Terah of the families of Shem (Sem), one of the sons of Noah. Note, Abraham's own statement. "My father was a Syrian ready to perish when the Almighty took him by the hand and led him to the land of Canaan." Deut. 26:5; Gen. 28:1–5.

Then Isaac the father of Jacob sent him to Padanaram in Syria, where he married his cousin, his uncle's daughter, and had twelve sons and a daughter whose name was Dinah. Then Jacob and his family returned to Canaan and there remained until the famine of that day and time when all Israel went into Egypt to buy corn, and became stranded there for four hundred and thirty years (430) until the birth and maturity of Moses, who was the son of Amram and Jecobed, 46:20. His brother and sister were Aaron and Miriam. Then by some strange coincidence, Moses went out one day to take a look just to see how his first born were doing. When he saw an Egyptian unmercifully beating one of his Hebrew brothers, whom he had come to see. Then he being trained in all the ways of the Egyptians looked this way and that way. Then he dismounted from his beast and slew the Egyptian and buried him. But the next day he had the urge to return to the scene of the defense, only to find the same fellow whom he rescued the day before, involved in another fight with a Hebrew, one of his own blood brothers. Moses then tried to make peace, as a good peacemaker, but the man whom he had befriended the preceding day, said to him, "who made you a ruler over us. Do you think you are going to kill me as you did the Egyptian yesterday?" Then Moses realized if this thing became known to the King that he and all his people might perish. So he fled to Midian, 42:11–22, where he married Jethro's daughter, whose name was Zeporah. Jethro was the high priest of Midian, and Zeporah brought forth two sons. After this the eternal took Moses up into the mountain and gave him the first three steps of his initiation by the burning bush, the Holyground, the Serpent and the Mystic Voice. (Ex. 3). After this he was sent back into Egypt, and the ten plagues followed, which was the prelude to Israel's deliverance. After four hundred and thirty years of servitude, Israel's first rebuff was by his twin brother, Esau. (Num. 20:14–21), who did not go into Egypt, but remained in Canaan and inhabited that section which is on this side of the Jordan, which was called Seir, and made it the kingdom of Edom who is Essau. Then Essau established the capital of Edom, which is Seir, which in the time of David became Jerusalem. Edom also built roads and highways, and the main highway from Egypt to Canaan which he called the King's Highway. Israel therefore, when he came to Kedesh, sent messengers to the king of Edom and said, "let me, I pray thee pass through the border of your land to go to the place which the Lord our

God has appointed us." But the king of Edom said, "Thou shalt not pass through my land." But again Israel begged for passage but this time Essau came out with the sword. So he, Israel, took the long and perilous way that took forty years before they came to Canaan.

Essau did not become Jewish until, David, king of Israel in order to avoid war with his twin brother had the Scribes to look at the record left by Moses, where it was written that Israel should not have war with Edom, "Because," said he, "He is thy brother." (Deut. 23:7). Thou shall not abhor the Edomite. This precept was accepted by both brothers, and a treaty was entered into in the year 1042 B.C.E., and Edom became a part of the house of Judah and Benjamin, and was governed by Israel to the reign and death of Solomon. From then unto this day, Edom has been known as the Jewish people or families. The Falasha Jews are the true representatives of the House of Judah. This branch of the House of Israel is from Solomon, the Son of David and Sheba, Queen of Ethiopia. (2 Chron. 21:8). From Menelieck the 1st to Menelieck the great to Haille Selasie 1st, 613 kings in an unbroken strain.

The monarchy of the Ethiopian Kingdom is the oldest monarchy in the world today. Ethiopia is the true home of the Falasha Jews, indisputably. However, the land of Canaan is the true home of all Israel. If Edom must fight for Palestine or Seir, he has a right to do so, and it is the duty of all Israel to help him. However Essau must be made to realize that his mother and father were black but he was born red and hairy. How come? Our brothers must not be allowed to make the black Jews to believe that Edom is the only true Jew of Arian blood because this is what Hitler wanted for Germany. All Israel are brothers. We should not allow the ancient enmity between the brothers to divide us. And no black Jew should allow a white Jew to berate a black Jew leader and let him go unchallenged.

Additional reading

Chireau, Yvonne and Nathaniel Deutsch, eds., *Black Zion: African American Religious Encounters with Judaism* (New York: Oxford University Press, 2000).

Dorman, Jacob S. *Chosen People: The Rise of American Black Israelite Religions* (New York: Oxford University Press, 2013).

Parfitt, Tudor. *Black Jews in Africa and the Americas* (Cambridge, MA: Harvard University Press, 2013).

Weisenfeld, Judith. *New World A-Coming: Black Religion and Racial Identity during the Great Migration* (New York: New York University Press, 2016).

11

Moorish Science Temple of America

E*ditors' Introduction*: Following a brief existence in New Jersey in the 1910s as the Canaanite Temple, the Moorish Science Temple of America, founded in the 1920s in Chicago, offered African Americans an alternative religious and racial identity. According to leader and prophet Noble Drew Ali, black, colored, and negro were all incorrect terms to describe America's African-descended population. Rather, Ali argued that they were Moorish, which was an ethnic or racial identity, based in Morocco and the Middle East, and it was a Muslim identity. Ali described how Allah originally created all Moorish people to be Muslims, but when Europeans enslaved them, slavery disconnected the Moors from their authentic identity and past. Only with reclaiming that identity would salvation be achieved. God had prepared Christianity for Europeans and their descendants while Allah had prepared Islam for Moors. This Moorish identity connected members of the Moorish Science Temple to a community that spanned national borders and scriptural texts. It was a respectable identity as old as the Bible. Their claim of this transnational identity was an attempt to remove themselves from Jim Crow racism by claiming an identity outside America's white-over-black racial hierarchy. The group was most popular under the leadership of Ali, who died under somewhat mysterious circumstances in 1929. In the wake of his death there was a scramble for authority, as more than one claimed that Ali's spirit worked through them. Still active today, there is a small network of temples around the country.

According to the organization's founding documents, including the Constitution and By-Laws, "Love, Truth, Peace, Freedom, and Justice" are at the center of their teachings. The organization's two newspapers, the *Moorish Guide* early on and the *Moorish Voice* after Ali's death, frequently cited their mission as to "uplift fallen humanity." In the US context, that fallen humanity was those American society labeled as "black," "negro," or "colored." Like salvation, social uplift would require a recognition of that Moorish, Muslim identity.

The new, yet old, religious and racial identity offered by the Moorish Science Temple had great appeal to black Americans during and in the wake of the Great Migration (the mass movement of southern blacks to more northern cities in the early twentieth century). It offered a respectable identity in the face of racism and encouraged them to take control of their identity. Moorish Science Temple members changed their names to connect with the historical narrative offered by Ali, they wore clothing that marked themselves as Moorish-American (fezzes, turbans, long dresses, suits, and more), and used healing teas and tonics made specifically for their bodies by the prophet himself.

Starting in the 1930s, the Federal Bureau of Investigation began to monitor the Moorish Science Temple, classifying them as a violent "extremist Muslim group." The FBI understood the Moorish Science Temple to be a "part of a worldwide Organization" to "unite the dark races" and "take over" the United States during the Second World War. As such, the FBI files on the Moorish Science Temple should be read with a grain of salt, realizing that a biased perspective was writing these. The Moorish Science Temple was not trying to take over the United States and Ali had set clear rules to follow the laws of the US Government. The FBI files indicate that they often did not understand the movement's theology, practice, or their program of racial uplift. There were members who filed as conscientious objectors when reporting for the draft due to their emphasis on peace. While there were a few cases where it seems some pro-Japanese sentiment was expressed, the agents in the field cleared the majority of temples under investigation citing no evidence of any anti-American behavior. On the contrary, many field agents found that many Moorish Science Temple members emphasized the American component of their Moorish-American identity.

The documents here include an excerpt from the group's official text, *The Holy Koran of the Moorish Science Temple* and excerpts from the declassified FBI files on the movement. Included here is part of the final chapter of *The Holy Koran*. Ali plagiarized the first forty-four chapters of the text from esoteric texts, popular in the early twentieth century. He only wrote the final four chapters and these detailed the historical origin of the Asiatic and Moorish race, describe the movement's prophetic significance, and explain the movement's relationship to Christianity. As a whole, those chapters outline the relationships and connections between non-white populations throughout Asia, the Middle East, Africa, and the Americas, with Chapter 48 focusing on the organization's place in the US Document Two is excerpts from the declassified FBI files collected during their monitoring of the Moorish Science Temple. These proclaimed historical and religious ties likely drew increased attention from the FBI. The excerpts include two field reports.

Documents

Document One: Noble Drew Ali, *The Holy Koran of the Moorish Science Temple*, excerpt from Chapter 48

Chapter 48. The End of Time and the Fulfilling of the Prophesies

1. The last Prophet in these days is Noble Drew Ali, who was prepared divinely in due time by Allah to redeem men from their sinful ways; and to warn them of the great wrath which is sure to come upon the earth.

2. John the Baptist was the forerunner of Jesus in those days, to warn and stir up the nation and prepare them to receive the divine creed which was to be taught by Jesus.

3. In these modern days there came a forerunner of Jesus, who was divinely prepared by the great God-Allah and his name is Marcus Garvey, who did teach and warn the nations of the earth to prepare to meet the coming Prophet; who was to bring the true and divine Creed of Islam, and his name is Noble Drew Ali who was prepared and sent to this earth by Allah, to teach the old time religion and the everlasting gospel to the sons of men. That every nation shall and must worship under their own vine and fig tree, and return to their own and be one with their Father God-Allah.

4. The Moorish Science Temple of America is a lawfully chartered and incorporated organization. Any subordinate Temple that desires to receive a charter; the prophet has them to issue to every state throughout the United States, etc.

5. That the world may hear and know the truth, that among the descendants of Africa there is still much wisdom to be learned in these days for the redemption of the sons of men under Love, Truth, Peace, Freedom, and Justice.

6. We, as a clean and pure nation descended from the inhabitants of Africa, do not desire to amalgamate or marry into the families of the pale skin nations of Europe. Neither serve the gods of their religion, because our forefathers are the true and divine founders of the first religious creed, for the redemption and salvation of mankind on earth.

7. Therefore we are returning the Church and Christianity back to the European Nations, as it was prepared by their forefathers for their earthly salvation.

8. While we, the Moorish Americans are returning to Islam, which was founded by our forefathers for our earthly and divine salvation.

Document Two: Excerpt from the FBI monitoring files of the movement. This particular field report comes from April of 1940 in New York City. These files are available publicly from the FBI's online "vault." Unlike other primary sources in the volume, brackets around the word redacted here denote what the FBI blacked out from the document before declassifying it.

New York City Area Report, 4/8/40; Suspicious Matters

Synopsis of Fact: Information received that Japanese Chamber of Commerce officials have on several occasions spoken before the Hartford, Conn. Chapter of the

"MOORISH SCIENCE TEMPLE OF AMERICA," a Negro organization claiming over 8,000,000 members who describe themselves as Moors and not Negroes. Series of six articles prepared for a Hartford newspaper about this Moorish organization obtained and forwarded to Bureau.

Report: The informant further advised that this organization was believed founded for the purpose of "uplifting the lot of the poor negro in the United States." He stated further that this organization claims to have over 8,000,000 members at the present time throughout the United States.

Informant stated that the reason he thought this matter would be of interest to the Federal Bureau of Investigation was the fact that on several occasions members of the Japanese Chamber of Commerce were reported to have spoken at meetings held by the Hartford Chapter and that, therefore, there was the possibility the Japanese Government might be spreading propaganda at these meetings. Informant advised that he has a negro informant who attends the meetings held and who has given him information about what transpired at the various meetings. He informed that this organization has not been very active recently and the summer of 1939 was the last time that Japanese officials spoke at the Hartford meetings. He stated that in the event he receives further information about the activities of this organization he will immediately notify the writer.

Informant furnished the writer a photo of the cover of the "Holy Koran of the Moorish Science Temple of America," and also photos of three inside pages of this same book. In addition to this the informant furnished the writer rough draft proofs of six short articles he had prepared for possible publication in a Hartford newspaper. Photostatic copies were made of the above material and one set of these photostats are being forwarded to the Bureau and another set is being retained in the New York file on this matter. The originals of the above were returned to the informant.

No further investigation will be conducted on this matter by the New York Division unless the Bureau directs to the contrary. Two copies of this report are being forwarded to the Chicago Division inasmuch as the main headquarters for this organization is given as "Noble Drew Ali, founder, Moorish Science Temple of America, 930 N. Townsend St., Chicago, Ill."

Document Three: Excerpt from the FBI monitoring files of the movement. This particular document is a memo from the Military Intelligence Service to the FBI, dated February 26, 1943. These files are available publicly from the FBI's online "vault."

Moorish Science Temple of America
(Moorish Holy Temple of Science)

This Negro cult, which has been reported as active in many sections of the country, shows strong traces of Japanese influence, and is known to have influenced its members to refuse to comply with the provisions of the Selective Service Act because of their "Mohammedan Religion." Meetings of the organization, which restricts its membership to members of the so-called darker races, are known to have been held at the homes of Japanese nationals.

Generally taught doctrines of the order are that its members are not Negroes but Moorish Americans, entitled to full rights and privileges of any American without the slightest racial discrimination, and that the Negro should favor the Japanese cause because a Japanese victory would insure for the Negro complete equality with other races.

The actual degree of Japanese instigation in the origin and teachings of this organization remain uncertain. MIMO DE GUZMAN, known to have been an active propaganda agent for Japan among the Negroes of this country, has said that the movement is patterned upon the PACIFIC MOVEMENT OF THE EASTERN WORLD and that its activities are very pro-Japanese. It is further reported from reliable sources that the instructors of this society have been in the past been largely Japanese and Filipinos. In this connection it is noted that the MOORISH VOICE, official publication of the order, in its August, 1941, issue, stated: "It is significant that many years ago when Japan won freedom from mental slavery, we gained physical freedom, and when Japan won her first battle over the Europeans, we won our first mental battle, and gained the right to become a National Unit through our Prophet Noble Drew Ali. Now Japan has reached a position where she can hold her own with all European nations, say and do when and what she pleases, and our people are aroused to the need of sticking together."

. . .

The MOORISH SCIENCE TEMPLE OF AMERICA is said to have been organized in Chicago in 1925 by a North Carolina Negro named TIMOTHY DREW, known variously as NOBLE DREW ALI, PROPHET DREW ALI, and NOBLE DERW ALLAH. Associated with him in its founding was a Negro who called himself MOHAMMED BEY. The organization was incorporated in Cook County, Illinois, in 1928, at which time PROPHET NOBLE DREW ALI was stated to be treasurer of the temple. Other officers then registered were L. BARNES, C. HIGHBAUGH, ALBERT STRICKLAND, and C. CURTMAN BEY. In 1928, the order had an estimated membership of 15,000. Since that date, the organization's activities have been marked by considerable rivalry among its leadership, in one incident of which NOBLE DREW ALI is said to have succumbed to a terrible beating and died. At present the following individuals are reported to regard themselves as the true successor to the prophet, and maintain individual organizations: CHARLES KIRKMAN BEY, RHODES EL, GIVENS EL, J. SHELBY EL, and DELIA EL. The largest of these groups is that controlled by KIRKMAN BEY, leader of the MOORISH SCIENCE TEMPLE OF AMERICA in Detroit, Michigan. BATES is believed to have been formerly active with SATOHASHI TAMAHASHI, previously mentioned as a promoter of pro-Japanese Negro groups in this country.

. . .

With regard to the pseudo-Moslem nomenclature of this sect, an informant has stated that the tribal names always follow the actual names on all documents, and that there three known tribes. Members of one of the tribe adds "Allah." These surnames are assumed by members when they join the organization, and in filling out applications for employment these "Moslems," as they call themselves, have refused to use their proper names and to list the religious name as an alias. Inasmuch as the organization teaches its members that they are not colored, they have been known to refuse to write the word "black" after "color" in application questionnaires.

At meetings of the lodge in Detroit, Michigan, all of the members are said to wear red fezzes with black tassels and some of the officers wear two-toned colored pants of green and red and a jacket of Asiatic pattern.

A membership card is issued to all members. This card is white with a red rim around it. In the upper left hand corner is a three-quarter moon with a start in the upper center with the word "Islam" under it. In the upper center of the card are two hands clasped with the word "Unity" over them. In the upper right hand corner is a black circle with the figure "7" in it and the world "Allah" under it. Beneath this the card reads as follows: "This is your nationality and identification card for the Moorish Science Temple of America, and Birthrights for the Moorish Americans, etc. We honor all the Divine Prophets, Jesus, Mohammad, Buddha, and Confucius. May the blessings of the God our Father Allah, be upon you that carry this card. I do hereby declare that you are a Moslem under the Divine Laws of the Holy Koran of Mecca . . . NOBLE DREW ALI, The Prophet, 1104 Sedgwick Street, Chicago, Illinois."

The organization also uses a round blue pin made of celluloid with a three-quarter gold or silver moon and a star in the upper right hand corner of the moon. Above the moon in red letters are the initials M.A. Under the moon in red or silver letters is the word "Allah."

Document Four: Excerpt from the FBI monitoring files of the movement. This particular field report comes from January of 1944 in Chicago. These files are available publicly from the FBI's online "vault." Unlike other primary sources in the volume, brackets around the word redacted here denote what the FBI blacked out from the document before declassifying it.

Chicago Area Report, 1/31/44; Internal Security – Security Matters

Synopsis of Fact: Subject presently under indictment along with [redacted] for violation of Sedition Laws of State of Mississippi. Subject is the minister of the [redacted] Branch of the Moorish Science Temple of America, Inc. [redacted] Chicago, Illinois. Has registered for Selective Service and filed C.O. Form which he says he filed because he was advised to do so by his local board inasmuch as he was a minister. He says that he is willing to serve in the armed forces and denies in any way that he or his organization are favorable to Japan. He stated that he and [redacted] had gone to Mississippi for the purpose of organizing an auxiliary branch of the Moorish Science Temple of America but had discontinued the enterprise because of the difficulties which they had become involved in with the State of Mississippi. He claims that they have no auxiliary branches in Mississippi or elsewhere. Subject employed as garage mechanic where he has a good employment record. No criminal or credit record.

Report: [Redacted] Branch of the Moorish Science Temple of America, Inc., which is located at [redacted] Chicago, Illinois, and also because of the information reflected in the report of Special Agent [redacted] May 26, 1942, Jackson, Mississippi, wherein it was disclosed that the State Grand Jury had indicated [redacted] and [redacted], along with several others, for a violation of a state statue making it a criminal offense to teach any belief that indicates the overthrow of government by force or violence. The statute is carried under the sedition laws of the State of Mississippi. The report reflects that [redacted] and [redacted] returned to Chicago without having been tried under the indictment.

On December 31, 1943 the records of the Draft Board No. 2, 3104 South Michigan Avenue, Chicago, Illinois, reflected that Brother [redacted] EL SHEIK, [redacted] was registered under Order No. [redacted]. The following physical description and background information was reflected in the files:

Age	[redacted]
Born	[redacted]
Birthplace	[redacted]
Race	Asiatic
Weight	165 pounds
Eyes	Brown
Hair	Black
Complexion	Black
Marital Status	married—two children
Occupation	Ordained minister of the Divine Gospel Moorish Science Temple of America
Employment	[redacted] Chicago, Illinois
Social Security No.	[redacted]

Subject filed a C.O. Form in which he stated "I am a minister of the Divine Gospel of the Almighty God ALLAH of the Moorish Divine and National Movement, Prophet NOBLE DREW ALI, Founder and Head." He stated that he had acquired such belief at a public meeting of the members of the Moorish Holy Temple of Science, [redacted]. He gave the Prophet NOBLE DREW ALI, 3229 Indiana Avenue, as the one on whom his religious guidance was dependent.

With reference to the use of force, the subject stated, "I believe that force is the will of ALLAH and is omnipotent in power that will not manifest destruction between brothers." With respect to the acts and behavior demonstrating consistency and depth of the religion which he professes, the subject gave "love, truth, and obedience." He stated that such beliefs were publicly expressed in a public meeting of the Moorish Divine and National Movement of the Moorish Holy Temple of Science Hall every Friday and Sunday from 8:00 p.m. until 10:00 p.m. at [redacted]. He gave as the school where he had acquired this belief as the Moorish Science Temple of American, Inc., 3229 Indiana Avenue, which he classified as a divinity school. He stated that he had attended this school since he had become a member in 1937 until the present date. He gave as a former place of employment the [redacted] from 1928 to 1936; the [redacted] 1937 to 1941; [redacted].

He gave as former addresses the following: [redacted]

With respect to the view of the organization towards the war the subject gave the following answer: "My creed is Moslem. Islamism was prepared by our ancient forefathers and mothers for earthly and divine salvation in the Garden of Eden, the Holy City of Mecca, under the principles of love, truth, peace, freedom, and justice and human equality—peace on earth, good will towards men." He gave the name of Brother [redacted] EL, [redacted] minister and brother-in-unity, as one who could supply information as to the sincerity of his belief against participation in war. Subject is present classified as III-A.

On December 31, 1943 [redacted] advised that the subject was no longer in his employ. He said that [redacted] had left their employ approximately a year ago, that the subject was an intelligent, loyal, and obedient worker, that he was believed to belong to a Moslem Cult with which he was familiar. [redacted] that subject had been interviewed by the Federal Bureau of Investigation over a year ago concerning the activities of the cult of which he was a member. [redacted] stated that he had never heard the subject make any remarks which would indicate that he was anything but a loyal and patriotic citizen [redacted] that he subject was presently employed at the [redacted] Chicago. The reason for the subject's leaving their employ [redacted] stated was that he had an offer of higher wages at his present place of employment and that he would very much like to have subject back in his employ.

[redacted] stated that the subject was presently employed by that company, that he was an honest, loyal, and constant worker and was buying ward bonds and cooperating in every way with the war effort. [redacted] is definitely sure that the subject was not of a radical nature but rather the direct opposite of that. He stated that the subject insisted on the title of "EL" following the name on his checks, war bonds, and any other matter in which he dealt with the company. [redacted] that the subject was a member of a cult in which the belief was that the members were not Negroes but rather Moors or Moorish Americans. The subject had been employed intermittently by that company for the last eight years. It was during this time that [redacted] that the subject made a short trip to Mississippi on behalf of the organization to which he belonged. [redacted] could furnish no further details concerning the trip to Mississippi, however.

On January 12, 1944 subject was interviewed by the reporting agent at the [redacted]. Subject related the following story: He said that he was minister of the Moorish Science Temple of American, Inc., v that [redacted] El was the [redacted] and that meetings were conducted regularly at that address on Friday and Sunday evenings; that the average attendance was from twenty-five to thirty-five people. He said that to the best of his recollection that there were over fifty members of the group but that only a little over half of these members were presently active. He said that [redacted] is presently very ill with rheumatism, and is unable to preside over the meetings, and that in his absence [redacted] Bey presides. He said that his brother, [redacted] EL, is the [redacted] of the organization and keeps order at meetings. [redacted] is employed at a potato chip shop on [redacted] just east of Halsted on the south side of the street.

Subject stated that he would be willing to serve in the armed forces if called or would perform any other duty that he should be called upon to do in furtherance of the war effort. He said that he was presently buying war bonds also. He said that the welfare of the government was his welfare and that his belief was that of the organization of which he was a minister. He stated that he did not object to war but that he had filed the C.O. Form because he had been informed at his local board that he was entitled to file such a form inasmuch as he was acting in the capacity of a minister.

In reference to the trip to Mississippi, he stated that he, along with [redacted] EL and Sister [redacted] EL, had traveled to [redacted] Mississippi, February 23, 1941 for the purpose of organizing an auxiliary branch of the Moorish Science Temple; that such enterprise was discontinued at Milestone after they had become involved in difficulties with the officials of the State of Mississippi. He said that the organization had no auxiliary branches in the State of Mississippi, nor do they have any such branches elsewhere in the United States.

When questioned concerning the difficulty and friction which exists between the [redacted] Branch and that of CHARLES KIRKMAN BEY, 1032 Orleans Street, Chicago, Illinois, he denied any friction did exist between the two organizations. He stated that the Prophet NOBLE DREW ALI had handed down certain rules and regulations by which all members and branches should abide. The fact that other branches are organized independently should be no concern of the various other branches so long as there has been no violation of the by-laws and rules set down by the Prophet.

In answer to the question as to whether or not he or the organization were favorable to Japan or claimed themselves to be brothers of Japan, he stated that he or the organized definitely were not in sympathy with the Japanese. He did say that he believes that he is a descendant of the Asiatics and not necessarily Japanese. He compared their belief and descendants to the people of the United States who are descendants of Europeans. He stated that he was of the Mohammaden faith, believing in the God ALLAH, that their Bible was the Holy Koran which was not identical with that of the true Mohammaden but rather a modified concept called a Koran, which had been designed by the Prophet NOBLE DREW ALI.

In conclusion the subject expressed his desire to be of any assistance in the war effort that he might be called upon to do and that his belief was shared by every member of the organization to the best of his knowledge. He said that if it ever came to his attention that any member of his organization was not cooperating with the war effort or had not the best interests of this country at heart, that he would immediately report it.

[Full paragraph redacted]

Unless advised to the contrary, no further investigation is contemplated at this time.

Document Five: Excerpt from the FBI monitoring files of the movement. This particular field report comes from 1944 in Chicago. These files are available publicly from the FBI's online "vault." Unlike other primary sources in the volume, brackets around the word redacted here denote what the FBI blacked out from the document before declassifying it.

Age	58
Height	5'11"
Weight	150 lbs.
Race	Moorish (Negro)
Eyes	Brown
Hair	Black
Complexion	Light Brown
Marital Status	Single

On February 26, 1944, the Reporting Agent interviewed the Subject at his residence at [redacted] third floor, rear, room No. 5. He stated that he was the [redacted] Chicago, Illinois. He had acted in his capacity for the last three or four years. In indicated that C. KIRKMAN BEY was the Supreme Grand Moderator and Advisor over this temple. According to the Subject the meeting place had originally been in the 1400 block on North Clybourn Avenue and was later moved to the corner of Oak and Franklin Streets. He said that at the present time the meetings of the organization are conducted only on Sunday afternoon and evenings inasmuch as the hall is in use at other times during the week. The Subject stated that the purpose of the organization was to uplift fallen humanity, to proclaim the nationality of the members, and that any members so doing automatically uplifted themselves and proclaimed their nationality and were therefore no longer Negroes. He said that all of the members were not Negroes, but Moorish-Americans, descendants of Morocco. In the Subject's room was displayed the American and Moroccan flag. Upon being asked by the Reporting Agent the significance of the two flags, he stated that the American flag indicated the country of which the members were citizens and the Moroccan flag indicated the country from which they were descendants. By virtue of the fact that they were descendants of Morocco, they were therefore Asiatics. When asked whether or not he considered himself a blood brother of the Japanese, he indicated that they were of the same general race but that the attitude taken by the organization was the same as that of the Europeans and Americans or the white race. He indicated that neither he nor the organization favored the Japanese in any way. He merely stated that the brief of the organization is love, truth, peace, freedom, and justice, and because of this fact, they believe in being at peace with everyone through the world. He emphasized the fact that he and the members firmly believe in the United States Government and that all members are registered for

Selective Service; many of them are presently serving in the Armed Forces. He stated that the members of Temple No. 9 number approximately 200 . . .

On February 26, 1944, [redacted] was interviewed at [redacted]. He stated that the Subject had a favorable employment record with them and was a very good worker. He stated that the Subject had been employed since December 30, 1943, and that there was no indication of any un-American or un-patriotic tendencies on the part of the Subject.

Additional reading

Clark, Emily Suzanne. "Noble Drew Ali's 'Clean and Pure Nation': The Moorish Science Temple, Identity, and Healing," *Nova Religio: The Journal of Alternative and Emergent Religions* 16.3 (February 2013): 31–51.

Johnson, Sylvester. "The Rise of Black Ethnics: The Ethnic Turn in African American Religions, 1916–1945," *Religion and American Culture: A Journal of Interpretation* 20.2 (Summer 2010): 125–163.

Turner, Richard Brent. *Islam and the African American Experience* (Bloomington, IN: Indiana University Press, 2003), 71–108.

Weisenfeld, Judith. "Spiritual Complexions: On Race and the Body in the Moorish Science Temple of America," in *Sensational Religion: Sense and Contention in Material Practice*, Sally Promey, ed. (New Haven, CT: Yale University Press, 2014), 413–428.

12

International Peace Mission Movement

Editors' Introduction: In 1914, a man known as Major Jealous Father Divine, typically called Father Divine, founded the International Peace Mission Movement. Preaching that he was God in a body, Divine taught listeners that they all possessed the spirit of God within them. Thus, the movement believes that all are equal, despite how society defines their gender identity, racial identity, or class identity. Based on his interpretation of 1 Corinthians 3:16, that God's spirit dwells within you, Divine understood himself to be incarnate divinity. He encouraged followers to "acknowledge God in matter" and see him as the materialized, tangible God. He preached that his followers should feel Christ in "every joint" of their bodies. Christianity was thus a huge influence on Father Divine's movement, though, like most alternative religious movements, he splintered off and melded new revelations with the long accepted. Divine's teachings are reminiscent of Baptist and Pentecostal ideas and his ideas also intersect with the New Thought Movement, in particular its focus on the power of positive thought. (In fact, after hearing Father Divine preach, singer-songwriter Johnny Mercer wrote the song "Accentuate the Positive.")

The movement denies the ontology of racial identity, and this claim to be God held great significance in the context of American race relations. Occupying a body that outsiders would identify as short, hefty, balding, and black, Divine's identification as God carried much import. Additionally, because everyone should recognize that the spirit of God (not the same level as God himself) resided within them, Divine's movement proclaimed a form of racial and gender equality. These were radical claims during the era of Jim Crow. Additionally, followers of Divine's International Peace Mission Movement often lived together in interracial communities called "heavens." An earlier version of this was Divine's home in Sayville, New York (on Long Island). When local whites brought suit against Divine for disruption of the peace (their complaints likely prompted by the movement's interracialism), the judge in the case suddenly died, an event for which Divine apparently claimed responsibility, reportedly stating "I hated to do it."

In Divine's "heavens," followers used the Sermon on the Mount to structure much of their everyday lives. They focused on the needs of each other and the poor. According to Divine, in these heavens, "life, liberty, and the reality of happiness" were a possibility. In a decision reminiscent of the Shakers, the core community of the movement followed Divine's call to be sexually celibate. Around the time of the movement's founding, he married his first wife, an older woman named Penninah, who became the movement's first Mother Divine. In accordance with his teachings, Divine's marriage to Penninah was abstinent. Divine's love feasts and Peace Mission banquets were also important, particularly during the Great Depression. During these, followers and those who came to the community could take part of a fine meal, for free or for a very low cost. Divine argued that he was trying to unify people, in comparison to the general support for segregation that could be found in many southern and northern white churches. To financially support the movement Divine embarked on business ventures that supported it and its ideals. The movement created a number of businesses, such as grocery stores and hotels, which offered their services at affordable prices. Social discrimination, be it racial or gendered, was not accepted at any of the movement's businesses, which allowed for a rich avenue of recruitment for the movement as well as strong business potential.

Father Divine died in 1965, though many followers emphasize that only his physical body failed. Leadership of the movement fell to his second wife, also called Mother Divine. (After Penninah's death, Divine married again.) Mother Divine was formerly known as Edna Rose Ritchings and had worked as Divine's secretary. She was more than forty years Divine's junior and society classified her as white, unlike Divine or Penninah. Like Divine's marriage to Penninah, his marriage to Ritchings was celibate and for reasons of companionship and partnership. Divine's second marriage underscored the group's dedication to racial equality. The second Mother Divine died in 2017, though membership of the movement had been dropping ever since Father Divine's death.

The following three documents come from International Peace Mission Movement publications and each of them comprises transcripts of messages delivered by Father Divine. Document One comes from the movement's earlier periodical, *Spoken Word*. In these excerpts from Father Divine, he emphasized the equality of humanity and shared part of his vision for a "Righteous Government." This particular sermon came at the close of the International Righteous Government Convention, a three-day event hosted by the movement attended by its members, local politicians, and local community leaders. The language of emancipation and freedom would remind listeners of slavery's abolishment. Document Two contains excerpts from a Father Divine message published in *The New Day*, the movement's second periodical. Here, Father Divine focuses again on the "Righteous Government" and the importance of himself in that vision. Along with the equality emphasized in Document One, the personification of God in Father Divine was central to the possibility of the "Righteous Government." Finally, Document Three puts the focus squarely on racial issues and racial prejudice. Father Divine emphasized how racialized terms and categories supported racial prejudice and racial violence. Instead, he stressed the importance of equality, recognizing the universality of humanity, and the personal importance of each of his listeners. Not only God, Father Divine also identified himself with American liberty.

Documents

Document One: "FATHER DIVINE Delivers Message to Mighty Throng, Heralding the Glad Tidings of the New Day," *Spoken Word* 2.14 (January 14, 1936).

A Real Emancipation

Hence each of you should Praise GOD for the Victory. I would like to Say to My hearers, and those that are true Believers, Co-Workers and Friends—by the recognition of the Body in which I am Dwelling, you will receive your physical, and mental, and spiritual, and social Emancipation. You will receive your political emancipation and every other social expression. You will receive your deliverance from every angle and receive your Real Emancipation, for your Emancipator has Come. Remember, this is not confined nor bound to materiality . . .

Putting Righteousness Into Practice

We don't know anything about lacks, and wants and limitations, we are free, and FREE indeed; and I lift up this Standard for others, that I might emancipate them through the recognition of GOD'S Presence as a Living Reality and as a Living Factor in their hearts and in their lives. Then I Say, we shall have a RIGHTEOUS GOVERNMENT manifestly, materially, politically, socially, and otherwise, for the Righteousness which we are expressing through the Life and Teaching of the Fundamental has been materialized. Through the materialization of Righteousness by those that will observe Righteousness a Living Reality, they can become to be the "tangibilators" of RIGHTEOUSNESS, by putting RIGHTEOUSNESS, TRUTH and JUSTICE into practice. We must, as I heard one of our honored Speakers say this Evening, become Righteous ourselves and put it into practice daily, and we will be qualified to transmit it to others in fulfillment of the Gospel. First take the beam out of your own eye, that you might see clearly to take the mote out of thy brother's eye. These My Following, and millions of others throughout the Universe, have become Righteous, Truthful and Just, through the Words and Teaching of the Master. They have returned all stolen goods, they have paid their old debts that were due. Such debts and such bills they would have never paid, and did not intend to pay by any means, but through this great conversion they have returned the stolen goods and they have gone back to repay the old bills to whom they were due. By becoming Righteous firstly within, hence they will extend it to the children of men by doing unto them as they would have others do to those that may be concerned. Now isn't that Wonderful!

Appealing To All Men

I will not detain you very much longer at this juncture, for the time is fast approaching that we will be on the air. There are thousands of the radio audience listening and waiting even at this time, to hear the Voice of . . . ("GOD"—shouted the vast Audience.)

But just before we go very much further on this point, I will stop and pause for consideration. We wish to stress the significance of this RIGHTEOUS GOVERNMENT CONVENTION, this Evening. We have not organized merely to be seen and heard of men, but we meant to put the issue through by our Righteous Government Forum and by My PLATFORM, and all the Countries of our present Civilization must sit up and take notice.

We are calling for RIGHTEOUSNESS, TRUTH, and JUSTICE, and we must HAVE it. I appeal to the people of the United States of America to cooperate if they will to, that they might enjoy the Limitless Blessings that I will put through. If they do not, I will put it through without them. I appeal to the Administration of this CITY—to cooperate with ME if you desire the issue of RIGHTEOUSNESS, JUSTICE and TRUTH to go through. If you desire that which is Just, and Good, and Right, and True, I will be with you. I appeal to the great Nations of the world – consider this RIGHTEOUS PLATFORM which we have drafted for consideration, and recognize the Constitution of this great Country, and you will find all Nations will be blessed accordingly, as Myself as an Individual and this Peace Mission Movement that is actually under My Personal Jurisdiction.

. . .

A Real Emancipation

Abraham Lincoln could not give the slaves of America Emancipation it was not in his power to do it. Abraham Lincoln desired to bring about an emancipation but this was only a sketch and a reflection of the reality of this Emancipation that I am bringing. Then I Say let this Truth be established in YOU and you and all the Nations of the Earth will realize once and forever, "You are in another Day," and you as well as I, will be able to shout the Victory. As I have Victory over these conditions, I am endeavoring to transmit it to the Nations. I am endeavoring to get behind the Politicians and other Officials, to transmit and reincarnate My Spirit of RIGHTEOUSNESS, TRUTH, and JUSTICE in them, that they might become to be Righteous and Justice among the children of men.

Document Two: "The Righteous Government Platform is a Foundation on Which Men Can Build Who Have Been Hungering and Thirsting After Righteousness and Finding None," *The New Day* 2.37 (September 15, 1938).

PEACE, EVERYONE:
I rise at this instance to say, this evening has been set apart for our RIGHTEOUS GOVERNMENT MEETING. As MY Spirit Alone is the chairman, the chairlady, the master of ceremonies and the other official duties, MY Spirit will fill them. For this cause I have arisen, permitting MY Spirit to speak within at this particular time, after which I will allow MY Spirit to speak in others—to move in the act of the expression of the chairlady, the master of ceremonies, the chairman or whatsoever would be needful in such an organization.

Since this is not an organization, but merely a movement which will envelop the world, we do not customarily have the different officials in the divers meetings as the organizations do; however we carry on with the same spirit and the meaning of our endeavors as much as we would have different persons as individuals to fill such official duties. For this cause MY Spirit will carry on. Not only in this particular meeting at this particular time, but at all other times, as this evening is a sample and an example of what can be without the customary form of organizing and without the customary form of setting apart different officials to fill official duties; as GOD IS ALL AND IN ALL. GOD can and will speak through you all if all self and selfishness will get out of the way.

I have arisen at this time to say those words and to stamp them in your memory. From now, henceforth and forever, see that the Spirit of MY PRESENCE be just as expressive and just as active and as appreciated at MY PRESONAL Absence as it is in MY PERSONAL PRESENCE. If this is done with the recognition and the realization of MY PRESENCE when I AM apparently absent, I will be as expressive in SUCCESS and PROSPERITY, in WISDOM, in KNOWLEDGE and in UNDERSTANDING at MY PERSONAL Absence as when I AM Personally Present. I will also be as an abstract expression as a center of attraction to attract and draw others when I AM PERSONALLY Absent, the same as when I AM PERSONALLY PRESENT.

. . .

A Living Sacrifice

How marvelous it is to live in such a recognition; to get this thought stamped in your memory; as a living sacrifice I CAME, to create an atmosphere and an environment whereby God's PRESENCE could be reckoned. You cannot count GOD'S PRESENCE wheresoever the "other fellow" is in evidence and is expressing. Wheresoever there is evidence of wickedness, vice and crime and sin and debauchery of every kind, it is a matter of impossibility for you to reckon GOD'S PRESENCE in such an environment.

Create for yourself an environment whereby GOD'S PRESENCE can be reckoned. You cannot count GOD'S PRESENCE in an audience where there are doubts and fears, where there is swearing and obscene language used, effectively. GOD'S PRESENCE will not express itself evidently, but if you relax your conscious mentality from those tendencies and create for yourself an atmosphere in which GOD'S PRESENCE can be reckoned, GOD'S PRESENCE will be observable in such an atmosphere and in this environment of which we are now expressing and stressing will be the evidence of GOD'S ACTUAL PRESENCE, and GOD'S PRESENCE will be reckoned in such an atmosphere. YOU ALL KNOW GOD IS HERE, I SAY! Why then, know the same thing tomorrow morning. Know the same thing at all times, for:

"His Name shall be called IMMANUEL, being interpreted GOD IS WITH US."

. . .

Only Talk

You read it in the Bible about the RIGHTEOUS GOVERNMENT and RIGHTEOUS and JUDGMENT being the habitation of GOD'S Throne, but you did not see the enactment of RIGHTEOUS GOVERNMENT until I CAME. Did you? They would talk about

RIGHTEOUS GOVERNMENT, but they did not mean to enact a RIGHTEOUS GOVERNMENT as transmitted and as reincarnated and as exemplified by your HUMBLE SERVANT.

How glorious it is to reckon such a PRESENCE! Stress it vividly, emphasize it, advocate it and demonstrate it until others reincarnate it by concentration. Can you not see others are reincarnating the RIGHTEOUS GOVERNMENT I AM advocating and AM stressing by concentrating on the FUNDAMENTAL and recognizing GOD as being PRESENT with them? It is transmitted and inculcated through transmission. It is emphasized and advocated by them through harmonizing with ME. When this is done, it becomes to be a living factor in the hearts and lives of the children of men, and when this is established among them in a practical way of expression in all of their activities they become to be the personification of that of which they have been emphasizing, advocating and demonstrating. Aren't you glad?

Hence the Word of TRUTH is made real—no longer a supposition. Your conscious recognition will be established in you and you are the personification of the TRUTH among the children of men. Now that is what I AM doing here today.

. . .

Living in Him

I heard you say that Jesus said:

"I AM HE that liveth and was dead, but BEHOLD, I AM alive forevermore."

One said:

"Ye are dead and your life is hid with CHRIST in GOD."

He also said, on another occasion:

"Reckon yourself to be dead indeed unto sin and alive unto GOD through JESUS CHRIST our LORD."

"In that you die, you die unto sin; in that you live, you live unto GOD." Your life is quickened and your soul is revived and now you live in ME. Aren't you glad! As live wires, as live rails, as live coals—you are as live coals of fire; no longer from Elijah's ALTAR after the manner of Melschisedec. Aren't you glad! I AM making you alive daily! I AM causing you to recognize MY ACTUAL PRESENCE as being with you when I AM apparently absent from you. This is what we should do—recognize GOD's PRESENCE continually. Lo, I will be with you and the RIGHTEOUS GOVERNMENT, the RIGHTEOUS GOVERNMENT of which I have exemplified and Am demonstrating in the lives of the children of men.

Document Three: "Those Who Use Segregated Terms are Endorsing Lynch Mob Murders Even if They are Not Conscious of It," *The New Day* 3.43 (October 26, 1939).

How blind creation is to the fact that all men are created equal! Blind to the knowledge of even the substance of the Constitution and its Amendments and the Declaration of Independence wherein it declares such, and blind to the fact that Uncle Sam has declared E. PLURIBUS UNUM, which means ONE COMPOSED OF MANY!

There are those who are against segregation and race discrimination and wish to see it broken down, that all men might enjoy the freedom and the privileges afforded them without regard to so-called race, color or creed; but still in their ignorant intelligence they cut off their nose to spite their face, so to speak.

Such was the case on this night of the Righteous Government Meeting held in the auditorium at One Hundred and Twenty-sixth Street. A visiting friend, one of many who were present, arose to speak on the bad treatment given a certain class of people because of their complexion. Instead of speaking generally concerning the evil of prejudice, he continued to repeat a lowrating vulgar name by which so many have been robbed out of their rightful inheritance and the privilege of equality and the exercise of their citizen rights. This of course does not tend to abolish prejudice, but rather it tends to establish same and instill it in the minds of children of men. For this cause our beloved SAVIOR Arose and delivered this vital Message, explaining the mystery of how such distinctions are as thieves and robbers to humanity and how such must be completely eliminated from amongst us.

(The foregoing statements are those of the transcriber, after which FATHER Speaks as follows:)

PEACE, EVERYONE: Here you all are and there I sit and stand. As one of the human race, through MY Condescension I came, but representing whatsoever you may be called, as I AM "E PLURIBUS UNUM," as I AM the United States of America, as I AM the spirit of a true democracy, I come, I come, I come! At this instance I would just like to say, the reason for MY Followers and those who are being educated out of what they have been educated into, making such emotions as they do when you see a segregated term, especially those whom you call Afro-Americans—to get down to the real point of which I AM especially stressing I will call your attention to MY Followers buying some property up in Yonkers. Now why was it they did not want MY Followers to own property in Yonkers? It is not what they want, it is what they get! Nevertheless, they did not want it.

Some of MY Followers bought a large park, Greenkill Park, right near Kingston, New York. They did not want MY Followers to buy the park; which is true, I did not buy it. It has been said, "I do not want to sell to FATHER DIVINE." I did not buy the park, it is true, and I AM not expecting to buy any land, since the earth is the LORD'S and the fullness thereof!

MY Followers bought some property in Brooklyn and out on Long Island, in Connecticut, in Pennsylvania, in Massachusetts and in many of the different states. They did not want MY Followers to buy the property. Why was it they did not want them to buy that property?

Endorsing Murder

The Followers bought some property in New Rochelle. They did not want them to buy that property there. Why was it? Now I will tell you why we hate that name that you called a little while ago: because it is a thief, a robber and a murderer! Those who use such segregated terms, if they are not conscious of it, they are endorsing murder! They are endorsing lynch mob murders, if they are not conscious of it!

It is not that every man is conscious of it, but I know it is a segregated term that is used and it is a vulgar name. The same as if a man would meet you out in the street and just call you the "son of a" something! It is just as vulgar, I say, as if a man was to call you a son of something but not the Son of GOD! You would be ready to fight him too, would you not? The name is just as vulgar!

When you have been lowrated, when you have been disgraced, when you have been disenfranchised, when you have been isolated, when you have been segregated, when you have been mobbed by violence because of such a name, do you think we will tolerate it! The very name in itself is vulgar.

Look in your dictionary and see where they saw "cracker" concerning Irish-Americans in the South, where they say "cracker" concerning French-Americans in the South, where they say "buckra" concerning an English-American in the South. Is that not vulgar? Such cursed names should not be used, for they have been used for the purpose of lowrating and for the purpose of disgracing individuals and distorting and disrespecting such ones as are called by such names. These are hard sayings but yet they are true. Especially those names I mentioned there a little while ago, such as they are called, they have been named such names for the purpose of distortion in consciousness as well as you would distort one's features as a cartoon to discredit the individual. That is why we dislike the usage especially of that vulgar name. There are other vulgar names that have not robbed the people as much as those vulgar names have.

. . .

Do Not Brand Anyone

Oh, how glorious it is to know the truth, that the truth might set you free and give you your real emancipation, with Life, Liberty and the reality of Happiness, for which we all allegedly are seeking! Now let these thoughts abide with you and feel free to speak, each and everyone, but try to deny yourselves of branding anyone with a segregated term of lowration, a vulgar name for the purpose of lowration, in the act of lowrating the person or persons in these divers congregations. It is an expression of embarrassment and it reflects a sense of embarrassing and an embarrassment on those who are sensitive to such usage when they know definitely those names are detrimental and robbers in themselves.

Just think of thousands of men and women today, yea, millions of them. Because they are called by a vulgar name and the usage of such a segregated term concerning them, they have been robbed out of millions and billions of dollars, out of houses and lands, out of comfort and convenience, and even out of the privilege of living in decent and respectable homes because of the segregated and prejudicial, malicious and undermining of all lowrated terms men have used concerning them and imposing the vulgar name on them until they are classed as being vulgar people. Can you not see it is essential to take a stand in opposition to such tendencies?

I would just like to digress here for an instance. MY attention was called to the state employment agency somewhere in this community. I have been informed they had advertised, they wanted a stenographer some place and one of MY Followers went to get the position, and with that same old vice-versalted prejudicial mind, because that person did not look as this complexion does, that person, the agent there who thought he looked like ME said, "Who are you and what race are you?" or words to that effect. She said, "What matter is that? I came to get the position." He did not give it to her! Well, we will not tolerate it on the right hand nor on the left! **I will shake creation first!** They must deal justly and honestly, and if men seek office, unless they get away from races, creeds and colors and partisan parties I will throw them out of office! Those who are in such offices, unless they get those prejudicial and segregated tendencies out of their system by getting them out of their mentality and out of their characteristics, I will move them out of office if I do not cast a ballot!

The People Must be Judged with Equity

Oh, what a privilege to live in such a recognition! That which I have declared I will do it with or without a Body! I need not have a body to do it. You need not think that anything can stop it.

We shall have a Righteous Government and the people must be judged with equity! Everybody must be squarely and fairly dealt with!

Oh, what a privilege to live in such a recognition and to know from whence I AM speaking! I AM not speaking from the Body, I AM speaking without the Body. I AM speaking without any Body! That which I have declared I will accomplish with or without a body!

What said I through the Scripture, in other words, in the Scripture, concerning the mystery?

"It is not by power nor by might but by MY Spirit, declares the LORD!"

Then if it is by the spirit of GOD, let GOD'S Spirit do it!

I did not mean to say so much. The more I talk, the more I can talk. The deeper it gets and the broader. The higher the heights and the deeper the depths, for GOD is infinite, and when you get in HIS infinite Spirit, when you get in it, of you apparently and of your access and expression, it will apparently be no end!

Now I want these thoughts stamped in your memory, and considered. People who have been branded by that vulgar name and called by that vulgar name for the purpose of lowration, they have been lowly rated and the lowest rated persons in creation, and more vulgarly classed as a vulgar people because of the lowrated name by which they have been called and by the usage of vulgarity concerning them. They have been robbed, they have been spoiled, they have not had the privilege others have had. Even as I afore said, financially, when all such who had not been lowly rated or branded as a lowrated person would get one hundred and fifty dollars a month, the majority of those who were branded with a lowrated name, a lowrated, vulgar name, they would get fifty. That lowrated name had lowrated them regardless to the classification or qualification, and they were robbed by that old cursed name, of one hundred dollars a month!

Qualify Yourselves

That is just a parable, just one witness speaking of what it has done universally throughout all of this land and this country and throughout other lands and countries, where the prejudice of the English-speaking people have conveyed it.

Live in this recognition and build upon this foundation and study and prove yourselves workmen! Qualify yourselves for registering and voting and remain qualified. Even if you do not cast a ballot, know within yourself you are qualified intellectually to pass the literacy test on every hand. Know within yourself you are qualified to pass the civil service code wheresoever you may be and whatsoever position you may desire. Nevertheless you do not have to commit yourselves to something that is law because of a position, for GOD is Omnipotent and Omniscient and Omnipresent. God can and will, as HE has been doing, make a way where there is no way, and will build you up where you had been torn down—will establish your going in the land of the living and will develop HIS Omniscience within you that you might produce the spirit of superintelligence is concerned.

Additional reading

Fauset, Arthur Huff. *Black Gods of the Metropolis: Negro Religious Cults of the Urban North* (1944; Philadelphia, PA: University of Pennsylvania Press, 2002), 52–67.

Primiano, Leonard Norman. " 'The Consciousness of God's Presence Will Keep You Well, Healthy, Happy, and Singing': The Tradition of Innovation in the Music of Father Divine's Peace Mission Movement," in *The New Black Gods: Arthur Huff Fauset and the Study of African American Religions*, edited by Edward E. Curtis, IV and Danielle Brune Sigler (Bloomington, IN: Indiana University Press, 2009), 91–115.

Satter, Beryl. "Marcus Garvey, Father Divine and Gender Politics of Race Difference and Race Neutrality," *American Quarterly* 48.1 (March 1996): 43–76.

Weisenfeld, Judith. *New World A-Coming: Black Religion and Racial Identity during the Great Migration* (New York: New York University Press, 2016).

13

Nation of Islam

Editors' Introduction: Master Fard Muhammad (a man known by many names) created The Lost-Found Nation of Islam in Detroit, Michigan, in 1930. After he mysteriously disappeared four years later, an acolyte named Elijah Poole (later renamed Elijah Muhammad) became the group's leader, a position he held until he died in 1975. The Nation of Islam differed from the vast majority of religions popular in early twentieth-century America as it rejected Christianity in favor of a racialized form of Islam. Under the leadership of both Fard and Elijah Muhammad, the Nation of Islam appropriated some beliefs, texts, and rituals associated with more traditional forms of Islam and taught their theologies primarily to black Americans in urban spaces, primarily those who recently moved north during the Great Migration.

Elijah Muhammad taught his followers that Fard Muhammad was Allah incarnate and that he, Elijah Muhammad, was not only Allah's prophet, but that he continued to communicate with Allah. He taught that black Muslims are true Muslims; that they are morally, ethically, and religiously superior to white people (or "white devils," as he often called them); and that they should separate in America from white people to the fullest extent possible. To facilitate this separation, the Nation of Islam opened a variety of businesses, and the Nation's ministers preached that the members of the Nation should, to the fullest extent possible, only support Nation-owned businesses and other businesses owned by members of the Nation of Islam. The Nation's newspaper, *Muhammad Speaks*, was one such business. It not only provided the Nation of Islam with a forum for spreading its theology and for criticizing white America, but it provided a source of income for the thousands of male members who sold it on the streets.

The combination of black nationalism and Islam proved highly offensive, both to Muslims who believed in more traditional forms of Islam, and to mainstream civil rights leaders who favored racial integration and racial equality. It proved attractive, however, to many urban black Americans, including Muhammad Ali, the world heavyweight boxing champion, and a petty criminal named Malcolm Little (renamed Malcolm X), who became the Nation's most influential and famous minister. Malcolm X left the organization in 1964 and subsequently embraced Sunni Islam, a more traditional form of Islam, although he was soon murdered in February 1965, and many people believed that the Nation of Islam sanctioned or even orchestrated the killing.

Malcolm X's departure is often cited as a turning point for the Nation of Islam, as it began to lose members and influence. Elijah Muhammad continued to lead the organization until his death in 1975, when one of his sons led the Nation of Islam into what he hoped would be a mass conversion to Sunni Islam. Several disaffected members then resurrected the old Nation of Islam, which continues to exist today under the leadership of Louis Farrakhan.

The following documents include two speeches by Malcolm X and excerpts from *Message to the Blackman in America*, one of Elijah Muhammad's many books. The first speech by Malcolm X is one of his more famous speeches, where he criticizes black civil rights leaders who favored desegregation and racial equality between the races. Instead, Malcolm X argued that a new type of "negro" is becoming the majority, one who wants to distance and separate himself not only from white people but also from black leaders who represent the old mentality. In his second speech, he offers a brief but comparably comprehensive summary of Nation of Islam theology. The excerpts from *Message to the Blackman in America* repeat several of these themes, but they also highlight the practical application of Muhammad's teachings, particularly as they relate to gender. Together, these documents provide the reader with a brief glimpse into the Nation of Islam prior to Elijah Muhammad's death.

Documents

Document One: Malcolm X, Harvard Law School Forum Speech (March 24, 1961).

Mr. Chairman, Ladies and Gentlemen. We thank you for inviting us here to the Harvard Law School Forum this evening to present our views on this timely topic: The American Negro, Problems and Solutions. But to understand our views, the views of the Black Muslims, you must first realize that we are a religious group, and you must also know something about our religion, the religion of Islam.

The Creator of the Universe, whom many of you call God or Jehovah, is known to the Muslims by the name Allah. Since the Muslims believe there is but one God, and that all the prophets came from this one God, we believe also that all prophets taught the same religion, and that they themselves called that religion Islam, an Arabic word that means the complete submission and obedience to the will of Allah.

One who practices this Divine Obedience is called a Muslim (commonly known, spelled, and referred to here in the West as Moslem). There are over 725 million Muslims on this earth, predominantly in Africa and Asia, the non-white world . . . and we here in America who are under the Divine Leadership of the Honorable Elijah Muhammad, are an integral part of the vast World of Islam that stretches from the China Seas to the sunny shores of West Africa.

A unique situation faces the 20 million ex-slaves here in America because of our unique condition, thus our acceptance of Islam, and into Islam, affects us uniquely . . . differently than all other Muslim "converts" anywhere else on this earth.

Mr. Elijah Muhammad is our Divine Leader and Teacher here in America. Mr. Muhammad believes in and obeys God 100 per cent, and is teaching and working among our people to fulfill God's Divine Purpose today.

I am here at this Harvard Law School Forum this evening to represent Mr. Elijah Muhammad, the spiritual head of the fastest-growing group of Black Muslims in the Western Hemisphere.

We who follow Mr. Muhammad know that he has been divinely taught and sent to us by God Himself. We believe that the miserable plight of the 20 million black people in America is the fulfillment of divine prophecy. We believe that the serious race problem that our presence here poses for America is also the fulfillment of divine prophecy. We also believe that the presence today in America of the Honorable Elijah Muhammad, his teachings among the 20 million so-called Negroes, and his naked warning to America concerning her treatment of these 20 million ex-slaves is all the fulfillment of divine prophecy.

Therefore, when Mr. Muhammad declares that the only solution to America's serious race problem is complete separation of the two races, he is fulfilling that which was predicted by all of the biblical prophets to take place in this day.

But, because Mr. Muhammad takes this uncompromising stand, those of you who don't understand biblical prophecy wrongly label him as a racist, a hate teacher, or of being anti-white, and of teaching black supremacy.

But, this evening, we are all here at the Harvard Law School Forum together: both races, face to face. During the next few moments we can question and examine for ourselves the wisdom or the folly of what Mr. Muhammad is teaching.

Many of you who classify yourselves as "white" express surprise and shock at this truth that Mr. Muhammad is teaching among your 20 million ex-slaves here in America, but you should be neither surprised nor shocked.

As students, scholars, professors and scientists you should be well aware that we are living in a world and at a time when great changes are taking place. New ideas are replacing the old ones. Old governments are collapsing, and new nations are being born. The entire "old system" which has held the Old World together has lost its effectiveness, and now that Old World is going out. A new system or New World must replace the Old World.

Just as the old ideas must be removed to make way for the new, God has declared to Mr. Muhammad that the evil features of this wicked Old World must be exposed, faced up to, and removed in order to make way for the New World that God Himself is getting ready to establish.

The Divine Mission of Mr. Muhammad here in America today is to prepare us for this New World of Righteousness, by delivering to us a message that will give us a better understanding of this Old World's many defects, and then we will all agree that God must remove this wicked Old World.

We see by reports in the daily press that even many of you who are scholars and scientists think that this message of Islam that is being taught here in America among your 20 million ex-slaves is "new," or that it is something Mr. Muhammad himself has made up.

Mr. Muhammad's religious message is not "new." All of the scientists and prophets of old predicted that a man such as he, with a doctrine or message such as this that Mr. Muhammad is spreading among your 20 million ex-slaves, would make his appearance among us at a time such as we are living in today.

It is also written in your own scriptures that this prophetic figure would not be raised up from the midst of the educated class, but that God would make His choice of a man from among the lowly, uneducated, downtrodden and oppressed masses, among the lowest element of America's 20 million ex-slaves.

Just as it was in the days when God raised up Moses from among the lowly Hebrew slaves, and missioned him to separate his oppressed people from a slave master named Pharaoh, and Moses found himself opposed by the scholars and scientists of that day, who are symbolically described in the bible as "Pharaoh's Magicians," and just as Jesus, himself a lowly carpenter, was also missioned by God in that day to find his people . . . the "lost sheep" . . . and separate them from their Gentile enemies, and restore them back among their own people, Jesus also found himself opposed by the scholars and scientists of his day, who are symbolically described in the bible as "scribes, priests, and pharisees."

Just as the learned class of those days disagreed and opposed both Moses and Jesus primarily because of their humble origin and status, today Mr. Elijah Muhammad is likewise being opposed by the learned, educated intellectuals from among his own kind primarily because of his humble origin and status in their eyesight, and efforts are made by these modem-day "magicians, scribes, and Pharisees" to ridicule Mr. Muhammad by magnifying the humble origin of his many followers.

Moses was raised up among his enslaved people at a time when God was planning to remove the power of the slave master and bring about a great change by placing the slaves in a land of their own where they could give birth to a "New Civilization," completely independent of their former slave master. Pharaoh opposed God's plan and God's servant, so Pharaoh and his people were destroyed.

Jesus was sent among his people again at a time when God was planning to bring about a great change. The new dispensation preached by Jesus 2,000 years ago ushered in a new type of civilization, the Christian civilization, better known as the Christian world.

The Holy Prophet Muhammad, may the peace and blessings of Allah be upon him, came 600 years after Jesus with another dispensation that did not destroy or remove the Christian civilization, but it did put a dent in it, a wound that has lasted even until today.

Now today, God has sent Mr. Elijah Muhammad among the downtrodden and oppressed so-called American Negroes to warn us that God is again about to bring about another great change . . . only this time, it will be a Final Change! This is the day and the time for a Complete Change.

Mr. Muhammad is teaching that the religion of Islam is the only solution to the problems confronting our people here in America, but he also warns us that it is even more important for us to know the base or foundation of that which we must build upon tomorrow.

Therefore, the way in which Mr. Muhammad teaches us the religion of Islam, and the particular kind of Islam he teaches us, may appear to be different from that which is taught in the Old World of Islam, but the basic principles and practices are the same.

You must remember: the condition of America's 20 million ex-slaves is uniquely pitiful. But, just as the old religious leaders in the days of Moses and Jesus refused to accept Moses and Jesus as religious reformers, today many of the religious leaders in the Old Muslim World may also refute the teachings of Mr. Elijah Muhammad, not realizing the unique condition of these 20 million ex-slaves, and by not understanding that Mr. Elijah Muhammad's teachings are divinely prescribed to rectify the miserable condition of our oppressed people here, but as God made Pharaoh's Magicians bow before Moses, and the Scribes and Pharisees bow before Jesus, it is God's plan today to make all opposition, both at home and abroad, bow before this truth that is now being taught by the Honorable Elijah Muhammad.

We are 4,000 years from the time of that great change which took place in Moses' day. We are 2,000 years from the time of that great change that took place in Jesus' day, and if you will but look around you on this earth today it will be as clear as the five fingers on your hand that we are again living at the time of a great change right now.

God has come to close out the entire Old World, the Old World in which for the past 6,000 years practically the entire earth has been deceived, conquered, colonized, ruled, enslaved, oppressed and exploited by the Caucasian race.

The Black Muslims who follow Mr. Muhammad are not only making our exit out of the door of the Old World, but the door to the New World is yet to be opened and what is inside that door is yet to be revealed.

This present teaching of Mr. Muhammad among your 20 million ex-slaves is only to prepare us to walk out of this wicked Old World in as intelligent, pleasant, and peaceful a way as is possible.

This present teaching among the so-called American Negroes is designed only to show proof to us why we should give up this wicked Old House. The roof is leaking; the walls are collapsing, and we find it is no longer able to support the tremendous weight caused by our continued presence in it.

And since the knowledge of the deterioration and eventual collapse of this Old Building has come to Mr. Muhammad from Almighty God Himself, whose proper name is Allah, the Lord of all the Worlds, the Master of the Judgment Day, the Honorable Elijah Muhammad is pointing these dangerous present conditions and future events out to you who have enslaved us, as well as to us.

With the proper support and guidance our people can get out of this sagging Old Building before it collapses.

Do justice by your faithful ex-slaves. Give us some land of our own right here, some SEPARATE STATES, so we can separate ourselves from you, then everyone will be satisfied, and perhaps we will all be able to then live happily ever after, as your own Christian Bible says . . . "every one under his own vine and fig tree."

Otherwise: all of you who are sitting here, your government, and your entire race will be destroyed and removed from this earth by Almighty God, Allah. I thank you.

Document Two: Malcolm X, The Race Problem Speech (January 23, 1963).

So you have two types of Negro. The old type and the new type. Most of you know the old type. When you read about him in history during slavery he was called "Uncle Tom." He was the house Negro. And during slavery you had two Negroes. You had the house Negro and the field Negro.

The house Negro usually lived close to his master. He dressed like his master. He wore his master's second-hand clothes. He ate food that his master left on the table. And he lived in his master's house—probably in the basement or the attic—but he still lived in the master's house.

So whenever that house Negro identified himself, he always identified himself in the same sense that his master identified himself. When his master said, "We have good food," the house Negro would say, "Yes, we have plenty of good food." "We" have plenty of good food. When the master said that "we have a fine home here," the house Negro said, "Yes, we have a fine home here." When the master would be sick, the house Negro identified himself so much with his master he'd say, "What's the matter boss, we sick?" His master's pain was his pain. And it hurt him more for his master to be sick than for him to be sick himself. When the house started burning down, that type of Negro would fight harder to put the master's house out than the master himself would.

But then you had another Negro out in the field. The house Negro was in the minority. The masses—the field Negroes were the masses. They were in the majority. When the master got sick, they prayed that he'd die. [Laughter] If his house caught on fire, they'd pray for a wind to come along and fan the breeze.

If someone came to the house Negro and said, "Let's go, let's separate," naturally that Uncle Tom would say, "Go where? What could I do without boss? Where would I live? How would I dress? Who would look out for me?" That's the house Negro. But if you went to the field Negro and said, "Let's go, let's separate," he wouldn't even ask you where or how. He'd say, "Yes, let's go." And that one ended right there.

So now you have a twentieth-century-type of house Negro. A twentieth-century Uncle Tom. He's just as much an Uncle Tom today as Uncle Tom was 100 and 200 years ago. Only he's a modern Uncle Tom. That Uncle Tom wore a handkerchief around his head. This Uncle Tom wears a top hat. He's sharp. He dresses just like you do. He speaks the same phraseology, the same language. He tries to speak it better than you do. He speaks with the same accents, same diction. And when you say, "your army," he says, "our army." He hasn't got anybody to defend him, but anytime you say "we" he says "we." "Our president," "our government," "our Senate," "our congressmen," "our this and our that." And he hasn't even got a seat in that "our" even at the end of the line. So this is the twentieth-century Negro. Whenever you say "you," the personal pronoun in the singular or in the plural, he uses it right along with you. When you say you're in trouble, he says, "Yes, we're in trouble."

But there's another kind of Black man on the scene. If you say you're in trouble, he says, "Yes, you're in trouble." [Laughter] He doesn't identify himself with your plight whatsoever.

Document Three: Excerpts from Elijah Muhammad, *Message to the Blackman in America* (Chicago, IL: Muhammad Mosque of Islam No. 2, 1965).

Chapter 2: "Allah is God. Who is that Mystery God? Part 2"

Did God say that He was a Mystery God, or did someone say it of Him? Did God say that He was only a Spirit, or did someone say it of Him? The most important question of all questions that one could ask is, "Who is God?" It is like a child who does not know his father asking his mother to tell him the name of his father, wanting to know what his father looks like and if he favors his father. Can we not ask the same question who are seeking the knowledge of Our Father, God? Should we be called disbeliever's or infidels, just because we seek the truth or knowledge of Our Father, God? The mother may, in some cases, think it best to keep the name of her child a secret, as it was in the case of Mary and Joseph, 2,000 years ago. But, in the case of God, one would say that we all should know Him, but at the proper time.

It has been for the past 6,000 years that we had to wait for the proper time to learn just who is Our Father, for the false god (the devil) would not dare tell us lest he lose his followers. Naturally, the child will leave a foster father for his real father, especially when he is a good father. The real father by nature loves his own flesh and blood regardless of how it looks or acts, for it is his own child. So it is with us, the so-called Negroes, "lost-found members of the Asiatic nation." He who has found us is Our Father, the God of love, light, life, freedom, Justice, and Equality. He has found his own, though His own does not know Him. They (the so- called Negroes) are following and loving a foster father (the devil) who has no love for them nor their real father but seeks to persecute and kill them daily. He (the devil) makes the lost and found children (the American so-called Negroes) think that their real father (God) is a mystery (unknown) or is some invisible spook somewhere in space. The only chance that the children have to know their real father is that He must come and make Himself known by overpowering and freeing them from Him whom they fear.

The devils reared the poor so-called Negroes for 400 years and put fear in them when they were babies. They (the devils) kept them apart from their own kind coming in from abroad, so as to deprive them of any knowledge other than what he (the devil) has taught them. As soon as they hears of a so-called Negro learning and teaching his own people that which they (the devils) would not teach them, the devils then seek to kill that one or trail him wherever he goes, threatening those who would listen to him, believe him and follow him. Knowing that their very presence and inquiries might frighten or scare Negroes they ask, "What is this you are listening to and believing in?" This will frighten most of them away from accepting his or her own salvation and keep them from returning to their own God, religion and people.

My people, if you only knew the time and presence of your God, Allah, there should be no fear for you nor grief. But, you are deceived in the knowledge of your God. If your God were a mystery, you and I would be a mystery people. If He were a Spirit and not a man, we would all be spirits and not human beings! If He were a mystery or only a Spirit, the prophets could not have predicted the coming of that which no one has knowledge of or of a spirit which cannot be seen, only felt.

Because of the false teaching of our enemies (the devils), God has made Himself known; (for I teach not the coming of God but the presence of God, in person.) This kind of teaching hurts the false teachings of the devils, for they knew that God would come in person after you. They, (the devils) also are aware that God is present among us, but those of you who are asleep they desire to keep asleep.

The enemies of God today are the same as they were thousands of years ago, thinking that they will be the winner against Him. America, for her evil done to me and my people, shall he isolated and deceived by her friends. The heavens shall withhold their blessing until America is brought to a disgraceful ruin.

Chapter 18: "Original Man: Know Thyself"

It is knowledge of self that the so-called Negroes lack which keeps them from enjoying freedom, justice and equality. This belongs to them divinely as much as it does to other nations of the earth.

It is Allah's (God's) will and purpose that we shall know ourselves. Therefore He came Himself to teach us the knowledge of self. Who is better knowing of who we are than God, Himself? He has declared that we are descendants of the Asian Black Nation and the tribe of Shabazz.

You might ask, who is this tribe of Shabazz? Originally, they were the tribe that came with the earth (or this part) 66 trillion years ago when a great explosion on our planet divided it into two parts. One we call earth and the other moon.

This was done by one of our scientists, God, who wanted the people to speak one language, one dialect for all, but was unable to bring this about. He decided to kill us by the destroying our planet, but still He failed. We were lucky to be on this part, earth, which did not lose its water in the mighty blasting away of the part called moon.

We, the tribe of Shabazz,, says Allah (God), or the first to discover the best part of our planet to live on. The rich Nile Valley of Egypt and the present seat of the Holy City, Mecca, Arabia.

The origin of our kinky hair, says Allah, came from one of our dissatisfied scientists, 50,000 years ago, who wanted to make all of us tough and hard in order to endure the life of the jungles of East Asia (Africa) and to overcome the beasts there. But he failed to get the others to agree with him.

He took his family and moved into the jungle to prove to us that we could live there and conquer the wild beasts, and we have. So, being the first and the smartest scientist on the deportation of our moon and the one who suffered most of all, Allah (God) has decided to place us on the top with a thorough knowledge of self and his guidance.

We are the mighty, the wise, the best, but do not know it. Being without the knowledge, we disgrace ourselves, subjecting ourselves to suffering and shame. We could not get the knowledge of self until the coming of Allah. To know thyself is to know all men, as from us came all and to us all will return.

I must keep warning you that you should be give up the white race's names and religion in order to gain success. Their days of success are over. Their rule will last only as long as you remain asleep to the knowledge of self.

Awake and know that Allah has revealed the truth. Stop believing in something coming to you after you are physically dead. That is untrue, and no one can show any proof of such belief.

Again, know that Jesus was only a prophet and cannot hear you pray any more than Moses or any other dead prophet. Know too, that this white race was created to be the enemy of black mankind for 6,000 years, which makes their number to be six. That is not your number or mine. We do not have a number, because we have no birth record. Do not let anyone fool you. This is the separation and the War of Armageddon.

Chapter 32: "The Black Woman"

The woman is the man's field to produce his nation. If he does not keep the enemy out of his field, he won't produce a good nation. If we love our vegetable crops we will go out and turn up the leaves on that vegetable stalk and look carefully for worms that are eating and destroying the vegetables. We will kill that worm—right?

Again, we will go out into the cotton field and look for the enemies of our cotton and try to kill that enemy. We study poisons and chemicals of the earth and we pour these chemicals on the enemies of our crops to keep their enemies from destroying them. We love a crop that we can produce every year, every season, so well that we will kill every enemy that we find seeking to destroy it.

We will even kill one another if we find the other one out there trying to steal that crop.

Is not your woman more valuable than that crop of corn, that crop of cotton, that crop of cabbage, potatoes, beans, tomatoes? How much more valuable is your woman than these crops that you should keep the enemies from destroying the crops. Yet you are not careful about your women. You don't love them. Why? It is because you have allowed visitors to run in and out of your house, thus they have destroyed your love for your woman and your woman has not the love for you that she should.

That is a good sign. Until we learn to love and protect our woman, we will never be a fit and recognized people on the earth. The white people here among you will never recognize you until you protect your woman.

The brown man will never recognize you until you protect your woman. The yellow man will never recognize you until you protect your woman. The white man will never recognize you until you protect your woman.

You and I may go to Harvard, we may go to York of England, or go to Al Ahzar in Cairo and get degrees from all of these great seats of learning. But we will never be recognized until we recognize our women.

On visiting with a couple of my sons in what they call the Near East, in 1959, I began in Turkey. We traveled from Turkey down to Africa to Ethiopia and the Sudan. We visited Arabia (Mecca and Medina), and we visited Pakistan. We returned home from Lahore, Pakistan, on or about the 6th of January, 1960. We didn't even find on that entire tour such a thing as not recognizing the black woman.

Everywhere we went, the Black man recognized his woman. He had great respect for her. We dined in many of the "top (as you say in slang) homes". We dined with some of the most influential people of these countries—government people. In some of their homes, we never did see any of their family, only men.

The waiter was a man or a boy, not any woman. My beloved brothers in America, you have lost the respect for your woman and therefore you have lost the respect for yourself. You won't protect her; therefore you can't protect yourself.

She is your first nurse. She is your teacher. Your first lesson comes from your mother. If you don't protect your mother, how do you think you look in the eyes of other fellow human beings?

Chapter 78: "A Program for Self Development"

We must remember that we just cannot depend on the white race ever to do that which we can and should do for self. The American so-called Negroes are like the Bible story of Lazarus and the rich man, the story that Jesus must have foreseen at the time. This Bible beggar was charmed by the wealth of the rich man to whom he was a servant, and he could not make up his mind to go seek something for self.

This beggar was offered a home in Paradise but could not make up his mind to leave the gate of his master, the rich man, wishing for that which God had in store for destruction along with its owner. The beggar's eyes could not turn from that perishable wealth. So it is with the American Negroes; they are charmed by the luxury of their slave-master, and cannot make up their minds to seek for self something of this good earth, though hated and despised by the rich man and full of sores caused by the evil treatment of the rich man. On top of that he is chased by the rich man's dogs and still remains a beggar at the gate, though the gates of Paradise were ever open to him and the gates of hell were open to receive his rich master.

The American Negroes have the same gates of Paradise open to them but are charmed by the wealth of America and cannot see the great opportunity that lies before them. They are suffering untold injustices at the hands of the rich; they have been and still are being lynched and burned; they and their women and children are beaten all over the country, by the rich slave-masters and their children. The slaves' houses and churches are bombed by the slave-masters; their girls are used as prostitutes and at times are raped in public. Yet the Negroes are on their knees begging the rich man to treat them as the rich man treats himself and his kind. The poor beggar kindly asks for the crumbs, a job and a house in the neighborhood of the rich man.

The Negro leaders are frightened to death and are afraid to ask for anything other than a job. The good things of this earth could be theirs if they would only unite and acquire wealth as the masters and the other independent nations have. The Negroes could have all of this if they could get up and go to work for self. They are far too lazy as a Nation—100 years up from slavery and still looking to the master to care for them and give them a job, bread and a house to live in on the master's land. You should be ashamed of yourselves, surely the white race has been very good in the way of making jobs for their willing slaves, but this cannot go on forever; we are about at the end of it and must do something for SELF or else.

The slave-master has given you enough education to go and do for self, but this education is not being used for self; it is even offered back to the slave-masters to help them to keep you a dependent people looking to them for support. Let us unite every good that is in us for the uplifting of the American so-called Negroes to the equal of the world's independent nations. Ask for a start for self and the American white people, I believer, are willing to help give us a start if they see you and I are willing to do for self. It would remove from them not only the worry of trying to give jobs and schools to a lazy people but also would get them honor and sincere friendship all over the Asiatic world and God, Himself, would prolong their time on the earth.

We must stop relying upon the white man to care for us. We must become an independent people. So-called Negroes should:

1. Separate yourselves from the slave-master.

2. Pool your resources, education and qualifications for independence.

3. Stop forcing yourselves into places where you are not wanted.

4. Make your own neighborhood a decent place to live.

5. Rid yourselves of the lust of wine and drink and learn to love self and your kind before loving others.

6. Unite to create a future for yourself.

7. Build your own homes, schools, hospitals, and factories.

8. Do not seek to mix your blood through racial integration.

9. Stop buying expensive cars, fine clothes and shoes before being able to live in a fine home.

10. Spend your money among yourselves.

11. Build an economic system among yourselves.

12. Protect your women.

Stop allowing the white men to shake hands or speak to your women anytime or anywhere. This practice has ruined us. They wink their eye at your daughter after coming into your home—but you cannot go on the North side and do the same with his women.

No black man feels good—by nature—seeing a white man with a Negro woman. We have all colors in our race—red, yellow, brown, and jet black—why should we need a white person?

Africans would not dare allow their women to be the targets that we allow ours to be.

If I were not protected by Allah (God), how would I be able to stand before this white man unafraid and speak as I do.

You educators, you Christian ministers should stop preaching integration. The most foolish thing an educator can do is to preach interracial marriage. It shows the white man you want to be white.

Educators should teach our people of the great history that was theirs before they were brought to America in shackles by slave-masters.

Our children should be trained in our own schools, not dropped into the schools of the enemy where they are taught that whites have been and forever will be world rulers.

I am the first man since the death of Yakub commissioned by God directly. I say no more than what Jesus said. The [sic] said that he came from God. I say that I am missioned by God.

Additional reading

Cregg, Claude Andrew III. *An Original Man: The Life and Times of Elijah Muhammad* (New York: St. Martin's Press, 1997).

Curtis, Edward E. IV. *Black Muslim Religion in the Nation of Islam, 1960–1975* (Chapel Hill, NC: University of North Carolina Press, 2006).

Lee, Martha F. *The Nation of Islam: An American Millenarian Movement* (Syracuse, NY: Syracuse University Press, 1996).

X, Malcolm and Alex Haley, *The Autobiography of Malcolm X* (New York: Grove Press, 1965).

14

Peoples Temple

*E**ditors' Introduction**: In 1954, the Reverend Jim Jones founded the Peoples Temple Full Gospel Church in Indiana. From his earliest years, Jones, a white man, preached a version of Christianity centered on racial justice and social equality. Motivated both by his message and by Jones's personal example (Jones and his wife adopted several children who were racial minorities), white and black congregants filled the pews in his church.

In 1962, *Esquire* magazine published an article that identified Eureka, California, as one of the nine safest places in the event of a nuclear war. Motivated by the article, in 1965, Jones moved to Eureka, taking many of his followers with him. Jones thrived in California, where he created several churches, although his church in San Francisco served as his official headquarters. Outsiders knew him as an advocate of social justice, civil rights, and marginalized communities in general, and Jones became a powerful political force in San Francisco and was appointed chairman of the San Francisco Housing Authority Commission.

Over time, the content of Jones's sermons changed as he focused less on Christianity and the Bible. Instead, Jones fancied himself a prophet that would usher in a multiracial socialist or communist utopia. Jones also began to expect strict and unquestioning obedience from his followers, many of whom lived in apartment complexes owned by the Peoples Temple and who signed their welfare checks over to the church. Jones also started practicing "White Nights," where he would instruct his followers to drink a liquid that might include poison. If they fully trusted them, he argued, they had nothing to worry about.

For these and other reasons, rumors began to spread that Jones was a fraud who exercised an unhealthy level of control over his congregation, and his detractors believed that many of his followers were either brainwashed or scared to leave the community. Jones leveraged his political connections to silence many of these rumors, but in 1977, journalists ran a shocking exposé that argued that Jones was a tyrannical charlatan. To avoid the backlash, Jones and several hundred congregants fled to Guyana, where Jones promised that the jungle's isolation would allow them to create a multiracial communist utopia free from racism, capitalist exploitation, and other forms of injustice that Jones had preached against during his public ministry. Both insiders and outsiders referred to the community as Jonestown.

Jonestown came to an abrupt end on November 18, 1978, when US Congressman Leo Ryan visited the community. After what seemed at first to be a pleasant visit, several people indicated that they wished to leave Jonestown, and they accompanied Ryan to his plane. In the meantime, several of Jones's followers followed Ryan to the airstrip where they executed Ryan and several of the people in his entourage. Jones must have realized that the murders would bring a premature end to his community. Instead of taking that risk, Jones instructed his followers to drink cyanide-laced Flavor Aid. Those who refused to drink were shot. Jones, along with over 900 of his followers, died during the final White Night.

The following readings contain four separate passages designed to capture, first, the evolution of Jones's message; second, his activist version of Christianity; and third, his ongoing commitment to race and racial justice. The first reading is a one-page flyer written either by Jones or by someone writing in the first person for Jones probably in the late 1960s or early 1970s. While the text does not explicitly reference race, it appears in this anthology because it characterizes the commitment to activism that came to define Jones. What it omits is that racial and economic justice would become the primary foci of his activism. The second text was written in 1972 not by Jones, but by one of his supporters, Evangelist S. D. Peter. Peter describes Jones as the majority of his supporters saw Jones at the height of his ministry; that is, as a Christian minister devoted to a host of social causes such as racial equality.

The third text is a sermon Jones delivered in 1973, where he attacked the prominent black minister Frederick J. Eikerenkoetter II, or Reverend Ike. Ike was known as an extravagant black minister and unrepentant capitalist who, according to Jones, delivered a false message to his black followers. In this sermon, Jones had either completed the transformation or was in the final stages of that transition from Christian minister to messianic socialist. In this sermon, Jones provided his theory of "race" in the era of capitalist and racial exploitation. The final text is an interview with Jones from 1977, the year before Jones led his followers to commit mass suicide. In hindsight, the text is quite chilling, not because it describes Jones's racial and socialist ideology toward the end of his life, but because several of the interviewer's questions foreshadow the final "White Night" that ended the Jonestown community.

Document One: "A True Follower of This Activist Christian Ministry." Flyer distributed by The Peoples Temple sometime between 1965 and 1974.

Jim Says:

. . . ATTEMPTS TO BECOME JEALOUS OF NONE . . . GIVING OF GREAT MERCY . . . one who treats friends and foes alike, never allows emotions to rule, has no special loves, and treats all the same. Love all people, but no individual above this Principle.

. . . ATTEMPTS AT ALL TIMES TO BE FREE . . . free from jealousy, free from egotism, free from any need for exultation, free from pride, free from sorrow and self pity, free from fear of any man or any thing.

. . . LOVES THE SILENCE . . . He can be at peace and bliss with no one present, and can enjoy times of introspection.

. . . SHOULD HAVE A DISCIPLINED REASON . . . and not do things impulsively. His actions should be of such a character as not to cause dread. He renounces his accomplishments and takes no thought for the fruit of his work. "But his delight is in the law of the (Good Shepherd); and in his law doth he meditate (and act upon) day and night." (Psalms 1:2)

. . . DOES NOTHING FOR REWARD, BUT RATHER FOR THE SHEER JOY OF DOING . . . If you made a mistake, don't go about defending yourself. Take thought for your intent, that you are trying to do the right thing, but after it is done, do not dwell on the action. (If I fell down yesterday, today I can stand up erect again.)

. . . OWES NO MAN ANYTHING BUT TO LOVE ONE ANOTHER . . . As I have said before, "The highest worship to Deity is service to your fellowman." "By this shall all men know that ye are my disciples, because you have love for one another."

. . . ASKS NOTHING FROM GOD (GOOD) . . . that is, asks nothing for himself. He lives a life of Principle and has no difference in attachments. This way of life precludes one thing. You cannot have any strong superficial attachments (me and mine attitude). Attachment forming is self-serving.

. . . DOES NOT WORSHIP THINGS . . . Do not talk about them. Eliminate fretting and pride. Do not allow yourself to be offended. This includes intemperance of eating habits that are ailing your bodies.

. . . TREATS HEAT AND COLD ALIKE . . . pain and blessing just alike, in order to avoid the vulnerability of that which destroys most from being a channel of truth, such as flattery, bribery, and intimidation. Have firm convictions. Do not vacillate! Always find gratitude in whatever state you find yourselves at the time. Treat prosperity and misery alike.

. . . IS ONE FOR WHOM ALL THINGS HAVE LOST THEIR ATTRACTION . . . If you find yourself in boredom to such a degree it is difficult to contemplate on esoteric values, it is not something to be discouraged about necessarily. It can be a sign that the detachment you have been working for has come. If you find the greatest peace in the smile of a child, or the feel of a breeze, or the myriad formations of the sky, it is not because you are a vain dreamer, but because you have begun to reach that place of self-denial or detachment that one must attain to, to be free of ego and self love. As scripture has stated, one must deny self and take up his one cross in order to follow the Christ. (Luke 9:23)

Document Two: Evangelist S. D. Peter, "Thy Kingdom Come," *The Living Word: An Apostolic Monthly* 1 (July 1972): 4.

Thy Kingdom Come . . .

For years our Pastor, Jim Jones, had the great inner urge to free the people from superstition, lacks, wants, and limitations, to free them from mental and spiritual stagnation. His highest intuition gave him a still greater urge to bring back to the people their rightful inheritance of true Christian fellowship as shared by Christ and expounded by His Disciples at Pentecost.

This great infinite urge to bring all people together, regardless of their race, color, or creed, on one common level of communal fellowship, each one sharing alike of food, clothing and shelter, was endeavored and practiced by the first early Christians. In such living and sharing they created a happy harmonious atmosphere in which for many years there was neither sickness nor death . . . until selfishness crept in.

Our Pastor's great desire to serve as a channel for the Spoken Word and to lead his people out of bondage became such a passionate urge that he sacrificed the Individual for the Universal Principle. Through this unselfish and unfeigned passion the Holy Spirit fell upon him; the Gift of Prophecy became a living reality; and the Principle of Christ was renewed in him. Pastor Jim Jones has come to personify this Infinite, Spirit and Mind that was in Christ Jesus.

With his coming in the One Hundred Fold degree of expression, manifesting the will of the Father in the Spirit of Prophecy, the Word becomes incarnate anew. Our bodies are made whole, and our minds are renewed as on that Pentecostal day. What you see in Jim Jones he will transmit to you. He is the living witness of the Christ life for people to think upon harmoniously and in deep faith. Gazing at his example, you will have no occasion to say: many are sick among you and sleep the sleep of Death for not discerning the Body of Love.

By manifesting His Greatest Infinite Supernatural Presence through our beloved Pastor, Jim Jones, Christ is here and now renewing the people's minds and bodies with that New Life; and He is doing it here in Redwood Valley.

This is the clarion call: Reach out for Christ. Prophet Jim Jones is answering that clarion call. Let us all arise in Christ!

Document Three: Sermon by Jim Jones (1973), The Jonestown Institute, Annotated Transcript Q957.

Jones: I hope you understand the point and why you should resist [Reverend Ike], and you should write [] television stations and tell them to get the stinking mess off the air, because it's doing us harm. Everything that comes up for proposal, we've heard his name whipped around. Our attorneys has heard his name whipped around. They'll say, look at that Reverend Ike, when they want to get improvement for housing, or want to get urban renewal or a special back– black business program, they'll say, look at him, they're already doing it. They're getting all the money anyway. They're getting the best federal jobs. Look at Reverend Ike. I tell you, we oughta look at him until he gets out of the way.

Congregation: Applause

Jones: 'Cause any old white man or bigot, whoever they are, any bigoted person, they want to look for reasons to justify their bigotry. So you open up a great picture– I wouldn't show 'em, I wouldn't show the bigots all we black people have. I wouldn't take a TV camera up to Redwood Valley and show them our children's home. No, I wouldn't. I wouldn't take a TV camera to show them our greens or our cave or our catfish. I wouldn't take a camera– a television camera up there to show them our children's home, our forty acres, or our four senior citizen homes, or our two convalescent sanatoriums, or our four college dormitories, or our one hundred and nine students, because if we did, they would try to do everything they could to stop us. I don't want anything but to get out of our way. I want them out of the way.

Congregation: Applause

Jones: They look at Jones' family, this precious black family. Say, well, I'm not black, I'm white. Oh, no, you're black, you're in here, you're lifting the burden, you identify with the people that're oppressed, you're black. I don't care if you are as white as the driven snow. You're black if you're in here.

Congregation: Applause

Jones: Say, I'm Mexican, I'm not black. Well, you go down and see how they've killed a few of these Mexicans off these days, and you watch what's [] happening to Mexicans, you'll decide you're black too.

Congregation: Applause

Jones: Somebody told me, said– Sister said, I was resentful because I'm Mexican. Says Governor [Edmund "Pat"] Brown– and I've been on that ever since I heard that– said Governor Brown said we were not black, and the black were black and we were not. They'd list us as being white. Does it get you white jobs?

Congregation: No.

Jones: Does it get you nice white housing? Does it get you nice white money? Then honey, I don't care what Governor Brown put on your birth record, you're still just one of us.

Congregation: Applause

Jones: They did that to divide the poor people anyway. They afraid of all that Mexican– And actually, Mexicans suffer greatly, terribly. In Texas, they're more discriminated against than any people. But a lot of 'em still sayin', I'm white. Huh? When they gonna wake up and find out?

Congregation: Scattered laughter

Jones: Yeah, there're folk [stumbles over words], I got some blacks in here think they're white too. But honey, you just gonna have to look in the mirror again.

Congregation: Applause

Jones: Racial consciousness have to be developed. Sure, a Reverend Ike moves along smoothly. He's in no danger, because he's being a puppet of the system, he's being promoted by the lying dogs of the oppressor. But I'll tell you one thing. The liberators will find this kind one day. They'll find this kind one day. He degraded

Black Power today, he degraded everything that stands for black progress, he made light of it, and laughed. That's an enemy. That is an enemy of the cause of righteousness. I hope you are he– I hope you're hearing me.

Congregation: Applause

Jones: Now do you understand the question? I– I know I was taking offering, but all our offerings won't do us any good unless we have a consciousness. Unless we know what we're doing, we can take all the money till our s– Well, I won't say that.

Congregation: Laughter

Jones: You've gotta know what you're doing, you've gotta know what you're working for, you have to know what your purpose is. We have this discussion of King Alfred Plan here, we have the discussion of there is a choice, that the pra– past cabinet just approved, which will be the total annihilation of the black race. We had this man, Nussbaum, come to me and say, Jones, you and [Ralph] Nader are the two most feared people in this country. I thought, well, if this isn't something. All we've got, just a little church here, and a little church in L– San Francisco, a few thousand people and a little bit of land, and they fear us. That speaks bad if there's only two left that they fear. Man that'd worked with the CIA told us that. (Pause) I just gave you his name. Peace. (Pause) I hope you're listening, 'cause I'm telling you that there's a plan to destroy the black man, and Reverend Ike is helping them pick up the dagger. He's helping them pick up the sh– up the guns that will do it. The man who hates looks for reasons to justify his hatred, so he looks in all that glorious Ike's uh, trim on his clothes, they'll be made of gold, his s– kingly seat, he's got a royal crown over his seat in gold. (Pause) And they look in and see all that, and they say, black people don't need any more money for education, black people don't need any more money for jobs, black people don't need any more uh, money for h– health, welfare, black people don't need any more money, period. And you tell me, he's not a plan? He's a plant? Yes, he's a plant.

Document Four: "Five Sundays at the Peoples Temple," *Le Nouvel Observatoire* (1978): 51–54.

R: If you were going to die in a week, what would be the ultimate thing that you would take care of?

Jones: That's a pretty hard question, being that I have an enormous commitment to people, a large number of people that I would be responsible for. That would be enormously hard for me to answer. I want to give as much time to the people I love, not just limited to my "nuclear family," it's a much larger scope. There would be a priority. My children. I have adopted many, and have one natural born. I try to live every day as if it might be the last. Death is a reality. To a controversial person, it's a vivid reality all the time, so I try, when I pass people, my children, my companion, others . . . I try to extend as much love as I can every day because I would want to be sure that they knew I loved them as much as humanly possible to love. I deeply want them to know that. I try to do that on a daily basis because sometimes one doesn't have a week. So I guess built in to me is the thought I could die any time.

R: What's love?

Jones: It's genuine concern for people. I've tried to overcome needing people; it's a terrible burden. I haven't overcome it but I try not to impose my needs on others. There are a lot of people who are needy, so I try to be one of those persons who can respond to need as much as possible. And you never do it as adequately as you feel it should be done.

R: How is the ideal country that you would dream about?

Jones: A country that has a greater share of the wealth. Thank you for asking that. You're sensitive. I would consider ideal a country where race made no difference, where whether a person believed in God or didn't believe in God would be irrelevant. A country where there was equal opportunity, but a great deal of sharing of the resources . . . that's idealistic and utopian, I'm sure. But that would be my ideal. I would be happy to live in a society where I had a lot less than anyone else if I can see everyone else having enough.

R: How do you see yourself in 10 years?

Jones: Probably dead. I think at the pace I go, it's a possibility. I worked very extensively, have threats of my life from the Nazis, and threats of my life from the Ku Klux Klan, threats of my life from even certain militants of the far Left as well as the far Right. I think it's plausible that some time, someone will get me.

R: . . . unselfish attitude – you must look after yourself because people need you.

Jones: I try to do that and yet I am not doing it well enough. And yet when someone comes with needs, so many crises come from every angle, you don't know where to say "no." It's very hard to develop boundaries, but you're quite right . . . I have no argument for that. I think I get by with a lot less rest than most people can. I think that's been proven.

R: What about I was saying, just for the storybook, how do you see what will happen with the Indian people in this country?

Jones: It depends. If we continue to build, to evolve into a more democratic society, acceptance will take place. If we have an economic turn for the worse, I can see that we could have fascism. We have a rising trend of racism. You mentioned seeing 63 Nazis gathered together in the most liberal area of America. It's been clearly presented what Hitler did. But we even have a faculty member of Northwestern University who published a book but denies that the Holocaust ever took place. It's called The Hoax of the Twentieth Century. This book is a popular demand, and is being circulated by many right wing groups. It just depends upon which way things go. I have a feeling that no nation is immune to fascism. No nation is immune to the kinds of things Hitler did, partially as a result of public apathy. Germans right next door to the concentration camps said they didn't know what was happening. It's hard for me to conceive of that, but I think it's possible for people to rationalize . . .

R: What is happening in the city that makes you really mad?

Jones: Racism makes me very mad. Indifference by those that have so much property. The International Hotel situation, where people for 40 years have lived in one place. It's owned by a corporation that's been rumored to receive their funds from tax dollars that were given to aid people in the Far East, then that money ends up in the hands of people it was not intended for. They come over here and buy property, dispossess elderly, then go to the extent of using the machinery of the law and the courts to uphold it. I guess I am more incensed that there's still a prevalent attitude that we should put property rights above human rights.

R: If you'd like to go somewhere else, away from America, where would you go?

Jones: South America, carve out a little community there. Far away from civilized society. Impossible, really. An island in the sea someplace that hasn't been noted on any particular map, if you could find it.

R: But the least you would re-create what you have here; at least I hope you would.

Jones: I would. I didn't mean I would go it alone.

R: What do you think irritate you when you meet someone? Sometimes we get one feeling out of somebody. What stands out in your mind?

Jones: I've overcome that. I don't make immediate reactions to people anymore. I've learned, from too many mistakes, that it is very bad business to make an ideal judgment. We can't know all our own subjective reactions. I may react to a person because they subconsciously reminded me of a teacher I had in school. I'm careful not to let that bar me from going on. I don't think I'm critically irritated.

R: But deep down, there must be something, even if you overcome it, I'm sure you do.

Jones: Well, it's now looks or appearance. When a person opens his mouth and comes out with crass insensitivity about people, about the aged, or race, or shows intolerance—that bothers me. I think we need a great deal of tolerance and our society. I'm motivated heterosexually, and I don't have any homosexual and need that I am aware of, but recently someone made a crack about a gay person—that infuriated me. I don't think that sexual persuasion or orientation has a damn thing to do with what a person is. I don't think that it should enter in. I don't like these jokes about people. And there's a lot of it in America. Particularly some males are so insecure about their own sexuality that they have to make comments.

R: You are a very scary person.

Jones: I'm scary? Oh, dear, I don't want to be scary!

R: I don't know if you know it or not, but you are.

Jones: In what way? Elaborate. I'm interested.

R: Strength. Real genuine strength. It's scary. It's a huge tool . . .

Jones: It can be used for good or for evil.

R: You are sensitive. But, it's beautiful.

Jones: You're quite correct. Strength is beautiful. But, of course, Hitler had strength, too.

R: Yeah, but his sickness was as big as the amount of strength that he had, you could feel that.

Jones: I don't understand German but I could sense it in his delivery. It's very hard at least for me to determine a good person from a bad person, unless I understand the language. Fidel Castro is a strong person, I think a good person. He may be more autocratic than some would prefer. I can't ascertain that. I know Cuba . . . it's a good solution for the Cuban people. There's a general state of well-being there. But Castro, when he's wound up, and Hitler when he was wound up— it was very hard if you didn't understand the language to know the enormous difference.

R: But still you get some vibration from them . . .

Jones: I was just thinking that the general public would have some difficulty with strength—so I'm "scary," I suppose. I don't like to be. It's too bad.

R: Well, I think it's about power, and you are a very powerful person.

Jones: I wish people could see me as a good person, because I am a good person. Power . . .

R: Goodness is scary too. It's rare and everything rare to me is scary.

Jones: I love to find good people and I'm sure you're not scared of finding good people. You must find so many that are not; you're glad to find good people.

R: What's a good person?

Jones: Well, a person that's got their ego under some control, you know, and is willing to live and let live. Some people have such insatiable ego, a desire for power. I think the only person who's capable of leading is someone that doesn't like leading. Really doesn't basically like it. Then that person may be capable of being a representative of the people. I wish to see people someday moving on one level. I'm afraid of strong leaders. Strong leaders can be very dangerous. They can lead us to demagoguery. You got to know your own mind. You got to be aware of what's going on in your ego. Know yourself.

R: Describe to me one of your days—what did you do today? Seven AM on . . .

Jones: What did I do today? Counseled a woman going to commit suicide; talked to someone who was on drugs; talked to someone else who wanted to leave her husband; dealt with a host of problems I couldn't go into. Tried to get the newspaper distribution worked out. I went on a radio show for an hour. I interviewed with five reporters. I talked with the Public Advocates on what we could do about a number of problems, discrimination in the police department, discrimination on the various levels of the community, International Hotel, which seems to still not have a legal resolution; we got a postponement but there are a lot of things left to be done. I met with a group of truckers who felt they were not getting fair treatment in the mayor's office. I met with another group, NAACP, and Cecil Williams, on another matter to talk to the Mayor about. I met with a group of commissioners on housing. I wrote letters from one till six and have not been to bed since sometime Monday night. I didn't lay down last night. Numb. Not the best time for you, I'm sorry that you have to interview me now because I'm not as quick, you know. I'd be upstairs dealing with business otherwise. But that's alright, you're a nice person, so it's no problem. I like to be probed. It's good for the mind to have people ask you questions. Introspection, self-analysis is good, but others asking their very pointed questions . . . and you ask very good questions.

R: How do you see young people, under twenty, how do you picture them?

Jones: I have a very great deal of pain for them because the future is going to be very bleak. Many world scientists think we are not going to make it through the Thermonuclear Age. I don't know one nuclear scientist who doesn't say we are somewhere in the eleventh, near the midnight hour. We've got overpopulation and food shortages before us. It's very difficult, not to mention that some 90% of the world is under one form of dictatorship or another. I have a great deal of compassion for young people. It's not easy being young.

R: Let's talk a little bit about your family, your children.

Jones: Had 10, most adopted, some are grown. We have four still in the home, the others are grown, one was killed in a very tragic accident in 1960.

R: How old is the oldest?

Jones: I think 27. My wife and I adopted her when we were very young.

R: And how old is the youngest?

Jones: About 16.

R: What do you wish for your children?

Jones: The same thing I mentioned for the world. Peace. To be able to live in a society where they could plan for the future, with no dangers of oppressive government. To have enough to sustain a good life. To be able to pursue the kind of education or career they wished to. But I wish that for the whole world.

Additional reading

Chidester, David. *Salvation and Suicide: An Interpretation of Jim Jones, the Peoples Temple, and Jonestown* (Bloomington, IN: Indiana University Press, 1988).

Fondakowski, Leigh. *Stories from Jonestown* (Minneapolis, MN: University of Minnesota Press, 2013).

Moore, Rebecca, Anthony B. Pinn, and Mary R. Sawyer, eds., *Peoples Temple and Black Religion in America* (Bloomington, IN: Indiana University Press, 2004).

Scheeres, Julia. *A Thousand Lives: The Untold Story of Jonestown* (New York: Free Press, 2011).

15

Aryan Nations

Editors' Introduction: In the mid-1970s, Richard Butler established a twenty-acre compound in rural, northern Idaho for the Aryan Nations. Aryan Nations was a white, nationalist, hate movement that brought together Christian Identity theology and anti-Semitism with a paramilitary presence. Outside Hayden, Idaho, the Aryan Nations compound was the headquarters of the movement and many Aryan gatherings from the 1980s to the early 2000s. Butler's movement had the explicit intent of fashioning a "White People's Republic" where Neo-Nazis and the members of the Ku Klux Klan could share ideas, train, and strategize. By the early 1980s, pro-Aryan Nation pamphlets were common in nearby towns, and Butler felt so empowered that he began hosting Neo-Nazi rallies described as "world congresses," which often culminated in marches through downtown Coeur d'Alene, Idaho. Those parades were complete with Nazi memorabilia and participants flaunted guns. The movement disbanded when they lost a civil lawsuit (and the compound) brought on by their paramilitary actions and intimidation.

The Aryan Nations was a unified group and a meeting place for like-minded individuals. The "world congresses" included members of numerous white supremacist and white hate groups in the US and were complete with youth assemblies and leadership and paramilitary training. White power metal bands were also present at many of these events to attract and keep the interest of younger generations. Sermons during services at "world congresses" and other events emphasized white power/ pride, the demonization of Jews, and love of country. The fiery crosses of the Klan were a common sight on the Aryan Nations compound.

Butler's compound included a main office, a church, workshop, and bunkhouse for visiting members. Worship at the Aryan Nations church included numerous references to Adolf Hitler and a bust of Hitler on the altar from which Butler preached. (The compound also included a Hitler memorial room, complete with stained-glass windows featuring swastikas.) Aryan Nations prayers emphasized obedience to God's vision for the white world, their openness for violence (battling for the cause), and purity of blood. Christian Identity heavily influenced the Aryan Nations. Popularized by Wesley Swift, a Protestant minister whose works were popular among Aryan Nations members, Christian Identity became a white supremacist, Christian force in the 1960s. Christian Identity and the Aryan Nations used a particular interpretation of

Christian history and the Bible to argue that white Protestants in America were descended from the original twelve tribes of Israel. Followers called people of color "Mud People" and believed that people of color only exist to serve whites. Thus, followers considered white American Protestants to be God's real chosen people. Both the Christian Identity movement and the Aryan Nations deemed the Jewish people as descendants from Cain with no claim to the title of God's chosen people. Equating race with nation, the Aryan Nations believed that the United States should be a white ethno-nation state. They viewed Jews and people of color as not just inferior but also dangerous.

This introduction uses the past tense to describe the Aryan Nations because the group formally disbanded in 2001. They lost a lawsuit to the Southern Poverty Law Center and Victoria and Jason Keenan (who were attacked by the Aryan Nations), resulting in bankruptcy and the loss of their compound and intellectual property. However, fliers and pamphlets claiming affiliation with the Aryan Nations or groups with similar names have been spotted throughout northern Idaho and eastern Washington with increased regularity since 2016. Butler died in 2004, but his model of bringing together multiple smaller movements within Christian Identity and white nationalist/supremacy organizations in large celebrations and white pride festivals has been adapted by many white power communities across the nation. Recent use of the internet and prison outreach has helped galvanize contemporary iterations of Butler's original movement.

The documents included here were publicly distributed by the Aryan Nations in the northern Idaho/eastern Washington area in the late 1980s and early to mid-1990s. Strong dedication to white supremacy, white nationalism, and anti-Semitism are incredibly apparent throughout all the included pamphlets and texts. The first document, "Who What Why When Where: Aryan Nations," offers a summation of the Aryan Nations' chief beliefs and a biography of founder Richard Butler. The pamphlet brings together the movement's strong belief in white supremacy with a particular understanding of biblical history that places white history at the core of the scriptural story. The pamphlet ends with a version of the movement's fidelity statement, which reflects their main ideas. That statement appears on Documents One, Two, and Three. Document Two, "Where to Look in the Bible: Jews," offers a clear look into the community's anti-Semitism, pairing Bible verses that they used to interpret particular questions about Jewish history and the Jewish people. Document Three, "Where to Look in the Bible: On Negroes," follows a similar structure and equates African-descended peoples with the beasts and animals of the Bible. The fourth document is excerpted from Butler's undated text, The Aryan Warrior. It offers an explanation of the movement's main symbols and desire for a white ethno-state. Document Five is the text of a flyer distributed in northern Idaho in the 1980s by the Aryan Nations movement that reflected their concerns about the end of the white race and a decline in birth rate among white couples.

Documents

Document One: "Who What Why When Where: Aryan Nations," 1990s-era Aryan Nations tri-fold pamphlet, distributed publicly in northern Idaho (interior of tri-fold only), from personal archive of volume editor.

Who What Why When Where: Aryan Nations

[*Editors' Note*: Featured underneath the title is a picture of a crusader knight, slaying a serpent with a cross.]

This is *Aryan Nations*

This pamphlet is published to answer a few basic questions regarding the Kingdom Identity message. We pray fervently that those who read these words will do so in an objective manner and will allow God's Holy Spirit to penetrate and enlighten.

Aryan Nations is not a new right-wing organization which has suddenly appeared on the scene. Aryan Nations is the on-going work of Jesus Christ regathering His people, calling His people to a state for their nation to bring in His Kingdom! Hail His Victory!

WE BELIEVE the Bible is the true Word of God written for and about a specific people. The bible is the family history of the White Race, the children of Yahweh placed here through the seedline of Adam.

WE BELIEVE that Adam-man of Genesis was the placing of the White Race upon this earth. All races did not descend from Adam. Adam is the father of the White Race only. (Adam in the original Hebrew is translated, "to show blood; flesh; turn rosy.")

WE BELIEVE that the true, literal children of the Bible are the 13 tribes of Israel which are now scattered throughout the world and are now known as the Anglo-Saxon, Celtic, Scandinavian, Teutonic people of this earth. We know that the bible is written to the family of Abraham, descending from Shem, back to the man, Adam. God blessed Abraham and promised that he would be the "Father of Nations." This same promise continued through the seedline of Abraham's son Isaac, and again to Isaac's son Jacob, the Patriarch of the 12 tribes, whose name God changed to Israel (meaning "he will rule as God.")

WE BELIEVE that there are literal children of Satan in the world today. These children are the descendants of Cain, who was the result of Eve's original sin, her physical seduction by Satan. We know that because of this sin, there is a battle and a natural enmity between the children of Satan and the Children of The Most High God.

WE BELIEVE the Jew is the adversary of our race and God, as is attested by all of secular history as well as the word of God in scripture; that he will always do what he was born to do, that is, be the cancer invading the Aryan body politic to break down and destroy the dross from Aryan culture and racial purity; that those who are able to resist this satanic "disease" are the "called chosen and faithful."

WE BELIEVE there is a battle being fought this day between the children of darkness (today known as Jews) and the children of light (God), the Aryan race, the true Israel of the Bible.

WE BELIEVE that God created pure seed lines, races, and that each have a specific place in His order on this earth under the administration of His Life Law. We know that man (Adam) was given the command to have dominion over the earth and subdue it, but that, in great part, our race has been deceived into rejecting this divine order. They have forgotten the words of Yahweh to Abraham, "In thee shall all the families of the earth be blessed." (Genesis 13:3) There is no race hatred in this statement. It was and is the plan of Yahweh to bless all, through the seed of Abraham.

WE BELIEVE in the preservation of our race individually and collectively as a people demanded and directed by God. We believe a racial nation has a right and is under obligation to preserve itself and its members.

WE BELIEVE that the present world problems are a result of our disobedience to God's laws. God's intended purpose was that His racial kinsmen were to be in charge of this earth. Our race, within itself, holds divine power; and when we abrogate and violate divine law, we give power to our God's enemies. Evil is the result to all.

WE BELIEVE that the redemptive work of Jesus was finished on the cross. As His Divine race, we have been commissioned to fulfill His divine purpose and plans—the restitution of all things.

WE BELIEVE that there is a day of reckoning. The usurper will be thrown out by the terrible might of Yahweh's people as they return to their roots and their special destiny. We know there is soon to be a day of judgment and a day when Christ's Kingdom (Government) will be established on earth as it is in heaven. "And in the days of these kings shall the God of heaven set up a kingdom which shall never be destroyed; and the kingdom shall not be left to other people, but it shall break in pieces and consume all these kingdoms and it shall stand forever. But the stains of the Most High shall take the kingdom and possess the kingdom forever, even for ever and ever. And the kingdom and dominion and greatness of the kingdom under the whole heaven shall be given to the people of the saints of the Most High, whose kingdom is an everlasting kingdom and all his dominions shall serve and obey Him." (Daniel 2:44, 7:18, 7:27)

Further explanation of these basic ideas and their implications are available upon request from:

Church of Jesus Christ Christian
Aryan Nations
Post Office Box 362
Hayden Lake, Idaho 83835

Biography of Aryan Nations: Richard G. Butler

Who are we, and who is Richard G. Butler? We are the continuing direct line "Church of Jesus Christ Christian," as originally founded by Dr. Wesley Swift of Lancaster, California. After Dr. Swift's death, the church was carried on by Richard G. Butler.

Mr. Butler received his formal education and training in Southern California including Aeronautical Engineering at Los Angeles City College. His early experience in the aircraft industry included management of maintenance assembly and repair of major assemblies for Commerce and Military Aircraft in the United States, Africa, and . . . [*Editors' Note*: last location illegible on pamphlet.]

In 1946, and for the following 18 years, he organized, owned and operated a machine plant for the production and precision machining of automotive parts and engine assemblies and aircraft parts. Subsequently, from 1964 through 1973, Mr. Butler was a marketing analyst for new inventions and finally, in 1968, became a Senior Manufacturing Engineer for Lockheed Aircraft Company at their Palmdale, California plant where extensive development was underway for the L-1011 aircraft. He resigned from this corporate associationship to devote full energy and time to his greatest and all-consuming desire—serving God and nation.

Pastor Butler is a co-inventor for rapid repair of tubeless tires and holds both US and Canadian patents thereon. He is a pilot, and during WWII, was, among other things, a Flight Engineer Instructor in the US Air Force. His background reflects a broad experience in the US and foreign countries concerning alien races, their work habits, status of "culture" and "religions."

Returning home from wartime activities in 1946, Mr. Butler was deeply troubled concerning the future of his nation from the things observed first hand overseas and events resulting from governmental edicts that seemed to be always contrary to the best interest of the Nation and of the White Race in particular. While active in business life, the closest thing to his heart was the future of his nation, therefore, most all available spare time was spent studying and delving into various service and political organizations, trying to arouse attention of friends, acquaintance, members of fraternal organizations, and business associates to action concerning the threat of Jewish communism. The media publicity received from these efforts, while nearly disastrous to business and professional life, turned out to be the greatest of all blessings in that he was led to Kingdom Identity with the meeting and forming of the closest, most rewarding of all personal relationships with Dr. Wesley A. Swift, starting in 1961 and continuing until Dr. Swift's passing on.

The years of study were spent under Dr. Swift in his magnificent library with line upon line, precept upon precept, and revelations over the years from Dr. Swift and Rev. Bertrand Comparet. They shared the blows of the enemy from their combined efforts in the Christian Defense League, of which Pastor Butler was the National Director from 1962 to 1965.

Upon the passing of Dr. Swift, Pastor Butler continued holding services for the congregation of the Church of Jesus Christ Christian, until he moved to northern Idaho to expand the Kingdom Identity Program and to form the foundation for a "Call to the Nation" or Aryan Nations.

We seek to let every Aryan Son and Daughter of God know what their duty is to the Covenant (Constitution) that Yahweh their God has made with them as Nations of His people and as His blessings come to, or are withheld from, a Nation, so is it that each citizen of the Nation is either blessed or cursed. The rewards are in direct proportion to the ACTIONS and WILL of the Nation for our people have the "Law written on their hearts." We seek to live and establish a government under the Law of God for "Your Race is your Nation."

Fidelity

That for which we fight is to safeguard the existence and reproduction of our race, by and of our Nations, the sustenance of our children and the purity of our blood, the freedom and independence of the people of our race; so that we, a kindred people, may mature for fulfillment of the mission allotted to us by the Creator of the Universe, our Father and God. Hail His Victory!

Document Two: "Where to Look in the Bible: Jews," 1990s-era Aryan Nations pamphlet, distributed publicly in northern Idaho, from personal archive of volume editor.

Where to Look in the Bible: Jews

Where to Look in the Bible . . .
Who was the Bible written for? Read Genesis 5:1
Who did Jesus come for? Read St. Matthew 15:24
Are Jews Israel? Read St. John 10:24–26
Why Aren't the Jews Israel? Read St. John 8:44
Did the Jews come from Abraham? Read St. John 8:39
Were the Jews ever in bondage? Read St. John 8:33
Did Cain come from Adam? Read Genesis 3:1, 13–15
Who is this serpent? Read Revelation 12:9
Was Cain of the wicked one? Read 1 John 3:12
Is Israel at war with the Canaanite Jews? Read Genesis 3:15
What does the Bible say we are to do with these Canaanite Jews? Read Deuteronomy 7:1–6
Are we to "hate" the Jews since they are God's enemies? Read Psalms 139:19–22
Did God say he would call His people Israel by a new name? Read Isaiah 62:2
What was this new name that Yahweh would call us by? Read The Acts 11:26
Would Jew Babylon be thrown down by violence? Read Revelation 18:21
Should we give heed to Jewish fables? Read Titus 1:14
Are Jews anti-Christ? Read 1 John 2:22
Do the Jews deny that Jesus is the Christ? Read St. John 10:25
Will there by any Canaanite Jews in the House of Yahweh of hosts? Read Zechariah 14:21

What is to happen to false preachers that teach that the Jews are "God's Chosen"? Read Jeremiah Chapter 23

What is to happen to those who "overcometh"? Read Revelation 2:7

Do you know about the second mystery, the tares among the wheat? Read St. Matthew 13:24–30

Who are the tares? Is it not the devil and his children the Jews? Read St. Matthew 13:36–40

Aryan Victory Prayer

Our Father, Who is forever, grant that we may march in Thine Army, ever mindful of our need of Thee. Strengthen us to please Thee in all things through obedience to Thy Law. Give us the vision of true understanding so that we, Thy people, may become worthy to take our place within the framework of Thy Kingdom. And as the time of Battle comes, Oh, Father, and as the darkness deepens, open our eyes to Thy presence so that we may not turn away from Thee. Strengthen us to serve Thee faithfully that all fear will be removed, and we will see only that Light which is Thy effulgent Glory, The Victory of YASHUA OUR KING.

Think not that I am come to send peace on earth: "I came not to send peace, But a sword . . ." Jesus Christ Math. 10:34

Fidelity

That which we fight for is to safeguard the existence and reproduction of our race, by and of our Nations, the sustenance of our children and the purity of our blood; the freedom and independence of the people of our race; so that we, a kindred people, may mature for fulfillment of the mission allotted us by the Creator of the Universe: our Father and God. Hail His Victory!

For more information:
Aryan Nations Box 362
Hayden Lake Idaho, 83835

Document Three: "Where to Look in the Bible: On Negroes," 1990s-era Aryan Nations pamphlet, distributed publicly in northern Idaho, from personal archive of volume editor.

Where to Look in the Bible: On Negroes

Beast-Chayah-Negro

The worst beast appears throughout scriptures and often appears as simple "Beast," or "Beast of the Field," or "Beast of the Earth." Three different Hebrew words are translated into the English word BEAST in the Bible. The Hebrew word CHAYAH means LIVING

CREATURE, the word BEHEMA, meaning quadrupeds (like cattle), and BEIR meaning BRUTE BEAST. The Greek word ZOON translated BEAST means LIVING CREATURE.

In tracing this word down through scriptures, it is important to note that the Bible speaks of both quadruped (four-footed) beast and biped (two-legged) beasts. If you have failed to distinguish between beasts (quadruped) and beasts (biped) in the Holy Bible, you have missed a great deal of truth. We are concerned with the Hebrew word CHAYAH, which means LIVING CREATURE, and which we feel refers to the following biped (two-legged) beasts.

As you study the following scriptures and provide an answer to each question, perhaps the full implications of the Bible biped beast will become more clear to you.

It is interesting to note that in all these scriptures we find reference to a BEAST that is apparently biped (two-footed) and who can talk, riot, commit adultery, co-habit with man, work in vineyards, use his hands, wear clothing, cry unto his creator and sow his seed with other races. Those who have clearly traced this Hebrew word CHAYAH through the scriptures under the English word beast know it is speaking of the NEGRO! If this truth were known and taught from the pulpits of our American churches, it would stop the mad race toward racial suicide and mongrelization of the races dead in its tracks.

Was Joel speaking of a "beast" or field hand in Joel 2:22?
What kind of beast do you know that wears clothing (sack-cloth) as we read in Jonah 3:8?
What kind of beasts has hands as reported in Exodus 19:13?
What type of beast is capable of mixing or "sowing" his seed with the "seed of Adam" as described in Jeremiah 31:27?
What kind of male beast could a woman lust after and "lie down thereto" and cause God to have them executed in righteous judgment? Leviticus 20:16
What kind of female beast could a man lust after and cause penalty of death to be decreed by God? Leviticus 20:15
What kind of beast would have the ability to "keep the vineyard" as we find in The Song of Solomon, Chapter 1, who incidentally was Black?
What kind of beast "cries mightily unto God" in Jonah 3:8–10?
What kind of a beast would have "eyes full of adultery," as recorded in 2 Peter 2:12–14?
What kind of a beast can talk of or speak? 2 Peter 2:12
What kind of a beast was made to be taken and DESTROYED? 2 Peter 2:12

Our Fidelity

That which we fight for is to safeguard the existence and reproduction of our race, by and of our Nations, the sustenance of our children and the purity of our blood; the freedom and independence of the people of our race; so that we, a kindred people, may mature for fulfillment of the mission allotted to us by the Creator of the Universe; our Father and God.

That love, loyalty, spirit of sacrifice and discretion are virtues which our race, the armies of our Ever-living Father, absolutely need, and their cultivation and development are infinitely all important to the fulfillment of His Will, above the fallacious falderal, the travesty of anti-Christ, that submerges the law – Word of our God – and fictitiously – called Christian. Hail His Victory!

R. G. Butler

"Let The High Praise Of God Be In Their Mouth, And A Twoedged Sword In Their Hand" Ps. 149:6

For more information:
Aryan Nations Box 362
Hayden Lake Idaho, 83835

Document Four: Selected excerpts from Pastor Richard G. Butler, *The Aryan Warrior*, booklet distributed publicly in the 1990s in northern Idaho, from personal archive of volume editor.

Heraldry of the Aryan Nations Symbol

1. The Crown: The symbol of our Father's complete and immutable sovereignty over all things, the One and Only GOD, whose Name is YAHWEH.

2. The Three Jewels: Of the Crown symbolize the Divine and complete perfection, the Triune, absolute of our Father, the Everliving God.

3. The Shield: A symbol of our Christian Faith and Trust in His perfect Law and the Covenants He has made to them that keep the Faith.

4. The Two-Edged Sword: A symbol of truth that proceeds forth solely from Him and shall, by His Divine sovereign will, be the instrument of His vengeance upon all that hate Him.

5. The Revolving Resurrection Cross: Centered on the Sword of Truth, symbolizing the returning to righteousness of our Race, who yet one day will be placed on the right hand of Christ in Faith of the sure promise of resurrection.

6. The Cross of Jacob: Symbolizing the blessings to Israel that centers upon the Sword of Truth and Resurrection Cross: the three bars on each of the four corners symbolize the twelve tribes of His racial nation's inheritance in His Kingdom.

7. The Square: Outline symbolizes the Divinely appointed four square formation and order commanded by Yahweh of Hosts for the armies of the tribes of Israel in their beginning as His Nation and the symbol of the four-square city of His New Jerusalem with the twelve gates for the tribes of Israel, the Aryan Race of God.

. . .

The Twelve Foundation Stones

1. We recognize that there exists no place on earth in any branch of the Adamic Aryan Race a State of our Racial Nation.

2. An Aryan National State is an institution of God that has a single duty to itself and the people of the Racial Nation: the preservation of the race, culture, and people of the Nation.

3. There exists a Law Order that governs the life of men and nations of men in that obedience to this life law is life, disobedience is death.

4. The creative "life spirit" of the Adamic Aryan can only exist through the purity of the race in their generations.

5. No compromise or adulteration of this basic organic life-law principle can be made without violating all law.

6. The only hope for redemption of the Aryan racial household is the total return to the fundamental life law.

7. Life law is inseparable from the political government under which the Aryan racial family lives.

8. Only by the single united will of the people of the racial nation can there exist a State of Government for the Nation.

9. The people of the nation create the State and the State does not create the people.

10. A nation begins and ends as a race; everything else is predicated upon this fact.

11. There is, and can be, no separation of the "spiritual" worship state and the political state.

12. We have but one hope as a Racial Nation and that is the Life Law of our Father and God.

Document Five: "The Death of the White Race," flyer publicly disseminated in northern Idaho in the 1980s, from personal archive of volume editor.

The Death of the White Race
US Commissioner Confirms That White People Face Extinction

For years Aryan Nations has been warning our White kin that there was a conspiracy to Murder our White Aryan Race and that we were fast approaching the point of no return.

Now we have confirmation from US Government sources. On the back of this leaflet you will find a reproduction of an article from the August 4, 1981, Rocky Mountain News. When reading the article, please bear in mind the following things.

Considering the lower-than-replacement White birth rate, the high non-white birthrate, the colored immigration, and the fact that thousands of our young people (especially our women) desert their Race every day to marry non-whites, you can see that in ten years the child-bearing population of America will be less than ten percent White.

All history, as well as common sense, declares that no Race can survive without separation from others so they can promote, propagate, and protect their own kind.

There are over two dozen all-Black nations engaging in no integration or the inevitable resultant, miscegenation, which decrees the death of a Race. The population of one Yellow country alone, China, is nearly four times all the Whites on the Planet. They, too, are remaining racially pure. There are no all-White nations, at least in the Western world. We are the earth's most endangered species.

The famous American aviator Charles Lindberg, travelled America in the 30's warning that if we helped to destroy the tiny nation of Germany, which was the last and only White Racial Nation, then our Race was doomed. Was he right?

[*Editors' Note*: Next to these paragraphs is a picture of a young black man with a young white woman, in embrace and both smiling, with the caption: THE ULTIMATE ABOMINATION.]

Today YOU can escape the terror of the Black ghettos and the Brown barrios. Your children and your children's children will have no refuge. The DEATH OF THE WHITE RACE is neither imaginary nor far off in the distant future. History shows what "tender mercy" the few remaining Whites can expect from the colored hordes in the last days of our Race.

The JEWS, who have sworn to destroy our Race and who now own all three T.V. networks, the major movie companies, and nearly all newspapers and publishing companies, make it front page headlines, if they can find a non-integrated school or neighborhood anywhere.

Nations, economic systems, political systems, etc., will rise, fall, and evolve as long as man walks this planet. The DEATH OF THE WHITE RACE is eternal. Make no mistake, WHITEMAN, the death of our Race, the creators of Law, Justice, Technology, Medicine, Housing—virtually everything of value—spells the end of civilization.

Whiteman, look at the beautiful women you love. Whitewoman, think about the future of your children. WHITEMAN, THINK. The decision is for this generation. Your children will be outnumbered fifty to one by colored people, who have been inflamed to hatred of our people by the JEWSMEDIA. Nature's laws are as impartial as they are harsh. Love your own kind, fight for your own kind or perish, as have many thousands of other species.

YOUR FIRST LOYALTY MUST BE TO YOUR RACE WHICH IS YOUR NATION!

Additional reading

Balch, Robert W. "The Rise and Fall of Aryan Nations: A Resource Mobilization
    Perspective," *Journal of Political and Military Sociology* 34.1 (2006): 81–113.
Dobratz, Betty A. "The Role of Religion in the Collective Identity of the White Racialist
    Movement," *Journal for the Scientific Study of Religion* 40.2 (2001): 287–302.
Simi, Pete and Robert Futrell, *American Swastika: Inside the White Power Movement's
    Hidden Spaces of Hate* (Lanham, MD: Rowman & Littlefield Publishers, 2010).

16

The Nation of Yahweh

Editors' Introduction: The Nation of Yahweh began in 1979, when a black man named Hulon Mitchell, Jr. created the organization in Miami, Florida. Mitchell was born into a Christian family in Oklahoma and his father was a Pentecostal minister. He later moved and came of age in Chicago, where he became a prominent minister in the Nation of Islam. The historical record suggests he left the Nation of Islam and moved south after he had a falling out with senior ministers, ultimately settling in Florida where he created the Nation of Yahweh.

Mitchell taught that he was the messiah sent from "the Terrible Black God, Yahweh," and he adopted the name Yahweh ben Yahweh—meaning "God, Son of God" or "Lord, Son of the Lord" in Hebrew. Mitchell taught black Americans that black people are the Biblical Jews, that God and Jesus are black, and that God sent Yahweh ben Yahweh to lead black people to freedom in the promised land of Israel, contingent upon their obedience to him. Believing that they were the true historical Jews, the Nation of Yahweh kept several of the Jewish laws and followed some of the Jewish holidays.

Due largely to a series of infomercials, business interests, and community outreach, the Nation of Yahweh grew rapidly. By their own estimates, they had members in 1,300 US cities and in sixteen foreign countries. As they experienced financial success, Yahweh invested in various commercial enterprises in and around Miami, including several apartment buildings and a compound where many of the Nation's members lived communally. They also purchased a fleet of hundreds of white buses, vans, and cars, in addition to an eighteen-wheeler truck. According to the Nation of Yahweh, their assets totaled $250,000,000, although the *Miami Herald* estimated the group's net worth at $100,000,000.

Concomitant with the Nation's success, two narratives of the group developed. The first, the more dominant narrative, framed Yahweh as a civil rights hero who taught racial uplift, personal pride, and discipline in Miami's ghettos. The supporters of this narrative initially included the mayor of Miami, who declared October 7, 1990, "Yahweh ben Yahweh Day." A second group, however, fancied Yahweh ben Yahweh a charlatan. Not only did rumors begin to circulate about violence and intimidation associated with the Nation's members, but Yahweh ben Yahweh himself stoked controversy due to his extravagant and flamboyant dress and persona. Yahweh repeatedly reminded his followers that he embraced a life of poverty; however, he wore a white turban and long white robes, often adorned with jewels, leaving the appearance that he lived an extravagant life.

Yahweh ben Yahweh's critics felt vindicated when the police arrested him along with twelve of his followers in 1990 and charged them with fourteen murders, attempted murder, racketeering, arson, and extortion. After a controversial trial, Yahweh ben Yahweh and six of his co-defendants were acquitted of first-degree murder and found guilty of racketeering. Yahweh ben Yahweh served eleven years of his eighteen-year sentence before he was released on parole in 2001 and ordered not to reestablish any connection with his former congregation. Yahweh ben Yahweh died of prostate cancer in 2007, but the Nation of Yahweh continues to exist.

The following excerpts are from Yahweh's magnum opus, *You are not a Nigger! Our True History, The World's Best Kept Secret*, which contains a summary of his theology, this theory of history, some of his moral and ethical expectations for his community, and some of the scriptural justifications for his theories. It also describes the Hebrew God, and it summarizes God's plan for this chosen people. Yahweh ben Yahweh wrote this text early in the movement's history, and he circulated it for the dual purposes of education and recruitment.

Documents

Document One: God of Gods, *You are not a Nigger! Our True History, The World's Best Kept Secret* (Seguin, TX: PEESS Foundation, 1981).

Preface

Since being in America, we have been called "Colored," "Negroes," "Black," "Afro-American," "African-American," etc.; but before slavery, 400 years ago, we were somebody. **WHO?**

During slavery our foreparents were beaten and sometimes killed if they were caught reading or teaching their families to read (especially the Bible). WHY? Today, 80 percent of our youths graduating from the public school system are illiterate. Is this a coincidence? Or is it a conspiracy?

Chapter 1: "Our True History, The World's Best Kept Secret," LESSON #1

Shalom Aleichem. I am the Grand Master of the Celestial Lodge, Architect of the Universe, The Blessed and only Potentate. I am the Founder of the Nation of יהוה (YAHWEH), True Holiness and Righteousness, the Kingdom of Shalom, which is the most powerful knowledge of peace in existence. It is My pleasure to bring to you "Our True History the World's Best Kept Secret," Lesson Number One.

This lesson is to all so-called Negroes, and all so-called Black people. This is Lesson Number One of "Our True History, The World's Best Kept Secret" according to the Bible. Call your children and friends, sit down in a comfortable seat, study this with an open mind, and then discuss these facts which you have never been taught before.

This information will be shocking to you but it is true nevertheless. It is up to you to accept the truth or reject it. It is also up to Almighty God יהוה (YAHWEH) to accept you or reject you.

Have you heard people say that God יהוה (YAHWEH) is black? Have you heard people say that Jesus is black? Have you heard people say that the prophets were all black? That many of the events took place in Africa? Well, let us stop dealing with hearsay and see what the Bible has to say about these facts.

The first description of God Almighty יהוה (YAHWEH) can be found in Daniel, Chapter 7, verse 9, "I BEHELD TILL THE THRONES WERE CAST DOWN, AND THE ANCIENT OF DAYS DID SIT (the Ancient of Days is God Almighty יהוה [YAHWEH]. You can verify this in II Kings 19:25; also in the Book of Job 12:12–14; and Daniel 7:22), WHOSE GARMENT WAS WHITE AS SNOW, AND THE HAIR OF HIS HEAD LIKE THE PURE WOOL." Now reach up and feel your own head or look at the nappy heads of our people, the so-called Negroes, the so-called Blacks, and you have to admit that we (so-called Blacks) are the only people on the Earth who have hair like the pure wool. This lets us know beyond all shadow of doubt that the Ancient of days, God Almighty יהוה (YAHWEH), had nappy hair, thus being black.

The second Scripture that backs this up is found in the Book of Revelation 1:13–14, "AND IN THE MIDST OF THE SEVEN CANDLESTICKS ONE LIKE UNTO THE SON OF MAN (letting you know what Jesus, who is referred to as the Son of Man, looks like), CLOTHED WITH A GARMENT DOWN TO THE FOOT, AND GIRT ABOUT THE PAPS WITH A GOLDEN GIRDLE. HIS HEAD AND HIS HAIRS WERE WHITE LIKE WOOL, AS WHITE AS SNOW; AND HIS EYES WERE AS A FLAME OF FIRE." Verse 15 absolutely makes it clear beyond all shadow of doubt, "AND HIS FEET LIKE UNTO FINE BRASS, AS IF THEY BURNED IN A FURNACE." First of all, common sense lets you know that brass is brown naturally, and when you burn it in a furnace, it has to be black; therefore, here is a description of God's feet being black. If his feet are black then we know the rest of his body had to be black, for he also had nappy hair as we saw in verse 14. For more proof that the Son of God יהוה (YAHWEH) is black, read Revelation 2:18.

This truth that you have read about the description of God יהוה (YAHWEH) drives the gods of this world crazy. It drives them out of their minds. Why? Because they want you to worship the white man as God and as Jesus. They want to keep you and your children in slavery so they can continue to rob you. This description should make you take down all of those white lies that you have hanging in your churches and in your homes. Most especially in your homes because your children need to know the truth.

Now let us take a look at what Jesus had to tell you about his own color. Before we proceed, it is important for us to point out that all of the gods of this world today say color is not important. Color does not make any difference. Well, don't forget John 8:32 says, "AND YE SHALL KNOW THE TRUTH AND THE TRUTH SHALL MAKE YOU FREE." If these facts do not make any difference, then they should not mind you being told this truth. Why have they never objected to that white lie of a white man as Jesus? They should not get so upset about you learning this truth and reading this truth for yourself.

Now let us see what Jesus had to say about his own color. Turn to Revelation 22:16, "I JESUS HAVE SENT MINE ANGEL TO TESTIFY UNTO YOU THESE THINGS IN THE CHURCHES. I AM THE ROOT AND THE OFFSPRING OF DAVID. AND THE BRIGHT AND MORNING STAR." Now here Jesus has made it plain that he is the offspring of David. This was said with his own lips, no matter how these liars and those who love to make a lie will try to make you think differently. You can read for yourself, so, study for yourself. Jesus said with his own lips here in verse 16 that he is the offspring of David.

The Book of Lamentations lets us know that our forefathers, the precious sons of Zion (in the Book of Lamentations 4:2), THE TRUE HEBREWS, had faces blacker than coal. "THEIR VISAGE (meaning their faces) IS BLACKER THAN A COAL" (Lamentations 4:8). The day is come when "ALL" FACES SHALL GATHER BLACKNESS (Joel 2:6). Have you ever wondered why white people spend billions on lotions, laying on beaches, burning, catching cancer for hours trying to turn black?

Everybody in their right mind knows that Egyptians are black people, until this very day. Matthew 1:1 says that Jesus is the grandson of Abraham. Abraham married Hagar, the Egyptian, a black woman (according to Genesis 16:3). This is absolute clear proof that from Abraham to Jesus, we are dealing with BLACK PEOPLE. Thus it is clear that the OLD TESTAMENT IS OUR TRUE BLACK HISTORY. No wonder they only give you New Testament Bibles today: they don't want you to ever come into the knowledge of this truth. The great prophet Moses was not only a Hebrew by birth, but was described as looking like an Egyptian, a black man (in the Book of Exodus 2:11, 19–21). A black man delivered our forefathers, the CHILDREN OF ISRAEL, in the past. And only a black man is going to deliver us from the modern Pharaoh, the oppressors of today.

Don't forget that Our Great, Good and Terrible God, יהוה (YAHWEH) (in the Book of Psalm 68:4), made a promise to our black father Abraham, "AND I WILL MAKE OF THEE A GREAT NATION, AND I WILL BLESS THEE, AND MAKE THY NAME GREAT; AND THOU SHALT BE A BLESSING" (you may read this in the Book of Genesis 12:2, 22:17, 26:3–4, and 28:1–4).

Now we can understand why our oppressors want us to think the Old Testament is not important, or that it does not count today. The oppressors know the truth. IF THEY KNOW THAT YOU KNOW THIS TRUTH, they will admit to your face that they knew it all along. The oppressors are taught by their parents to never reveal this "secret" to you, the Black slaves, WHO ARE THE "TRUE HEBREWS." We will prove this to you in Lesson #2. When you learn this truth, you will become as Daniel and his Black Hebrew brethren, TEN TIMES BETTER IN WISDOM AND UNDERSTANDING THAN EVERYBODY (according to Daniel 1:20).

What do all of these facts have to do with us, the so-called Negroes, the so-called Blacks? Well, in the first place, we have proven that the Bible, the King James version, contains our true history. It proves beyond a shadow of a doubt that we, the so-called Negroes, the so-called Blacks, are God's chosen people. You must forever keep in mind that when you have not been taught the whole truth on a regular basis, it sounds very strange to you at first. These lessons are designed to make you think and study like never before in your life. There are many controversies about the Bible. No doubt you have tried to read it many times and you fail to understand it and it always seems somewhat of a mystery to you or hard to understand. The enemy has caused you to almost put it down and not read it at all.

The reason the enemy has caused you to have doubt about the Bible is because he knows that every promise in the Bible is directed toward us, the so-called Negroes, the so-called Blacks, and he knows that if we ever come into the correct knowledge of God יהוה (YAHWEH) and a proper understanding of the Bible, that we would become "free" of him and "free" from the material world, "free" from sin (the breaking of the laws of יהוה [YAHWEH]) and "free" from any entanglement as captives of this world. Although there are controversies about the Bible, if you study these lessons with an open mind full of questions, seeking answers, then all mysteries will become clear to you.

Having gone to church most of your life, led by ignorant teachers, it is indeed a shame that you know so little about "our book," the Bible. If you want to know all about this Great Book—the truth of it—then study these lessons with a serious mind.

First, it is important for you to remember that the Bible is past, present, and future at the same time. The Bible is written literally, figuratively, prose and poetically, symbolically and prophetically, metaphor and simile, as well as allegorically. Unless you are a religious scientist, you have no idea when to read the Bible as prose and poetry or whether to read it figuratively or literally or when to read it as a prophecy or how to understand the symbols such as found throughout the Book of Revelation. Thus you need a teacher from God. Don't leave it up to someone else to read it for you; get your Bible and follow these Scriptures for yourself. Read them, study them and ask questions for yourself. I have all of the answers for you to study.

Are you tired of tears, suffering, pain, hunger, poverty, sickness, disease, and death? Then write to Me, for in My Kingdom I shall wipe away all tears. There shall be no more sorrow, pain, and suffering. Write to Me, יהוה בו יהוה (Yahweh Ben Yahweh), today, now.

OUR MOTTO IS: ONE GOD! ONE MIND! ONE LOVE! ONE ACTION!

Chapter 2: "Our True History, The World's Best Kept Secret" LESSON #2

Shalom Aleichem, I am the Grand Master of the Celestial Lodge, Architect of the Universe, The Blessed and only Potentate. I am the Founder of the Nation of יהוה (YAHWEH), True Holiness and Righteousness, the Founder of the Kingdom of Shalom (Peace), and I am giving you the most powerful knowledge of peace in existence.

I am bringing to you "OUR TRUE HISTORY, THE WORLD'S BEST KEPT SECRET," Lesson Number Two. To all so-called Negroes, so-called Blacks, this is Lesson Number Two of "Our True History, The World's Best Kept Secret" according to the Bible. Call your children and friends, sit down in a comfortable seat, listen with an open mind and discuss these facts which you have never been taught before. This information will be shocking to you but it is true nevertheless. It is up to you to accept the truth or reject it. It is also up to God יהוה (YAHWEH) to accept you or reject you.

Our subject for Lesson Number Two is, "WHY ARE WE CALLED NEGROES? WHY ARE WE CALLED BLACKS?" If you ask a man from China his NATIONALITY, he will tell you CHINESE; that he has a CHINESE name; that he speaks CHINESE; and that he comes from and owns a land called CHINA. If you ask a man from France his NATIONALITY, he will tell you FRENCH; that he speaks the FRENCH language; that he has a FRENCH name; and comes from FRANCE, which he owns. If you ask a man from Germany what is his NATIONALITY, he will tell you GERMAN; that he speaks the GERMAN language; that he has a GERMAN name; and comes from and owns some land called GERMANY. If you ask a man from Spain his NATIONALITY, he will tell you SPANISH; that he has a SPANISH name; that he speaks the SPANISH language; and that he comes from and owns a land called SPAIN. If you ask a man from England his NATIONALITY, he will tell you ENGLISH; that he has an ENGLISH name; that he speaks the ENGLISH language; and that he comes from and owns ENGLAND. Now this is true for all the nations on the Earth.

However, if you ask the BLACK MAN of America, whose foreparents were slaves, what is his NATIONALITY, he will say such foolish things as NIGGER, NEGRO, BLACK, COLORED, AMERICAN, AFROAMERICAN, BILALIAN, ACE OF SPADES, JIGGS, COON, BAPTIST, METHODIST, MOSLEM. He names himself that way. How many of us speak NEGROESE? BLACKESE? COONESE? AMERICANESE? Or COLOREDESE? Yet how many of us have Negro names, or Black names, or Colored names? Where is a land called Coloredland, Negroland, Blackland, Bilalianland? It is clear that as so-called Negroes of America, we are LOST and cut off from the knowledge of our NATIONALITY; we are cut off from the knowledge of our LANGUAGE; we are cut off from the knowledge of our NAME; we are cut off from the knowledge of our LAND. Why? Because we are cut off from the knowledge of our God יהוה (YAHWEH), the only true and living God, our Creator, the Creator of all things seen and unseen.

Before slavery over 400 years ago we were somebody. Who? If America had to be given back to the Indians right now, and all races in America had to return to their native land, where would we, the so-called Negro, the so-called Blacks, go? Think about this. You are going to say, "Oh, I'll go to Africa," then you still have the same question and problem. Where in Africa? Africa is tribal. Everybody there has land according to his tribe. What is your tribe? What part of Africa would you settle in? This is one of the most important questions for our people today. Without this knowledge, we are lost and CUT OFF as a nation of people. We are suffering from an identity crisis.

In order to keep us dumb, ignorant slaves, and to be used as TOOLS and FOOLS, we are called Negroes and Blacks and many other proverbs and bywords, such as niggers. Again, I repeat, we are called Negroes and Blacks and many other names because we have been CUT OFF as a nation and have lost the KNOWLEDGE OF OURSELVES and the KNOWLEDGE OF OUR GOD יהוה (YAHWEH). We simply have not been taught this truth. And this is the truth which would set you free. It is not taught to you in your schools. It is not taught to you in your churches. It is not taught to you in your homes. It is not taught to you on your jobs. It is not taught to you by the politicians, and it is not taught to you by society. I am the only One bringing you the truth which would set you free.

WHAT IS OUR NATIONALITY?

Get your Bible and turn to Acts 7:6 which says, "AND GOD יהוה (YAHWEH) SPAKE ON THIS WISE, THAT <u>HIS</u> SEED SHOULD SOJOURN IN A STRANGE LAND; AND THAT THEY SHOULD BRING THEM INTO BONDAGE, AND ENTREAT THEM EVIL FOUR HUNDRED YEARS"; also Genesis 15:13 says, "AND HE SAID UNTO ABRAM, KNOW OF A SURETY THAT THY SEED (your children) SHALL BE A STRANGER IN A LAND THAT IS NOT THEIRS, AND THEY SHALL SERVE THEM (their oppressors); AND THEY (their oppressors) SHALL AFFLICT THEM FOUR HUNDRED YEARS."

The only people on this Earth who have served in a strange land in bondage for 400 years are we, the so-called Negroes, the so-called Blacks. History proves and shows that the first ones of us were brought here, to this country called America, in the year 1555. Subtract 1555 from the current year and you will see that we have served our time according to the Holy Bible. Our true history is in this book—the Holy Bible.

In order to trick us, the white race PRETENDED to free us in 1865. They only took the chains off our feet and hands, but our MINDS are more of a slave to white people now than ever. The Bible says that Abraham's seed (his children) would be brought into bondage. Since we, the so-called Negroes, the so-called Blacks, are the only people on this Earth to fit this description, WE ARE ABRAHAM'S SEED according to the Bible.

Genesis 14:13 says that Abraham was a HEBREW. Since Abraham was a HEBREW, we, as his SEED, as his children, are HEBREWS; therefore, our NATIONALITY IS HEBREW. To reject this fact is to reject your freedom. To reject this fact is to reject your riches and your heritage and your inheritance. Our NATIONALITY is HEBREW; our language is HEBREW; our culture is HEBREW; and our common last name is ISRAEL (which is a HEBREW name). And those are the kinds of names that you must have: like everybody else in this country and on this Earth have names after their own. You must have names after your own. You presently have names of your slave masters which are all from different parts of the Earth, so you are scattered one from the other; you are not a family, and can never be a family with names other than of your own kind. And God יהוה (YAHWEH) gave us Palestine, or all of North Africa, forever.

The FALSE JEW (those who pretend to be Jews) is in our land today because we are blind, deaf, dumb, ignorant and dead to the WHOLE TRUTH. The Holy Scripture says in Hosea 4:6, "MY PEOPLE ARE DESTROYED FOR LACK OF KNOWLEDGE: BECAUSE THOU HAST REJECTED KNOWLEDGE, I WILL ALSO REJECT THEE, THAT THOU SHALT BE NO PRIEST TO ME: SEEING THOU HAST FORGOTTEN THE LAW OF THY GOD יהוה (YAHWEH), I WILL ALSO FORGET THY CHILDREN."

This Scripture explains why we are on the bottom of civilization today. The only way we can get up as a people is to get the CORRECT KNOWLEDGE OF GOD יהוה (YAHWEH), and to get the correct knowledge of the Bible. All the knowledge that you have been exposed to in your spiritual institutions, political institutions, educational institutions, social institutions have all left you without this knowledge. The only way you are going to be free is with this knowledge. There is no other way. To reject this, again, I repeat, is to reject your freedom and your future.

Chapter 23: "False Leaders Must Go!"

The main problem of our poor people in America is FALSE LEADERS. They love our enemies beyond all reason. The FALSE LEADERS oppose all true efforts of freedom, justice, and equality for our people. Everything they do is in their own interests.

FALSE LEADERS MUST GO. The words of THE MOST HIGH are against them.

"WOE (serious trouble) BE UNTO THE PASTORS (and other false leaders) THAT DESTROY AND SCATTER THE SHEEP (the so-called Negroes) OF MY PASTURE! SAITH THE LORD, יהוה (YAHWEH). THEREFORE THUS SAITH THE LORD GOD יהוה (YAHWEH) OF ISRAEL (the so-called Negroes) AGAINST THE PASTORS (and false leaders) THAT FEED MY PEOPLE; YE HAVE SCATTERED MY FLOCK (the so-called Negroes), AND DRIVEN THEM AWAY (destroyed their unity), AND HAVE NOT VISITED THEM (with the truth): BEHOLD, I, יהוה (YAHWEH), WILL VISIT (bring) UPON YOU (false leaders) THE EVIL OF YOUR DOINGS, SAITH THE LORD, יהוה (YAHWEH)" (Jeremiah 23:1–2).

Chapter 31: "*Our Homeland*: The Richest Land on Earth"

As we wake up from our 400-year sleep here in America, we realize that we need some land of our own. We do not and cannot function as a NATION without our own land. This is the first thing OUR GREAT, GOOD, AND TERRIBLE GOD, יהוה (YAHWEH), did for our Black father, Abraham (gave him land).

"FOR ALL THE LAND WHICH THOU SEEST, TO THEE WILL I, יהוה (YAHWEH), GIVE IT, AND TO THY SEED (descendants) FOR EVER" (Genesis 13: 15).

"AND I, יהוה (YAHWEH), WILL GIVE UNTO THEE, AND TO THY SEED AFTER THEE, THE LAND WHEREIN THOU ART A STRANGER, ALL THE LAND OF CANAAN (called ISRAEL today), FOR AN EVERLASTING POSSESSION; AND I, יהוה (YAHWEH), WILL BE THEIR GOD" (Genesis 17:8).

The UNITY of our people up from slavery is part of the answer to our salvation. WE WILL NEVER HAVE LASTING UNITY WITHOUT OUR CREATOR, יהוה (YAHWEH).

We are suffering untold torture and murder at the hands of those who oppress us because of the lack of knowledge of OUR GREAT, GOOD, AND TERRIBLE GOD יהוה (YAHWEH).

"MY PEOPLE (the so-called Negroes/Blacks) ARE DESTROYED FOR LACK OF KNOWLEDGE: BECAUSE THOU HAST REJECTED KNOWLEDGE (of יהוה [YAHWEH]), I WILL ALSO REJECT THEE, THAT THOU SHALT BE NO PRIEST

TO ME: SEEING THOU HAST <u>FORGOTTEN THE LAW OF THY GOD יהוה (YAHWEH)</u>, I WILL ALSO FORGET THY CHILDREN" (Hosea 4:6).

The cause of this lack of knowledge and unity among us is due to the work and teaching of our oppressors. They have reared our fathers and mothers to be enemies of each other. They have destroyed our love of self and Blacks in general. They have educated us to hate each other and to refuse ALL that goes for Black people.

The lack of knowledge of OUR CREATOR, יהוה (YAHWEH), is the root cause of the lack of love for self and our Black kind, which keeps us divided. And being divided makes us a <u>MENTALLY DEAD NATION</u> of prey (fools and tools) at the hand of those who oppress us. Whatever the amount of education we receive from them, we are still their slaves due to this <u>lack of knowledge of</u> OUR GREAT, GOOD, AND TERRIBLE GOD, הוהי (YAHWEH); our "true" Black Hebrew history, culture, language, names; our land (ISRAEL); our enemy, the devil, Satan, serpent; self-pride; self-interest; independence as a people; the desire to be in our own country; a righteous government of our own under the laws, statutes, judgments, and commandments of the GOD of gods, יהוה (YAHWEH).

We should be ready to return to OUR MIGHTY GOD, יהוי (YAHWEH), after suffering over 400 years of hatred in America, where we are the victims of no justice, freedom, equality, and protection. We are truly suffering from the pains of being divided in this STRANGE LAND, CALLED AMERICA.

At present, after over 400 years of evil, wicked treatment, we are showing the world that we are the biggest fools on Earth. <u>HOW</u>? We have thousands of clubs and organizations; thousands of teachers, educators, scholars, scientists, technicians, doctors, lawyers, judges, congressmen, inventors, ambassadors, professors, tradesmen, engineers, herdsmen, agriculturists, cattlemen, fishermen, hunters of wild game—with all this professional and leadership class, we use all of our knowledge to <u>KEEP OTHER PEOPLE ON TOP</u>, while our people sit around in poverty begging the oppressor.

What more do we need but the <u>UNITY</u> of our people for the benefit of the whole? <u>WHAT IS ACTUALLY PREVENTING THE UNITY OF OUR 60 MILLION BLACK PEOPLE IN AMERICA IS THE LACK OF KNOWLEDGE OF OUR GOD, יהוה (YAHWEH). WHICH CAUSES THE IGNORANT AND FOOLISH LOVE AND FEAR OF OUR ENEMIES IN THE PROFESSIONAL AND LEADERSHIP CLASS OF OUR 60 MILLION BLACK PEOPLE UP FROM SLAVERY.</u> Their lack of knowledge causes them to make excuses to depend upon our oppressors like little children.

We are disgraceful, "<u>UNCLE TOMS</u>" (and WILLING SLAVES) in a world of freedom, learning advanced science in every branch of study. <u>HOW LONG SHALL WE SEEK OUR ENEMIES' EDUCATION ONLY TO BECOME THEIR SERVANTS INSTEAD OF BECOMING BUILDERS OF A PROGRESSIVE NATION OF OUR OWN HOMELAND, ISRAEL</u>?

Why are we so foolish to think it cannot be done? We have OUR GREAT, GOOD, AND TERRIBLE GOD, יהוה (YAHWEH), on our side to accomplish this.

THERE IS NO HOPE FOR US UNDER THE RULE OF SOMEONE ELSE.

But our unity under the laws, statutes, judgments and commandments of יהוה (YAHWEH) will make us HIGH ABOVE ALL NATIONS ON EARTH (Deuteronomy 7:6; 14:2; 26:18–19).

OUR GREAT, GOOD, AND TERRIBLE GOD, יהוה (YAHWEH), has given us the ONLY SOLUTION to our problems here under our merciless oppressors.

Come and join with us (HEBREW ISRAELITES) and learn how to rule the world forever as the tribe of JUDAH (I Chronicles 28:4).

Chapter 33: "A Stone was Cut Without Hands"

According to Daniel 2:28, Our Great, Good, and Terrible God, יהוה (YAHWEH), revealeth secrets and maketh known what shall be in these last days of wicked rule.

Because of our disobedience, we were led into captivity here in modern Babylon (America). Our enemies cut us off from our name Israel (Psalm 83:4 and Daniel 1:6–7) and gave us slave names after themselves. They went a step further and cut us off from: The knowledge of our God, יהוה (YAHWEH), our history, culture, language, and land Israel.

Although our Great, Good, and Terrible God, יהוה (YAHWEH), chose us to rule forever (I Kings 9:5; Revelation 22:5), because of our disobedience, יהוה (YAHWEH) made our enemy ruler over all nations (Daniel 2:38) for a time (6,000 years). His time is now up. This is what is meant by "THE LAST DAYS." Different nations would rise and fall until the end of time (Daniel 2:38–43).

Chapter 34: "We Must Educate our own Children"

When we wake up as the original Hebrew Israelites, one of the first things we realize is that we must exercise our duty in teaching our children the whole truth about our history, culture, language, and God, יהוה (YAHWEH).

Instead of letting our children watch devil-vision (T.V.), or waste their time fussing or playing stupid games, we insist that they study "OUR TRUE HISTORY, THE WORLD'S BEST KEPT SECRET." The proper education of our children is not a joke.

The foundation of our Hebrew community is teaching our children the whole truth from the King James Version of the Bible concerning our history and culture. WE MUST TEACH OUR CHILDREN AT HOME (Deuteronomy 4:9–10). Any Hebrew mother who does not have to work should devote her energy to teaching her children at home. We, as Hebrew parents, are responsible for the training of future teachers, scientists, engineers, farmers, doctors, lawyers, merchants, industrialists, statesmen, and world rulers from among our children.

It is time that we, as Hebrew parents, promote the wisdom, knowledge, and understanding of our GREAT, GOOD, AND TERRIBLE GOD, יהוה (YAHWEH), in the same light as other nations promote those who excel in track, boxing, football, basketball, baseball, and various other sports. In essence, the accomplishments and discoveries of our Black Hebrew scholars (past and present, Daniel 1:20), contribute a great deal more to human progress than all of sports forever.

Our poor blind, deaf, dumb, ignorant, and dead people, called Negroes, are led to "sport and play" by the diabolical plots of those who oppress us. We are encouraged and tempted to place emphasis upon physical powers rather than "mental greatness." We thank and praise our GREAT, GOOD, AND TERRIBLE GOD, יהוה (YAHWEH), for making us aware of the fact that knowledge (Proverbs 1:7) of "OUR 'TRUE' HISTORY" is fundamental to our progress, development, freedom, and restoration as a nation. Always remember, "OUR PEOPLE ARE DESTROYED FOR LACK OF KNOWLEDGE" (Hosea 4:6).

Chapter 35: "The Truth is Here"

My people, the Truth is here to fulfill a promise made long ago, "AND YE SHALL KNOW THE TRUTH, AND THE TRUTH SHALL MAKE YOU FREE" (John 8:32). The "Truth" is here with a solution to the problems of the so-called Negro and his slave masters.

You are seeking solutions to your conditions. You are seeking an answer to your 400 year old problem of mental, economic, educational, and spiritual slavery at the hands of our oppressors. The "Truth" is here with the solution to those problems.

As Hebrews, we have One God, One Mind, One Love, and One Action. How good it is, then, for brothers and sisters of like minds and similar burdens to get together for a spiritual love feast. "BEHOLD, HOW GOOD AND HOW PLEASANT IT IS FOR BRETHREN (Hebrews) TO DWELL TOGETHER IN UNITY" (Psalm 133:1)!

For more than 400 years, your pleas for justice, freedom, equality, a decent place in the sun, have fallen on the ears of your hateful enemies. Yet there has been no answer. Our Great, Good, and Terrible God, יהוה (YAHWEH), said that we would be brought into bondage in this strange land and treated evil for 400 long years (Acts 7:6 and Genesis 15:13). Our time of serving this evil man is now up. And now we are getting the truth from our Great, Good, and Terrible God, יהוה (YAHWEH), which solves all of our problems.

Never in the history of human evil have so many asked for justice, so loud and so long, and received in return so little, if anything at all. Our oppressors prove their hatred for our people, no matter what sacrifices they (our people) make for them. They hate your dead body, even after you give your life for him. "YE HAVE CONDEMNED AND KILLED THE JUST (so-called Negroes); AND HE DOTH NOT RESIST YOU" (James 5:6).

Our Great, Good, and Terrible God, יהוה (YAHWEH), is ready to deliver you from all evildoers. THE TRUTH IS HERE!

Additional reading

Chireau, Yvonne and Nathaniel Deutsch, eds., *Black Zion: African American Religious Encounters with Judaism* (New York: Oxford University Press, 2000).

Dorman, Jacob S. *Chosen People: The Rise of American Black Israelite Religions* (New York: Oxford University Press, 2013).

Parfitt, Tudor. *Black Jews in Africa and the Americas* (Cambridge, MA: Harvard University Press, 2013).

17

Odinism

Editors' Introduction: Modern Odinism (sometimes call Asatru, Wotanism, Vanuatrú, or Dísitrú) emerged in nineteenth-century Germany amidst a growing nationalist movement that promoted the strength and independence of white Europeans and their ancestral polytheistic religion centered on the worship of Norse gods like Odin and Thor. Drawing largely from ancient Norse mythology and related poems, Odinists stressed the value of honor, strength, courage, independence, kinship, and bravery, particularly in opposition to foreign domination and subjugation. They taught that their ancestors were a proud and independent people who were displaced, killed, or forced to worship in private, primarily by Christians, who sought to eradicate the Odinists' paganism and polytheism. By returning to their ancestral religion and its accompanying values, the descendants of the original Teutonic or Germanic tribes would reclaim their lost pride, traditions, and—most importantly—their independence.

Odinism experienced a brief revival in Germany in the 1930s and 1940s, primarily among Nazis and Nazi sympathizers such as Alexander Rud Mills, an Australian Odinist who in the 1930s published Odinist literature and who established the First Anglecyn Church of Odin. Mills' writings included a more explicit valorization of whiteness as he rejected Christianity, Judaism, and miscegenation. This more explicitly racialized version of Odinism influenced a Danish woman named Else Christensen and her husband, who moved to Canada in the 1940s where they helped Odinism spread throughout North America. In 1969, she created The Odinist Fellowship as an organization that highlighted the association of whiteness and Odinism. Christensen adopted many of Mills's ideas, but based on her reading of Jungian psychology, she also argued that the white race possessed a collective unconscious and that a distinct whiteness comprises the authentic core of their genetic composition. She taught that Odinism can awaken this unconscious to help white Odinists overcome the alleged tyranny of Jews who supposedly control the global levers of power. Christensen eventually moved to the United States where she published *The Odinist* newsletter and other Odinist literature, helping the movement's ideas spread through white supremacist and white nationalist organizations in the US and beyond.

As Odinism increasingly circulated through various white supremacist organizations like skinheads and neo-Nazis, it attracted the attention of David Lane, a member of the Ku Klux Klan and Aryan Nations who in 1983 helped create The Order. The Order was not an explicitly Odinist organization, although The Order similarly taught that Jews and blacks threatened the purity of the white race. Lane, along with several Order members, was arrested and convicted for various charges including racketeering and the murder of Alan Berg, a Jewish talk radio host. Lane was sentenced to 190 years in prison where he coined the famous "Fourteen Words" slogan ("We must secure the existence of our people and a future for white children") popular today among various white supremacist organizations. Lane also created Fourteen Word Press, which published some of the most influential Odinist literature in the United States. Lane found a sympathetic audience for his version of Odinism both in prison and beyond before he died in 2007, leaving behind a racialized version of Odinism he helped create and nurture.

Odinism today exists in various forms in over 100 countries. Not all versions of Odinism stress racial purity, but racialized versions of Odinism are particularly common in the United States, primarily in prisons, where Odinism is recognized as a legitimate religion subject to First Amendment protections. Several Odinist prison ministries exist in the United States, run primarily by ex-convicts and sympathetic Odinists.

The following writings include five separate documents from various authors. In the first document, Alexander Rud Mills presents an early attempt to distinguish Odinism from Christianity and Judaism and to list its alleged virtues. The second document is from the influential magazine *The Odinist*. It summarizes an Odinist view of history, paying particular attention to the development of the different races. The third document is also from *The Odinist* and it argues that anarchism is the preferred system of governance for the Aryan race. In the process of defending anarchism, it posits a theory of Aryan virtues. David Eden Lane is the author of the final two documents, where he articulates Odinist values and where he argues against Christians who defend the United States. Collectively, these documents describe common Odinist beliefs as they relate to race, governance, history, and dominant religions.

Documents

Document One: Alexander Rud Mills, "The Odinist Religion Overcoming Jewish Christianity" (Melbourne, Australia: Mills), 1933.

Pamphlet one: The Odinist Movement

I.   A group has formed for the commencing of an Odinist Society. An Odinist is not a Christian.

II. Christianity (the basis of our culture) has failed. See Ancient Rome, Spain, United States of America and other nations. It fails, too, in other than national aspects.

III. Odinism shows the Great One as just and good, not as mean and bloodthirsty.

IV. Christianity seeks to substitute an Eastern outlook in place of our own native outlook.

V. Odinists reverence their own race and its father-spirit.

VI. If race "A," untrue to its own spirit, worships (with or without Self-renunciation as its ideal) another race "B," then race "A" will decay, and before its death will be ruled by the members of race "B."

VII. Differences of race evidently exist for divine purpose or expression. There are, in different degree, divisions and differences in the animal and plant worlds.

VIII. Christianity seeks to destroy race. May not this be as serious as the killing of an individual?

IX. The minds and outlooks of different men are in large degree expressed in their physical appearance and that of their forefathers.

X. Our own racial ideals and traditions (not those of another) are our best guide to health and national strength.

XI. The causes of the threatened extinction of our race, the economic unsoundness, the instinctive fear of to-day, can be traced to their origin. The real remedy is a spiritual one.

XII. About Odinism:

  a. Odin (put briefly) is the part of the Great One of Whom man can be aware in some degree.
  b. Odinists recognize race as an inescapable truth of Reality (or of What Is).
  c. Odinism was the outlook of the founders of our British race.
  d. Our Odinists reverence British heroes, British holy places, British traditions, British ideals, before those of any other race,
  e. The Odinist believes in the existence of his life, beyond the immediate physical expression of it.
  f. Odinists seek to be true to themselves and what is of them, and thus become better men for all the world.
  g. The Odinist sees himself as a part, and his race as a greater part of the life of Odin and the Great One.
  h. Odinism teaches men their high duties to each other, to their race and to Odin.

Document Two: "Overview," *The Odinist* 113 (1988): 1–4.

It was originally thought that one civilization had developed in one particular location, the Middle East, and from there spread like rings on still waters. This theory was tenaciously maintained for a while, but as more and more evidence of several civilizations close to the same age was found and other artifacts of a high level of craftsmanship were unearthed, the scientists had great trouble coordinating the time tables.

So the scientists agree, some reluctantly, that the special mixture of physical and mental intensity needed for these historic events to take place may be present at several locations at the same, or approximately the same, time, helped along by a strong evidence that a lively communication took place over long distances. Yet several thousand years went by before the right conditions and the needed dynamic fermentation were on hand and we have the first social complex we call a civilization.

Within the span of three thousand years from 3500 BCI to 500 BCI, the first five civilizations were born. Mesopotamia first; Egypt about 3100 BCI; the Indus Valley in 2500 BCI; the Menoan in Crete about 2000 BCI and China around 1500 BCI. The Meso-American and our own Western civilization came later.

The five early civilizations were concentrated in a rather small geographic area, the so-called Fertile Crescent; a coming and going of many different peoples were the order of the day. Eventually racial circumstances may have promoted intellectual growth, encouraging an interchange of ideas and knowledge, but in other ways the effect may also have been disruptive; be that as it may, possibly this process was exactly what was needed to get things rolling.

By 4000 BCI, before any of the civilizations actually had been spawned, the majority of the populations of the area belonged to the light-skinned family of man, still to this day commonly known as Caucasians, although true Caucasians come only from the mountainous regions of Georgia, now part of the USSR; these were the Indo-European nations to which we belong. The other two main racial groups coming into or living in the area were the Hamitic stock from Africa north of the Sahara and the Semites of the Arabian peninsula.

The main movers and shakers of the emerging civilizations were our ancestors. These early Indo-Europeans were divided into several groups, each coming into the area from different directions. By the year 2000 BCI the Hittites, coming from Europe pushed through into Anatolia (Asiatic Turkey) while from the east the Iranians came from the vasts of western Asia. From the north came others known as the Sea People. The various branches mingled with each other and with the people already living there and thus an early mixing with Hamites and Semites took place; the descendants of this process are still living in the area. However, the racial elements of the western European branches either went back home or became lost by absorption although still leaving their racial mark on the present population.

Whereas a mixing of racial stocks usually does not work to the advantage of the peoples involved, it must be admitted that the special mixture of environment and racial interaction at that particular time resulted in a dynamic concentration of a population able to foster the first known civilization—historically, intellectually and spiritually a tremendous accomplishment. It might also be noted that all these five civilizations, like every other organism, were mortal; it seems that the dynamic combinations that were at play in the early parts of these cultural exchanges soon (historically speaking) outlived their usefulness and productive effect; each participating element became exhausted, lost its cultural acumen and was unable to maintain its spiritual effectiveness.

Why should Odinists concern themselves with these old civilizations that seemingly hold no answer to present problems? The old dictum that "to every action there is a reaction" is also true today even when that action took place a long time ago; a ripple effect is still at play. These ancient civilizations were, as we have seen, mostly created or influenced by our forefathers although also shaped by other thought patterns and thus form an important part of our history; they are, in fact, the basis for much of modern thought and for the development of our own Western civilization.

Yockey was absolutely correct when he said "The realm of Thought is interested in the missing stages of past Cultures and the future of our own, but Action is interested in the Past as the key to effective performance."[1] Thus the higher importance of history-writing and history-thinking is that they serve effective action. History-reading gives us the necessary understanding of the folk soul, both our own and that of other peoples; and understanding is the main key to effective decision-making.

Document Three: "Anarchism," *The Odinist* 125 (1989): 1–2. The editor's note at the beginning of the document is internal to the document itself.

Editor's Note:

We are continuing our ongoing discussion of possible alternatives to capitalism and Marxism with a series of articles on what might be considered the original Third Force option: anarchism.

A reminder: THE ODINIST is a journal for critically-thinking individuals, not for weak-minded zombies who must be spoonfed a predigested ideology. We expect our readers to re-examine and refine their own ideological/political positions in light of the information and admittedly racial opinions we are presenting.

And, as always, the views expressed herein are those of the individual writers; they do not represent any sort of official policy declaration on the part of THE ODINIST or the Odinist Fellowship.

Aryan Anarchism

Anarchism attacks "authority" which is central to modern forms. Several elements make up the essential core of anarchism—rejection of dogma, deliberate avoidance of systematic theory, stress on the primacy of the individual, and extreme freedom of choice.

---

[1] The original source does not indicate the end of this quotation, but presumably, the quotation ends with the sentence.

Anarchism has existed in Aryan Europe since the 1840s—surviving while many stronger but less adaptable movements have completely disappeared.

Anarchism has a naturalistic Aryan view of society. Anarchists believe that man naturally contains all the attributes which make him capable of living in freedom and social peace among his racial kin. Anarchists may not believe that man is naturally good but they do believe that he is naturally social with his like kind. Hence, man is naturally capable of living in a free society, and if society is a natural growth, then those who attempt to create stable institutions of static control are the real enemies of society. Anarchists, who rebel against these institutions, are not antisocial—they are the true regenerators and responsible individuals striving to adjust the social balance back to its natural direction.

Anarchism's cult of the natural, the individual, the spontaneous, sets it against the entire highly organized structure of modern industrial, static society. The appeal of anarchism has always been strongest among the groups that remain outside the general trend toward mechanism and conformity in the industrial world—aristocracy, farmers, artisans and most rural people close to the soil. These "outsider" groups are united in their opposition to the modern state and its capitalist or communist economy. They represent a rebellion, not necessarily in favor of the past, but certainly in favor of an ideal of individual Aryan freedom which belongs outside the present in which they find themselves.

Anarchism does not view history as moving along steel lines of dialectical necessity. The pattern of history in anarchism's view emerges out of struggle—human struggle, the product of the exercise of man's will, based on the Aryan spark of free consciousness, respond to an impulse that provokes Aryan man's perennial urge to freedom. In reality the idea of anarchism is that of purified aristocracy. The spiral of history has turned full circle, and where aristocracy has always called for the freedom of noble men, anarchism has always declared the nobility of free men.

Anarchism is a comparatively recent phenomenon—at least as an organized movement of social protest. As a movement emerging in Europe in the late 19th and early 20th centuries it was mainly a reaction to quickening rate of economic and political centralization caused by the industrial revolution. Anarchism has no belief in social democratic reformism, republican parliamentarism or communist-Marxist doctrinarianism. Anarchists focused their attacks on the state and capitalism as the chief instruments of domination and exploitation. Anarchists called for a social revolution that would abolish all political and economic authority, bringing in a new decentralized society based on the voluntary cooperation of free Aryan individuals.

Document Four: David Lane, "88 Precepts." Accessed online at: https://ia800303.us.archive.org/3/items/88Precepts_937/88Precepts.pdf.

Until the white race realizes that there is only one source from which we can ascertain lasting truths, there will never be peace or stability on this earth. In the immutable Laws of Nature are the keys to life, order, and understanding. The words of men, even those which some consider "inspired" are subject to the translations, vocabulary, additions, subtractions, and distortions of fallible mortals. Therefore, every writing or influence, ancient or modern, must be strained through the test of conformity to Natural Law. The White Peoples of the earth must collectively understand that they are equally subject to the iron-hard Laws of Nature with every other creature of the Universe, or they will not secure peace, safety, nor even their existence. The world is in flames because Races, Subraces, Nations, and Cultures are being forced to violate their own Nature-ordained instincts for self-preservation. Many men of good will, but little understanding, are struggling against symptoms which are the result of disobedience to Natural Law. As is the Nature of Man, most take narrow, provincial stances predicated on views formed by immediate environment, current circumstances, and conditioned dogma. This is encouraged by that powerful and ruthless Tribe which has controlled the affairs of the world for untold centuries by exploiting Man's most base instincts. Conflict among and between the unenlightened serves as their mask and shield. A deeper understanding of the Fundamental Laws that govern the affairs of Men is necessary if we are to save civilization from its usurious executioners. The following are not intended to provide a detailed system of government, but as PRECEPTS which, when understood, will benefit and preserve a People as individuals and as a Nation.

1. Any religion or teaching which denies the Natural Laws of the Universe is false.

2. Whatever People's perception of God, or Gods, or the motive Force of the Universe might be, they can hardly deny that Nature's Law are the work of, and therefore the intent of, that Force.

7. Religion in its most beneficial form is the symbology of a People and their culture. A multiracial religion destroys the senses of uniqueness, exclusivity and value necessary to the survival of a race.

8. What men call the super natural is actually the natural not yet understood or revealed.

9. A proliferation of laws with the resultant loss of freedom is a sign of, and directly proportional to, spiritual sickness in a Nation.

10. If a Nation is devoid of spiritual health and moral character, then government and unprincipled men will fill the vacancy. Therefore, freedom prospers in moral values and tyranny thrives in moral decay.

14. In accord with Nature's Laws, nothing is more right than the preservation of one's own race.

18. There exists no such thing as rights or privileges under the Laws of Nature. The deer being stalked by a hungry lion has no right to life. However, he may purchase life by obedience to nature ordained instincts for vigilance and flight.

Similarly, men have no rights to life, liberty or happiness. These circumstances may be purchased by oneself, by ones family, by ones tribe or by ones ancestors, but they are nonetheless purchases and are not rights. Furthermore, the value of these purchases can only be maintained through vigilance and obedience to Natural Law.

19.   A people who are not convinced of their uniqueness and value will perish.

20.   The White race has suffered invasions and brutality from Africa and Asia for thousands of years. For example, Attila and the Asiatic Huns who invaded Europe in the 5th century, raping, plundering and killing from the Alps to the Baltic and the Caspian Seas. This scenario was repeated by the Mongols of Genghis Khan 800 years later. (Note here that the American Indians are not Native Americans, but are racially Mongolians.) In the 8th century, hundreds of years before Negroes were brought to America, the North African Moors of mixed racial background invaded and conquered Portugal, Spain and part of France. So, the attempted guilt-trip placed on the White race by civilizations executioners is invalid under both historical circumstance and the Natural Law which denies inter-species compassion. The fact is, all races have benefited immeasurably from the creative genius of the Aryan People.

21.   People who allow others not of their race to live among them will perish, because the inevitable result of a racial integration is racial inter-breeding which destroys the characteristics and existence of a race. Forced integration is deliberate and malicious genocide, particularly for a People like the White race, who are now a small minority in the world.

25.   A People without a culture exclusively their own will perish.

28.   The concept of a multi-racial society violates every Natural Law for species preservation.

We must secure the existence of our people and a future for white children. That the beauty of the White Aryan woman must not perish from the earth.

Document Five: David Eden Lane, "To: 'Christian Rightwing American Patriots,'" *Wotansvolk* (The WAU Sisterhood), 2017: 59–60.

My last article. Not because I am giving up the struggle. It appears that my destiny and role in this war for White Survival is to set an example of utter defiance until someday dying in the prisons of my enemies. So be it!

This is my last article, barring unforeseen circumstances, because everything necessary has already been said. If not by me, then Rockwell, Hitler, Yockey, and a host of others.

Thousands of our folk at least, and perhaps millions, know that our White race is facing extinction, and they know it is a plan of tyrants who are wealthy beyond conception, in a league with mindless universalists.

This genocide, meaning the murder of our race, has seldom been resisted except with words. It has been written about, read about, gossiped about, and sung about in millions of works. If words without swords had any value whatsoever, we would have beaten our enemies to death long ago.

But unfortunately, compromise, comfort, and cowardice are the predominate traits in the modern White male. They are a total disgrace to the memory of their ancestors. So now our race is little more than a walking corpse.

When the Supreme Court struck down the laws against interracial marriage, were there nine black robed devils found hanging by their necks the next day? No! Why not? Because the modern White man, the CRAP, is a castrated, selfish pussy.

When the US Military used bayonets to push White girls into colored schools, was there rebellion? No! Why? Because the modern White man is such a stinking maggot that he makes camel shit smell like roses.

Shall I continue with forced bussing, movies, and television, promoting interracial marriage, the destruction of the racial basis of our European homeland in World wars, etc. etc., ad nauseam without end? Why should I? It is only more words.

Once upon a time, when White men still had some integrity, words did have value. But speaking to walking, talking piles of camel shit is a waste of breath and ink.

I have told the CRAP for many years that in the wars, revolutions and assassinations that America has financed and participated in . . . the dead and maimed victims number 200 million or more, half of them white, many of them women and children.

But still the CRAP wraps logic five times around a crooked tree to proclaim themselves "American Patriots" who support "Our Boys" as they bomb helpless nations into the Stone Age and blow tens of thousands or millions of women and children into tiny fragments. Always looking for someone else to blame, the CRAP screams, it's the Jews, it's the Jews. Well I'd be the last to deny that the media is dominated by Jews who have an agenda of world domination and of extinction for White Aryans.

But it has been Christians who for centuries have been giving the White man's food, medicine, wealth, technology, and education to the colored races. It is the CRAP who now surrenders the last of the White man's women, power, and territory to the colored races.

White Christian Civilization is a catchy and idiotic phrase used by the CRAP. It was the Christians who destroyed our indigenous civilization and brought on the dark ages. It was the Christians who persecuted all men of science, philosophy, and reason for many centuries.

Two-thousand years ago, Julius Caesar said that as long as he could invent an enemy of the Empire, he could remain in power by employing calls to patriotism. The CRAP are so insane that they still fall for the same game as they go off to kill and make hundreds of millions for the Judeo-American/Judeo Christian empire.

Our race cannot survive without nations in which we are the only inhabitants. Anyone who claims that America can be made a White Nation is either totally insane or a deliberate deceiver. Unfortunately, almost all so-called White leaders since the civil war in America have been compromising deceivers.

As far as I know I am the only one who has ever told the whole truth about America, Christianity, philosophy, history, and natural law religion.

The well-known 14 WORDS are, "WE MUST SECURE THE EXISTENCE OF OUR PEOPLE AND A FUTURE FOR WHITE CHILDREN." My motivation is expressed in another 14 WORDS: "BECAUSE THE BEAUTY OF THE WHITE ARYAN WOMEN MUST NOT PERISH FROM THE EARTH".

If we are to accomplish the 14 words, then we must become revolutionaries. A revolution in fact is preceded by a revolution in the mind. We cannot continue to worship, or compromise with our executioners' institutions. Overthrow them or leave them, but you cannot procrastinate or compromise any longer.

14 WORDS and 88 PRECEPTS to Victory or Valhalla.

Additional reading

Dobratz, Betty A. "The Role of Religion in the Collective Identity of the White Racialist Movement," *Journal for the Scientific Study of Religion* 40.2 (2001): 287–302.

Gardell, Mattias. *Gods of the Blood: The Pagan Revival and White Separatism* (Durham, NC: Duke University Press, 2003).

Kaplan, Jeffrey. *Radical Religion in America: Millenarian Movements from the Far Right to the Children of Noah* (Syracuse, NY: Syracuse University Press, 1997).

Bibliography

Albanese, Catherine. *America: Religions and Religion*. Belmont: Wadsworth Publishing Company, 1981.

Asad, Talal. *Genealogies of Religion: Discipline and Reasons of Power in Christianity and Islam*. Baltimore: Johns Hopkins University Press, 1993.

Ashcraft, W. Michael. "Field Notes A History of the Study of New Religious Movements." *Nova Religio: The Journal of Alternative and Emergent Religions* 9.1 (2005): 93–105.

Baker, Kelly J. *Gospel According to the Klan: The KKK's Appeal to Protestant America, 1915–1930*. Lawrence, KS: University of Kansas Press, 2011.

Balch, Robert W. "The Rise and Fall of Aryan Nations: A Resource Mobilization Perspective." *Journal of Political and Military Sociology* 34.1 (2006): 81–113.

Bennett, Bridget. "Sacred Theatres: Shakers, Spiritualists, Theatricality, and the Indian in the 1830s and 1840s." *The Drama Review*, 49.3 (2005): 114–134.

Bennett, James B. "'Until This Curse of Polygamy Is Wiped Out': Black Methodists, White Mormons, and Constructions of Racial Identity in the Late Nineteenth Century." *Religion and American Culture: A Journal of Interpretation* 21.2 (Summer 2011): 167–194.

Blum, Edward J., Tracy Fessenden, Prema Kurien, and Judith Weisenfeld, "Forum: American Religion and 'Whiteness'." *Religion and American Culture: A Journal of Interpretation* 19.1 (Winter 2009): 1–35.

Bromley, David G. and Phillip E. Hammond, eds. *The Future of New Religious Movements*. Macon: Mercer University Press, 1987.

Brontz, Howard. *The Black Jews of Harlem*. New York: Free Press of Glencoe, 1964.

Bulter, Jon. *Awash in a Sea of Faith: Christianizing the American People*. Cambridge: Harvard University Press, 1992.

Chidester, David. "Anchoring Religion in the World: A Southern African History of Comparative Religion." *Religion* 26 (1996): 141–160.

Chidester, David. *Salvation and Suicide: An Interpretation of Jim Jones, the Peoples Temple, and Jonestown*. Bloomington: Indiana University Press, 1988.

Chireau, Yvonne. *Black Magic: Religion and the African American Conjuring Tradition*. Berkeley: University of California Press, 2006.

Chireau, Yvonne. "Conjure and Christianity in the Nineteenth Century: Religious Elements in African American Magic." *Religion and American Culture: A Journal of Interpretation* 7.2 (1997): 225–246.

Chireau, Yvonne and Nathaniel Deutsch, editors. *Black Zion: African American Religious Encounters with Judaism*. New York: Oxford University Press, 2000.

Chryssides, George R. and Benjamin E. Zeller. *The Bloomsbury Companion to New Religious Movements*. New York: Bloomsbury, 2014.

Clark, Emily Suzanne. *A Luminous Brotherhood: Afro-Creole Spiritualism in Nineteenth-Century New Orleans*. Chapel Hill: University of North Carolina Press, 2016.

Clark, Emily Suzanne. "Noble Drew Ali's 'Clean and Pure Nation': The Moorish Science Temple, Identity, and Healing." *Nova Religio: The Journal of Alternative and Emergent Religions* 16.3 (February 2013): 31–51.

Cregg, Claude Andrew III. *An Original Man: The Life and Times of Elijah Muhammad*. New York: St. Martin's Press, 1997.

Crow, John L. "Lemuria Rising: California in the Place-Making Imagination." Paper presented at the annual meeting of the Southeastern Commission for the Study of Religion, March 4–6, 2012.

Curtis, Edward E. IV. *Black Muslim Religion in the Nation of Islam, 1960–1975*. Chapel Hill: University of North Carolina Press, 2006.

Curtis, Edward E. IV., and Danielle Brune Sigler, eds. *The New Black Gods: Arthur Huff Fauset and the Study of African American Religions*. Bloomington: Indiana University Press, 2009.

Daschke, Dereck and Michael Ashcraft, eds. *New Religious Movements: A Documentary Reader*. New York: New York University Press, 2005.

DeMallie, Raymond J. "The Lakota Ghost Dance: An Ethnohistorical Account." *Pacific Historical Review* 51.4 (November 1982): 385–405.

Dennis, Matthew. *Seneca Possessed: Indians, Witchcraft, and Power in the Early American Republic*. Philadelphia: University of Pennsylvania Press, 2010.

Dobratz, Betty A. "The Role of Religion in the Collective Identity of the White Racialist Movement." *Journal for the Scientific Study of Religion* 40.2 (2001): 287–302.

Dorman, Jacob S. *Chosen People: The Rise of American Black Israelite Religions*. New York: Oxford University Press, 2013.

Dorman, Jacob S. "'I Saw You Disappear with My Own Eyes': Hidden Transcripts of New York Black Israelite Bricolage." *Nova Religio: The Journal of Alternative and Emergent Religions* 11.1 (2007): 61–83.

Farmer, Jared. *On Zion's Mount: Mormons, Indians, and the American Landscape*. Cambridge: Harvard University Press, 2008.

Fauset, Arthur Huff. *Black Gods of the Metropolis: Negro Religious Cults of the Urban North*. 1944. Philadelphia: University of Pennsylvania Press, 2002.

Fondakowski, Leigh. *Stories from Jonestown*. Minnesota: University of Minnesota Press, 2013.

Fett, Carla. *Working Cures: Healing, Health, and Power on Southern Slave Plantations*. Chapel Hill: University of North Carolina Press, 2002.

Gallagher, Eugene. *The New Religious Movements Experience in America*. Westport: Greenwood Press, 2004.

Gallagher, Eugene and W. Michael Ashcraft, eds. *Introduction to New and Alternative Religions in America*, 5 Vols. Westport: Greenwood Press, 2006.

Gardell, Mattias. *Gods of the Blood: The Pagan Revival and White Separatism*. Durham: Duke University Press, 2003.

Gordon, Linda. *The Second Coming of the KKK: The Ku Klux Klan of the 1920s and the American Political Tradition*. New York: Liveright, 2017.

Gordon, Michelle Y. "'Midnight Scenes and Orgies': Public Narratives of Voodoo in New Orleans and Nineteenth-Century Discourses of White Supremacy." *American Quarterly* 64.4 (December 2012): 767–786.

Harris, Cheryl. "Whiteness as Property." *Harvard Law Review* 106.8 (1993): 1707–1791.

Harrison, Peter. *"Religion" and the Religions in the English Enlightenment*. New York: Cambridge University Press, 1990.

Irwin, Lee. *Coming Down From Above: Prophecy, Resistance, and Renewal in native American Religions*. Norman: University of Oklahoma Press, 2008.

Johnson, Sylvester. *African American Religions, 1500–2000: Colonialism, Democracy, and Freedom*. New York: Cambridge University Press, 2015.

Johnson, Sylvester. "The Rise of Black Ethnics: The Ethnic Turn in African American Religions, 1916–1945." *Religion and American Culture: A Journal of Interpretation* 20.2 (Summer 2010): 125–163.

Kaplan, Jeffrey. *Radical Religion in America: Millenarian Movements from the Far Right to the Children of Noah*. Syracuse: Syracuse University Press, 1997.

Lee, Martha F. *The Nation of Islam: An American Millenarian Movement*. Syracuse: Syracuse University Press, 1996.

Lewis, James R., ed. *Cults in America: A Reference Handbook*. Santa Barbara: ABC-CLIO, 1998.

Lewis, James R., ed. *The Oxford Handbook to New Religious Movements*. New York: Oxford University Press, 2003.

Lynch, Don and Michael Hittman, with the Yerington Paiute Tribe. *Wovoka and the Ghost Dance*. Lincoln: University of Nebraska Press, 1990.

Maroukis, Thomas C. *The Peyote Road: Religious Freedom and the Native American Church*. Norman, OK: The University of Oklahoma Press, 2010.

McGarry, Molly. *Ghosts of Futures Past: Spiritualism and the Cultural Politics of Nineteenth-Century America*. Berkeley: University of California Press, 2008.

Melton, J. Gordon. *Encyclopedic Handbook of Cults in America*. New York: Routledge, 2014.

Mitchem, Stephanie. *African American Folk Healing*. New York: New York University Press, 2007.

Moore, R. Laurence. *Religious Outsiders and the Making of Americans*. Oxford: Oxford University Press, 1987.

Moore, Rebecca, Anthony B. Pinn, and Mary R. Sawyer, eds. *Peoples Temple and Black Religion in America*. Bloomington: Indiana University Press, 2004.

Moore, Steven C. "Reflections on the Elusive Promise of Religious Freedom for the Native American Church." *Wicazo Sa Review* 7.1 (Spring 1991): 42–50.

Mueller, Max Perry. *Race and the Making of the Mormon People*. Chapel Hill: University of North Carolina Press, 2017.

Newell, Quincy D. "The Autobiography and Interview of Jane Elizabeth Manning James." *Journal of Africana Religions* 1.2 (2013): 251–291.

Nongbri, Brent. *Before Religion: A History of a Modern Concept*. New Haven: Yale University Press, 2012.

Nye, Malory. "Race and Religion: Postcolonial Formations of Power and Whiteness." *Method & Theory in the Study of Religion* (2018): 1–28.

Parfitt, Tudor. *Black Jews in African and the Americas*. Cambridge: Harvard University Press, 2013.

Pegram, Thomas. *One Hundred Percent American: The Rebirth and Decline of the Ku Klux Klan in the 1920s*. Lantham: Ivan R. Dee, 2011.

Santucci, James A. "The Notion of Race in Theosophy." *Nova Religio: The Journal of Alternative and Emergent Religions* 11.3 (February 2008): 37–63.

Satter, Beryl. "Marcus Garvey, Father Divine and Gender Politics of Race Difference and Race Neutrality." *American Quarterly* 48.1 (March 1996): 43–76.

Scheeres, Julia. *A Thousand Lives: The Untold Story of Jonestown*. New York: Free Press, 2011.

Siegler, Elijah. *New Religious Movements*. Englewood Cliffs, N.J.: Prentice Hall, 2007.

Simi, Pete and Robert Futrell. *American Swastika: Inside the White Power Movement's Hidden Spaces of Hate*. Lanham, MD: Rowman & Littlefield Publishers, 2010.

Smoak, Gregory. *Ghost Dances and Identity: Prophetic Religion and American Indian Ethnogenesis in the Nineteenth Century*. Berkeley: University of California Press, 2008.

Stein, Stephen. "Alternative Religious Movements in American History." In *The Columbia Guide to Religion in American History*, eds. Paul Harvey and Edward J. Blum. New York: Columbia University Press, 2012.

Stewart, Omer C. *Peyote Religion: A History*. Norman, OK: The University of Oklahoma Press 1987.

Tooker, Elizabeth. "On the Development of the Handsome Lake Religion." *Proceedings of the American Philosophical Society* 133.1 (March 1989): 35–50.

Troy, Kathryn. *The Specter of the Indian: Race, Gender, and Ghosts in American Séances, 1848–1890*. Albany: State University of New York Press, 2017.

Turner, Richard Brent. *Islam and the African American Experience*. Bloomington: Indiana University Press, 2003.

Versluis, Arthur. *Magic and Mysticism: An Introduction to Western Esoteric Traditions*. Lantham: Rowman & Littlefield Publishers, 2007.

Wallace, Anthony. *The Death and Rebirth of the Seneca*. New York: Vintage Books, 1972.

Weisenfeld, Judith. *New World A-Coming: Black Religion and Racial Identity during the Great Migration*. New York: New York University Press, 2016.

Weisenfeld, Judith. "Spiritual Complexions: On Race and the Body in the Moorish Science Temple of America." In *Sensational Religion: Sense and Contention in Material Practice*, ed. Sally Promey. New Haven: Yale University Press, 2014.

X, Malcolm and Alex Haley. *The Autobiography of Malcolm X*. New York: Grove Press, 1965.

Index